# The Legendary RMs

JOHN PRICE WILLIAMS

THE CROWOOD PRESS

First published in 2005 by
The Crowood Press Ltd
Ramsbury, Marlborough
Wiltshire SN8 2HR

**www.crowood.com**

**British Library Cataloguing-in-Publication Data**
A catalogue record for this book is available from the British Library.

ISBN 1 86126 761 4

Typeface used: Bembo.

Typeset and designed by D & N Publishing
Hungerford, Berkshire.

Printed and bound in Great Britain by CPI Bath.

# Contents

# Introduction

The RM series of Rileys began in 1945 as one of the outstanding cars of the post-war era and ended, in some ignominy, in 1957 after just over 28,000 cars had been built.

The 1933 London Motor Show catalogue had called the Riley the 'most successful car in the world', though even at the peak of production in the mid-1930s, when about 5,500 cars a year were being produced in the works at Durbar Avenue, Coventry, the output was never more than 2½ per cent of Britain's car production.

Rileys were a niche product for the sporting driver – and had a considerable sporting heritage to back this up. But poor management allowed the family firm to fall into the hands of one of Britain's largest companies, the Nuffield Organization, which miraculously maintained the Riley identity until the chronic mismanagement of the British Motor Corporation brought the unhappy saga of the Pathfinder to an end in 1957.

The Riley RMs looked, as one writer put it, like 'an exercise in good taste' and this, combined with engineering innovation, made them exceptional cars that are much treasured and enjoyed today.

It is common for Riley RM enthusiasts to say that they have never seen two cars that are identical – such was the haphazard way in which they were built in both Coventry and Abingdon – and trying to document changes and the time at which they took place between the 1½-litre RMA and its successor the RME, and the 2½-litre RMB and RMF can test the patience.

Factory documentation such as the *Sales and Service Bulletins* can be contradictory, chassis and engine numbers never matched, so alas, there is no precise science in dating the cars. The figures in this book are based on the best information available but are not immutable.

The roadster is referred to in some chapters as the RMC and the drophead as RMD. These designations were never officially used by the factory and to this day some purists do not approve of them, though most Riley club members use them as convenient shorthand.

Victor Riley, son of the eponymous guiding genius of the famous firm, is still the president of the Riley Motor Club. He says that it is the engineering design and the 'sheer romance' of the cars that has kept the Riley magic alive.

This book attempts to capture some of that magic.

John Price Williams
Eastbourne

# Acknowledgements

There exists within the car clubs that cater for Rileys a wealth of knowledge about the history and technicalities of the RM series – information that has been absorbed over decades, so I am very grateful to the stalwarts of these clubs for their unstinting aid when I approached them about writing this book.

They have shared their expertise, filled in blanks, supplied material and most importantly told me when I had not got something quite right. If there are errors, they are mine not theirs. I have tried to make this book as accurate as possible by checking material with sources, but in some cases, just as it's said that there are no two RMs that are identical, there is no single correct opinion on some Riley matters.

RM Club registrar Nigel Trotman has played a major role in providing information and pictures. Riley wisdom came from marque historian *extraordinaire* Chris Hudson. RM gurus Gwyn Morris and John Joiner made sure I was properly briefed and supplied with contemporary material. Dave Rowlands, the fount of all Pathfinder knowledge, was keen to share it.

Alec Gatherer, editor of the RM Club magazine *RMemoranda* and David Pipes, editor of the Riley Motor Club's *Riley Record*, kindly gave permission to quote from their excellent magazines. David holds the very valuable Riley Motor Club archive, to which I was given open access. Alec also volunteered to read, correct and comment on the manuscript, which he did with his usual panache. Gordon Webster, who runs the RM Club's remarkable database, was very helpful in providing information on surviving cars.

Vernon E. Barker was painstaking in putting me right on the RMs' pre-war heritage, as was Denis R. Bell on Riley's sporting history. Phil Soden, who runs the *Rileys in Australia* website, provided facts relating to Nuffield exports. Gilbert Grace supplied the excellent pictures of his father's racing career.

Thanks are again due to Bryan Moylan, who has helped with previous books, for more reminiscences of Abingdon that also came from Peter Tothill.

Mike Thatcher of the Riley Motor Club kindly allowed me to photograph the restoration of Enid Blyton's RME, which has been done by Glen Kingham.

Much data has come from the British Motor Industry Heritage Trust at Gaydon, where Richard Brotherton is unfailingly helpful.

Many pictures have been supplied by Stephanie Sykes at Gaydon and by the National Motor Museum; they have also come from individuals such as Allan Fuller, Gilbert Grace, John Kirby, spares manager of the RM Club, Kees de Kock in the Netherlands, Colin Readey, Colin Peck and David Evans.

Alan Dixon, of Bratton Seymour, Somerset, who is a professional illustrator, kindly gave permission for me to use his excellent line drawings of the RM's wooden structure. Lynn Postle of the Institute of Cast Metals Engineers gave permission to reprint the appendix on repair times. Anyone left out of these lists by my thoughtlessness should also feel a warm glow of approbation.

FAMOUS IN FIVE CONTINENTS

# for Magnificent Motoring

"In very few cars, past or present, can one feel so keenly as with this Riley that here is

a car capable of ambling along a good main road at 60 to 70 m.p.h.  By ambling is meant

that there is no sense of mechanical effort or suggestion of moving quickly.  Yet this

speed represents to very many people a maximum seldom used in other cars.

The fact that at such a speed there is a good 20 m.p.h. in reserve means a great deal."

*vide "The Autocar"*

1½ litre Saloon £714.  Purchase Tax £199. 1. 8.  100 h.p. 2½ litre Salooon £958.  Purchase Tax £266. 17. 2

*Riley - as old as the industry - as modern as the hour*

RILEY MOTORS LIMITED COVENTRY. *London Showrooms:* "RILEY CARS" 55-56 PALL MALL, S.W.1

Overseas Business : Nuffield Exports Ltd. Oxford and 41 Piccadilly London

# 1  The beginning

It was an after-dinner handshake on the stairs of the Welcome Hotel in Stratford-upon-Avon in the late summer of 1938 that led to the birth of the Riley RM series.

Two of the British motor industry's most esteemed characters, William Morris, by now Lord Nuffield, and Victor Riley, head of his family's firm, were very old friends who had known each other through their interest in cycling and motoring since before the First World War. The Morris Motors empire was huge and thriving; the Riley family business was in debt and heading for bankruptcy, if not extinction. Attempts to sell it had failed.

As they made their way upstairs to their hotel rooms, Nuffield turned to Riley and said: 'Why don't you join me? You can be under my financial umbrella, but retain your design independence.' The two shook hands. The deal was done and after nearly forty years, Riley's independence came to an end as it became part of a conglomerate, but the name was saved and after the war a new line of sporting, elegant cars carried on the firm's tradition.

The RM series of cars was produced entirely during the days of the Nuffield Organization, Morris's creation that later became part of the British Motor Corporation. However, the link to the family firm of the 1930s is all-important; the RM cars were designed and built in the old pre-war Riley tradition and were not just another up-market sporting car from a large corporation.

Nevertheless, when it came to decisions affecting production and marketing of this outstanding range of cars, these were taken mainly at a corporate level, by people who were responsible for many other makes made at many different factories at the same time and who did not necessarily give Riley the attention it deserved.

It was not always so; there are those who argue that the glory days of Riley were before the Second World War when it was truly a family company – run by the brothers Riley after their father before them. From 1899 to 1939 the family produced about 55,000 cars, with some outstanding models like the Nine, that made the company's reputation, and the Brooklands that delivered competition success.

Riley's sporting prowess was legendary – in that period they took part in some 250 events and gained nearly 900 notable placings in everything from grands prix to Brooklands handicaps. Then there were the endurance runs: London to the Cape of Good Hope, and the Arctic Circle tour.

The Riley reputation for turning out exceptional cars from its works in Durbar Avenue, Foleshill, Coventry, was substantial and well-earned by its sporting cars and also for features such as promises of petrol consumption of 30mpg at 30mph – guaranteed in a certificate signed by Victor Riley, chairman and managing director, and by the factory's chief tester.

But due to family disputes, a proliferation of models and falling sales due to economic uncertainty before Munich, which affected all manufacturers, the firm was entering a crisis. But what tipped them over the edge financially was the investment in steel saloon bodies from Briggs Motor Bodies of Doncaster. Numbers were greatly over-ordered, Briggs refused to renegotiate the contract and the surplus bodies ended up being stacked around the factory.

There had also been a very expensive fiasco with what was called the Hi-charge induction system for the Nine and Twelve horsepower models – basically a system of tuned inlet tracts. It worked well on the test bed, promising a 20 per cent increase in power, but was a disaster on the road leading to what might be described literally as manifold carburettor problems and the recall of cars for modification.

Although the charismatic Victor had headed the company for some time, his influence had been vitiated by his father William, still on the board until his eighties. In his excellent book on Riley 16/4 production cars, Vernon Barker argues that the problems from the mid-1930s onwards were not of Victor's making since his obdurate father – who it has to be remembered wanted to produce wheels for the motor industry rather than cars of his own – opposed progress and would not let him run the business properly until he retired in October 1937.

During the 1930s Riley had produced more than 5,000 cars a year in some years from the Durbar Avenue factory. In the final 1938 season, that is beginning in October 1937, 1,200 were produced in about five or six months before the firm collapsed.

## The Autovia fiasco

At this crucial time in the company's fortunes, Victor had decided to compete in the luxury car market and to meet the threat of competition from companies that had started using large American engines like Jensen. He set up a company to make the Autovia, a substantial car using many Riley parts, notably in the engine, which was the company's small V8, an engine first schemed for the 8-90 Silver Streak Adelphi. It had two blocks set at 90 degrees, retaining the stroke of the Nine horsepower but using the 1½-litre's bore. C.M. van Eugen was recruited from Lea Francis to do the designing.

There was certainly spare capacity at Durbar Avenue to build it, so the Autovia chassis was constructed there from Riley parts, then driven to Northampton to be bodied.

'The presence of Mr Victor Riley as chairman and managing director is at least a guarantee that the Autovia will not be without pedigree', said the *Motor*. But it was not a guarantee of success, despite being an excellent car, in the overburdened luxury sector.

Victor thought a big luxury car could make big profits and Alan sided with him; Percy believed in small cars like the Nine in volume production as did brother Stanley.

In sharp contrast to the way the RM series was to be marketed, with only seven models on three chassis throughout its entire 12-year production run, in 1934 Riley offered 26 different models on nine different chassis. A Riley advertisement in September 1936 had said: '...we make far too many models of course. But then we have a pretty fertile design department, and we like making nice, interesting cars'.

There had been some attempts to rationalize production in late 1936 and by 1937 a single chassis was in use for the 15/6, V8 and Big Four.

But there was the usual bewilderingly large range of offerings announced ahead of the London Motor Show in the autumn of 1937 for the 1938 model year. It was as if the troops were being urged ever onwards towards Moscow even as the snow began to fall. As well as the Autovia, there were four chassis:

- 12 horsepower 1½-litre      1496cc
- 16 horsepower Big Four      2443cc
- 15 horsepower Six           1726cc
- 18 horsepower V8            2178cc.

There were four saloon bodies:

- Touring
- Adelphi
- Kestrel
- Close-coupled – on which the post-war RMs were to be based;

and two open cars:

- Sprite two-seater
- Lynx tourer.

Prices ranged from £345 to £475.

On the eve of the show there was a late entry, which seemed to indicate that the depth of the problem was beginning to be understood. It was the eponymous Victor, an all-steel saloon with the Briggs body, 'devoid of all unnecessary trimmings' as the *Motor* put it. It was offered with the 1½-litre engine as well as the disinterred Nine horsepower engine.

Losing those trimmings meant that the 1½-litre Victor could be priced at £299, considerably cheaper than the other Rileys on offer.

By 1937 Victor Riley, suffering badly from a duodenal ulcer and ordered to take six months off, was casting around for someone to save the company, now sliding into debt – production for the 1937/8 model year was to be only around 1,250 cars.

He tried Triumph, their neighbours in Foleshill, but they had severe problems of their own as their Dolomite range was losing money on every car sold. Like Riley and the Victor, they introduced a cheaper version to try to save the day. This was the 12 at £285, a

Dolomite without Walter Belgrove's famous waterfall grille. But they slid into the hands of the receiver in 1939 and were sold to Thomas W. Ward, the Sheffield engineering company, who sold the company on to Standard in 1944.

## The BMW connection

Riley had already been involved in major discussions with BMW, through the intermediary of the Aldington brothers, owners of AFN Ltd, who had bought Frazer Nash and who had been importing BMWs since the mid-1930s and re-badging them as 'Frazer Nash–BMW'.

There seemed to be what is now called a synergy between BMW and Riley. They had a similar culture and philosophy in the production of sporting cars.

There has been some suggestion that the Aldingtons, who held the BMW licensing rights for the UK, but had only small-scale production facilities where they made their own chain-drive Frazer Nashes, had proposed in 1936 that Riley should make the new BMW Type 326 six-cylinder 1971cc saloon under licence in Coventry[1].

Most of this model's four-door steel bodies were built by Ambi-Budd in Berlin and there several different styles followed: the 320/1, a two-door short-chassis saloon; the 327 – with

*The RMA was based on the pre-war Continental close-coupled saloon.*

two-seater coupé or convertible body – some by Autenrieth – and the 328, a sports two-seater with a highly-tuned engine.

The plan to manufacture under licence came to nothing, as did a later scheme to put the Riley 12 horsepower engine into a BMW chassis with a production rate of 5,000 per year, which could have led to BMW's light chassis being used with Riley's highly developed engines, particularly the Sprite, the 1½-litre twin carburettor unit that powered the 1935 and 1936 TT winner.

Later still, Victor proposed putting bodies built by their Midland Motor Bodies company onto BMW chassis. According to Nick Walker's excellent *A–Z of British Coachbuilders*: 'The only known example of a non-Riley body escaping from MMB is a single Frazer Nash-BMW', which suggests that serious thought was given to the proposal, but not for long, for in 1937, as Riley's woes deepened, there seems to have been a suggestion for a merger between Riley and BMW.

Much was discussed; BMW management came to Coventry and examined the Foleshill factory, and Victor went to Munich with his wife, Dorothy Champney, a former member of the Riley rally team. She was given a BMW to go sightseeing while Victor was taken around the factory.

His son, also called Victor, recalled for me that his father had told him that he was shown all over the works, apart from what was behind one locked door. It was said that only permission from Adolf Hitler would have enabled it to be opened for him[2]. Mightily offended by this, as he had shown the Germans everything at his works in Coventry, Victor senior left for home immediately, firing off a letter to the British Government on his return, warning of the possibility of war.

A few years ago Victor junior asked Bernd Pischetsrieder, then head of BMW and architect of the BMW takeover of the Rover group, whether there was any documentary trace of the unsuccessful attempt at a merger. None was found then and I have subsequently approached Herr Walter Zeichner of the BMW archive in Munich, who told me that there is no documentary evidence of it at all. It seems whatever existed was probably lost in wartime. The other curious aspect to the BMW connection is that nearly seventy years after Victor's visit, they actually own the name Riley, which came as part of the dowry of the Rover takeover.

What has all this to do with RMs? Victor might not have been enamoured of the Germans, but he certainly liked their cars and the RMs have definite overtones of the 1937 BMW 327, as we shall see.

## The end of the family firm

After attempts to find a buyer or a partner had failed, the family seems to have given up and in February of 1938, Lloyd's Bank forced Riley into receivership and for six months the factory struggled on assembling cars from parts already in hand. Production then halted completely and the Foleshill factory with its 700 feet long assembly hall began to be cleared of anything that was not bolted down, to raise cash for the receiver, Sir William Peat.

When Lord Nuffield, that inveterate snapper-up of bankrupt firms, bought the business in September 1938, he paid £143,000 of his own money for it. His biographer's version of the conversation on the stairs quotes him as putting the proposal thus: 'I think the best way out of your difficulties Victor, is for me to buy you out.' However, Nuffield, despite his philanthropy, was no altruist when it came to business and there was no place for any of the other Riley brothers on the board, or for Victor's Autovia that subsided into liquidation after making no more than about thirty-five cars; it was taken over by the London distributor Jimmy James and then wound up.

It's said that Nuffield wanted Riley so that no-one else could have it – given that in someone else's hands it could be a direct competitor to his MG cars – though there was not exactly a queue of buyers for a failed

*For the 1938 season, the close-coupled Continental body was offered on the new 2½-litre chassis. This car, chassis 38 BX 1240, was bought in March 1938, after the receiver had taken over.* Via R. Cameron

car company. But he did promise to preserve 'in every way the development of those characteristics that have made the Riley car so outstanding'. A promise he was to keep as long as he could.

Shortly afterwards, he sold Riley to his own Morris Motors Ltd for a nominal £1. The Nuffield Organization that Riley joined was an industrial giant, comprising Morris, Wolseley, MG, Morris-Commercial, Nuffield Tractors, SU Carburettors and various body and engine plants, that became known as Nuffield Products. Victor joined the board of directors.

Nuffield had rationalized all his many acquisitions into one group in 1935, but the main holding company since 1937 had been Morris Motors Ltd, which is where all the decisions relating to Riley were taken from now on. The headed notepaper of Riley Motors had a line underneath 'Proprietors: Morris Motors Ltd'. The company was, for the time being, in safe engineering hands; after all there was a saying that Mr Morris used three bolts where Mr Austin used two, though on the other side of the coin was the saying that Mr Austin designed and built cars, Mr Morris assembled them from other people's parts.

The Nuffield take-over led to two additional benefits: it ended the family bickering that had enervated the company in its declining years and restored some certainty to the staff at Durbar Avenue.

## The Nuffield Rileys

Even before the Nuffield takeover, as we have seen, Riley had begun rationalizing production to reduce the surfeit of models and this continued further when Morris Motors took charge. At the 1938 Motor Show samples were on show of what the public could expect from Riley under new ownership, a 1½-litre Twelve and 2½-litre Sixteen saloon and drophead, probably decided upon even before the takeover.

By the time serious production began early in 1939, the cars were rather different and had more of the Riley individuality that had been suggested in the early examples, although they were over-bodied. In a six-month season the Twelve sold 750 units and the Sixteen about 115.

But because of complaints by enthusiasts that the new range was too bland, the works had to bring back the 2½-litre Blue Streak Kestrel. The Kestrel body appeared only on the 2½-litre chassis because it would not fit the 1½-litre's.

*The Big Four Kestrel for 1938, standing next to an RM, was one of Riley's outstanding sporting cars. It was capable of 75mph cruising and a maximum of 90–95mph. This six-light saloon was lower than the Continental and the instruction to reduce the height of the RM prototype was probably to align it with the Kestrel's sporting image.* Via R. Cameron

So there were now only seven models on two chassis, the Twelve and Sixteen whose steel bodies were based on the previous Adelphi. Standardization of Nuffield components began such as the use of SU carburettors rather than the Zenith. 'Cost-cutting', cried the enthusiasts, as the dynamo was driven by belt rather than from the front of the crankshaft, air cushions in the seats were replaced by springs and wire wheels were dropped in favour of disc wheels.

The Rotax distributor was replaced by a Lucas item and another casualty was the Luvax chassis lubrication system that was replaced with Silentbloc bushes. However, all these 1930s items were becoming old-fashioned and would have gone in any event after the war.

Another disappearance was that of the preselector gearbox on the Twelve. Again, this was becoming redundant anyway as synchromesh was doing away with the terrible graunchings of the inexperienced using crash gearboxes. The options now were a manual Wolseley gearbox with a Borg and Beck clutch and something that prefigured an option on the Pathfinder fifteen years later – a gearbox with overdrive that cut in at between 38 and 42mph (61–68km/h). This was an option on the 12hp but standard on the 16hp.

Midland Motor Bodies, where the ash-framed aluminium Riley bodies were made, had also crashed – the last new bodies made there in 1938 were for the RM's predecessor, the Continental Touring Saloon of which some 150 were mounted on 1½-litre chassis[3].

The Nuffield bodies, now steel rather than aluminium, were made at the Morris Motors body plant at Quainton Road, Coventry, where MG bodies were put together. Vernon Barker, who has made a study of pre-war Rileys, thinks that the subsequent RM bodies were actually better built by Morris than they would have been by Midland Motor Bodies, as the basic construction was heavier and the ash frames were better.

The new range was not universally welcomed, even in the Foleshill works. 'They were one of the worst series of Rileys we ever built,' the-then service manager Arnold Farrar once told motoring writer Jon Pressnell. 'They weren't particularly reliable and they looked bloody awful' – thus the decision to bring back the Kestrel body. Some people referred to the Nuffield cars scornfully as Wolseleys and they are probably the least-loved of all Rileys.

*Motor* magazine had a different view: 'one of the finest cars to emanate from the Riley factory' it said at the time of the new Twelve. When the Sixteen began production in the summer of 1939, *Autocar* described it as 'a remarkable car – every inch a Riley in conception and individuality'. Despite the lowering clouds of war, the

British motor industry produced 341,000 cars in 1939, Nuffield contributing around 105,000. But not many of these were Rileys, as the Nuffield versions had hardly begun production before war broke out and in 1940 the Foleshill factory switched to making aircraft components.

The best guess – since all the production records were lost in the war – is that some 150 1½-litres and around thirty-five 2½-litres, or Big Four Continentals as they were dubbed, were built before production stopped.

Cars made before the Nuffield takeover were the only 'real' Rileys, according to a noisy group of those who owned them, some of whose voices can still be registered today. Then again, as the Pathfinder took over from the RMF in 1953, came the same refrain in a different form, since the RMA to RMF series had now acquired the status of 'genuine' Rileys and the Pathfinder was seen as a usurper that

*Nuffield's staid 16hp saloon of July 1939 lost the sporting élan of the previous Rileys, though it did reach 81mph (130km/h) on test. The gearbox was standard four-speed rather than the previous three-speed with overdrive. Motor*

was, to all intents and purposes, a Wolseley and not deserving of consideration.

In truth, this snobbery matters little to the post-war Riley enthusiast. Despite being built by a vast corporation, the RM cars are out-standingly good in many ways in design and engineering, a logical extension of the brilliant work done by the family in Coventry in the 1920s and 1930s.

There is a theory that had Victor Riley managed to hang on financially until 1939, the family firm would have recovered and pros-pered, thanks to the huge amount of war work that was to come the way of the Foleshill

factory. Many rocky enterprises of the 1930s were 'saved by the gun' when awarded War Office contracts, though a tale exists that Riley refused all profits from their First World War contracts.

But had Nuffield not saved the company late in 1938, at a time of great economic and political uncertainty, it is almost certain that yet another pre-war car manufacturer would have gone to the wall; Percy's PR head would be a pre-war memory; the Big Four engine, painstakingly developed in 1936–37, would probably have been lost forever and the RM series would never have existed.

### RM Rileys – a quick guide

| | | |
|---|---|---|
| RMA 1½-litre | four-door saloon | 1945–52 |
| RMB 2½-litre | four-door saloon | 1946–52 |
| RMC 2½-litre | two-door roadster | 1948–50 |
| RMD 2½-litre | two-door drophead coupé | 1948–50 |
| RME 1½-litre | four-door saloon | 1952–55 |
| RMF 2½-litre | four-door saloon | 1952–53 |
| RMH Pathfinder 2½-litre | four-door saloon | 1953–57 |

The RM series of cars were hardly ever called that when they were being made, and certainly not by the public. The categorization of RM for Riley Motors, and a following letter, was not introduced until after 1952 when the Nuffield and Austin empires were merged into the British Motor Corporation. It was used as a convenient way of delineating the cars for works purposes.

When they were being designed, the works followed the pre-war nomenclature of 12 horsepower for the 1½-litre and 16 horsepower for the 2½-litre, and indeed the first description of the 1½-litre by *Motor* in Feb-ruary 1946 described it as 'A New Riley Twelve'. By the time the larger-engined model was announced in November of that year it was described as being the 2½-litre and the Twelve became known in publicity and reviews as the 1½-litre.

However, the works continued to call them the Twelve and Sixteen chassis in documents as late as June 1947.

These rather boring appellations were a hangover from the Nuffield era just before the war. Until then, when Riley had been family-owned, the factory had always been very inventive in naming the cars, using no fewer than thirty-two.

The cars were largely named after birds – Kestrel, Gamecock, Falcon, Grebe and so on – and after places – Edinburgh, Grangeworth, Adelphi and even Foleshill – the area in Coventry where the Riley factory was situated in Durbar Avenue. Imp, Sprite, Victor and MPH were others.

A correspondent to *Motor* in the 1950s didn't like the RMA being called the Riley 1½-litre, because this was too much of a mouthful. A name like Merlin would be better, he announced.

Arnold Farrar often expressed his annoyance at the use of the names RMC and RMD; he pointed out that these had never been issued by the drawing offices at Coventry or Abingdon, but had come much later from Longbridge, the BMC headquarters, known in those days as the Kremlin.

Today's post-war Riley owners have adopted wholeheartedly the RM classification when talking of their cars, because it is much simpler than trying to explain which particular version of the chassis they are talking about.

**The life of Riley**

| 1896 | Riley Cycle Company |
|---|---|
| 1903 | Riley Engine Company |
| 1912 | Riley (Coventry) Ltd – set up to supply road wheels to 233 manufacturers |
| 1913 | Riley Motor Manufacturing Company – became Midlands Motor Bodies Ltd |
| 1916 | Nero Engine Company |
| 1918 | Riley (Coventry) Ltd |
| 1938 | Riley (Coventry) Successors – part of the Nuffield Corporation |
| 1940 | Riley (Coventry) Ltd |
| 1948 | Riley Motors Ltd |

After the BMC merger in 1951, it became the Riley Motors division of BMC, which disappeared in 1969 when BMC merged with Leyland to become the British Leyland Motor Corporation – BLMC.

The remarkable Riley brothers divided up their responsibilities between them:

| Victor Riley | salesman and business manager – eldest son – died 1958 aged 82. |
|---|---|
| Percy Riley | engineering genius, Riley Engine Co. – died 1941 aged 58. |
| Stanley Riley | chassis design and development – died 1952 aged 67. |
| Allan Riley | coachbuilder, Midland Motor Bodies – died 1963 aged 83. |
| Cecil Riley | export salesman, personal assistant to Victor, organized Riley Motor Club – died 1961 aged 66. |

Victor Riley's son, also Victor, is the current president of the Riley Motor Club, founded by the factory in 1925. The first issue of its magazine the *Riley Record*, was in November 1927 and it built a very successful reputation as a source of factory information on all things Riley until May 1950, when it was merged with the Nuffield publication *Motoring*, that covered all its marques. The *Record* though was revived and continues to be published as the magazine of the Riley Motor Club.

*Riley mottoes*

| | *First used* |
|---|---|
| *The King of Cars* | 1919 |
| *As Old as the Industry* | 1920 |
| *As Old as the Industry – As Modern as the Hour* | 1925 |
| *Magnificent Motoring* | 1945 |

1. BMW's superb six-cylinder engine, designed in 1936 by Rudolph Schleicher, had overtones of Percy's designs – a hemi head with opposed valves, though driven by a single rather than two camshafts. The exhaust valves on the opposite side to the camshaft were driven by transverse pushrods. This unit powered sporting BMWs until 1941 and after the engine came to Britain as part of wartime reparations, it was the mainstay of Bristol production until 1961.

2. The secrecy was connected with BMW's aero engine research and manufacture that was mainly based in Munich and where the engines for Focke-Wulf were being developed. BMW cars were made at a plant at Eisenach in eastern Germany, that later fell into the Soviet bloc after the war. The management at Eisenach had to change the name of their cars to EMW (Eisenacher Motorenwerke) and change the colour on the famous spinning badge from blue and white to red and white.

3. In 1938 the body was transferred to a different chassis and called the Close Coupled Saloon, which was only in 2½-litre form.

# 2    Into production

A New world and a New Riley – the car that is as Old as the Industry and as Modern as the Hour. That reputation will not be sullied when the days of peace return.

Riley advertisement 1943

When the war ended in 1945 there was a huge demand for new cars, which the motor industry was totally unable to meet. Although cars had been produced for the war effort by the British motor industry – more than 7,000 for the army alone – almost all productive capacity had been switched to making munitions and war materials, the country was broke and there was no steel.

But decisions on what sort of Rileys would be produced after the war were taken long before it ended and work had started even before hostilities began. However, the team in Durbar Avenue that had been developing Rileys together for years could not have known as they began their preliminary work for what was to become the RM series that it would be six years or so until their designs became metal.

Just like the 1939/40 model years, there would be Twelve and Sixteen horsepower cars. The Twelve would be in production first followed by the Sixteen and the new series would be an organic development of what had come before.

There were probably several prototypes and mock-ups. This version, with a Warwickshire registration number of the early 1930s, has a small badge on the radiator and a tiny badge on the starting handle plug. The horn grille was fortunately deleted.

Teasing advertisements appeared during the war like this one illustrated with a picture of a pre-war Six light saloon:

> The new Riley will be a new chassis, new body, yet to a degree the new Riley will be old; old inasmuch as those characteristics which made the Riley famous, superb performance and roadholding, with inherent quality will remain to give 'MAGNIFICENT MOTORING'.

The two pre-war Nuffield models were essentially stop-gaps; the new cars would have extra features, like independent front suspension that had been tested in 1937. The same production team probably started work in earnest in 1943. There is a belief that work on civilian car projects was not allowed during the war, but if this were the case, the regulation was widely avoided. Alec Issigonis and Jack Daniels for instance began work in 1942 on the Mosquito project that was to become the post-war Morris Minor.

The final development of Riley prototypes like EXP 12 had started by the autumn of 1944 under the direction of the chief designer Harry Rush and the chassis was probably put on one of the spare pre-war Kestrel bodies that had survived at Durbar Avenue.

The mock-up and prototypes had differing rear wings, headlamps, rear number plate, horn grilles and bumpers. There were four pre-production models, run mostly at night, but testing was greatly curtailed by the shortage of petrol.

Unlike almost all other British manufacturers, who staggered into production with slightly warmed-over versions of their pre-war offerings, the 1945 Riley was to look fresh and new, with a sleek low-slung body, largely because many of the jigs and drawings had been lost in the bombing of Coventry, and a new start had to be made.

Had the pre-war jigs been used from the 12hp, a tubby little car by comparison, the RMA would have been 4in (100mm) higher, 8in (200mm) shorter and have a wheelbase of 9ft (2,740mm) rather than 9ft 4in (2,860mm).

The only other brand-new car that year came from Armstrong Siddeley, of Parkside,

*The rear view has different profiles in each rear wing, a wider boot with an over-elaborate boot handle and protruding filler caps.*

*No door handles yet, but apart from the clumsy fuel filler cap, it's almost there.*

Coventry, makers heretofore of staid saloons, who astounded the motoring world by producing the Lancaster, a streamlined saloon of swooping lines that was announced the day after the war in Europe ended in May 1945. The Lancaster was followed shortly afterwards by the Hurricane drophead coupé and the Typhoon fixed-head – all of which created a styling sensation.

A marvel they might have been – Armstrong-Siddeley had worked on the design throughout the war years – but unlike the Riley engineering team they had not got their sums right and the underpowered 16 horsepower cars soon became known as the 'gutless wonders' until an 18 horsepower engine was substituted.

The month after the Lancaster's announcement, the Government began easing restrictions on the motor industry, now that it could be turned from war-work to producing cars again. The Board of Trade and Ministry of Supply sanctioned 200,000 cars to be built by the entire British motor industry in the following twelve months – and decreed that 50 per cent would have to go to overseas buyers. This figure was to go up to 75 per cent as the economic situation worsened.

The government were able to do this because they controlled the supply of steel that was to be rationed to car manufacturers, whose further steel supplies depended on how successful they were at exporting. The country was broke after a long war; 'export or die' became the watchword.

## The first press viewing

The first 1½-litre was shown to the motoring press in August 1945, before production began. It was a curious foretaste of the car, for the *Motor* and *Autocar* were not allowed to describe many of the new features of what they called 'the New Riley Twelve' when they reported on their afternoon with the car. There was not a proper road test, more of a genteel drive supervised by Victor Leverett, the sales manager. The only pictures they were able to use were publicity shots from Riley.

'There are a great many details of special interest in the construction', said the *Autocar*, 'but it is desired by the makers to withhold them until such time as cars are actually coming off the production line.'

Whatever the reason for this decision it was good for publicity purposes, as it ensured two lots of publicity in the motoring magazines – one for the announcement and another six months later for the description of the 'special features'.

But the *Autocar* was ecstatic at even a brief ride in the car. It described the performance as truly remarkable; 'the way this car can be taken round curves is astonishing. Not many racing cars would do better.' The Girling brakes were 'a revelation', being exceptionally smooth and powerful.

Then perhaps thinking that all this praise was a bit over the top, *Autocar* went on: 'Denied as one has been for so long the experience of trying out a new car, there may be a tendency to be over-enthusiastic but we feel that a similar verdict will come from every other experienced driver who handles this car'.

As it did from *Motor*, which praised the fine combination of highly accurate steering with unusually comfortable suspension. 'A car for the discriminating', it proclaimed, with spacious coachwork and 'abnormal luggage accommodation' – meaning that the boot was deceptively spacious by the standards of the day.

Though not all was rosy, as the 'general level of murmurous sound' seemed rather high.

But all in all, it was a car that not only justified, but inspired enthusiasm and was able 'to lighten the life of a motoring journalist' – praise indeed from this depressed class of hacks, who were not to be given any further information for another six months, when they were given a full description and allowed a brief run near the Coventry factory.

Production was due to start at the end of September 1945, but then only in tiny quantities until prototype testing had been completed. It is unlikely that the prototypes had production chassis numbers and the run began at 36S 10001. It seems that only eight cars were built before the end of the year as the first chassis of 1946 was 36S 10009, according to the contemporary *Glass's Guide*.

The first car, 36S 10001, may well have been running on trade plates for a while since it was not registered in Coventry as FRW 458 until August 1946 (this is why the chassis number is 36S rather than 35S. In those days *Glass's Guide* gave the chassis numbers in addition to other details and there are other instances where chassis numbers were overstamped when the year changed before registration).

This first RM was sold by the Park Gate Garage in Coventry and broken for parts in the 1960s. The other known car produced in 1945, 35S 10005, was registered in Essex as KHK 163 in December of that year.

For most of the public avid for a sight of the new Riley there was a wait until the summer of 1946 when the first RMAs were seen in Jimmy James's showroom in 55–56 Pall Mall in London.

In October 1945 Victor took a 1½-litre to Glasgow and back for a proving run. The journey of nearly 700 miles (1,125km) went well other than his sense of frustration due to the tyres. These were synthetic as rubber had been almost unobtainable since supplies were cut after the fall of Malaya and Singapore in June 1942.

'Dunlops tell me that their synthetic tyres should not be driven at higher speeds than 50mph' he wrote afterwards to Miles Thomas. 'Until something better is available, we shall be in the unfortunate position of putting a car into owners' hands that is crying out to be driven faster.'

Nevertheless, on the return journey of 330 miles (530km) he averaged 44mph (71km/h), but destroyed one of the tyres in the process.

Production was painfully slow. In January 1946, the factory produced only a handful of cars; the records describe them as being five Twelve horsepower saloons and one Sixteen horsepower saloon – the first 2½-litre, which was undergoing its first road test.

By April 1946, Nuffield alone had orders for more than 100,000 cars; 4,000 of them were for Rileys. The difficulty was that although Victor planned to build 7,000 cars in the first year of post-war production, he had materials for only 2,000.

There was to be no London Motor Show that year; the Society of Motor Manufacturers and Traders decided that it would 'seriously interfere with production' as all the factories were going as fast as they could to 'export or die'. By October 1946, exports had doubled compared with pre-war figures and exceeded the Government's targets by 175 per cent.

However, just as normality began to return, a succession of blows struck British manufacturing. The winter of 1947 was one of the coldest on record; huge amounts of snow fell for weeks in the snowiest winter since 1814; the railways came to a standstill, there was an acute shortage of coal, power stations ran out of fuel leading to massive electricity cuts. 'The whole country is in the grip of a coal shortage', wrote Miles Thomas, 'and it is rather like a car that has run out of petrol. Until somebody has walked to the garage and back with a two-gallon can, we cannot get going again.'

Car production stopped altogether in some places, in others the industry went on a three-day week. When the extreme cold finally ended in March, there was a very slow return to production, and Riley, like other manufacturers, was bedevilled by a lack of steel. There was also a considerable amount of industrial unrest that added to the problems.

The only bright spot in that gloomy spring was the Geneva Motor Show in March, the

---

### Victor's demise

Victor Riley joined on the board of Morris Motors Ltd two other men who had sold out to Nuffield – Carl Skinner of SU Carburettors and Harold Ryder of Osberton Radiators, both of whom had done well out of their struggling companies being taken over.

Skinner's name was in his firm's title – it stood for Skinner Union carburettors; one of the original Skinners was one of the Lilley and Skinner shoe family, but he and his brother Herbert, who invented the variable jet, were more interested in mechanics than footwear. The family sold out to Morris in 1926.

Pre-war Rileys had used Solex and Zenith as well as SU Carburettors, but one effect of the Nuffield takeover was that all RMs, like all Nuffield cars, were fitted with SUs as standard.

Ryder's firm was named after Osberton Road in Oxford where it was based in a former skating rink. Morris swallowed it up in 1923; it eventually became Morris Radiators and with SU went on, of course, to supply Riley and send millions of units to the other parts of the empire of Nuffield and his successors.

Riley, Skinner and Ryder lasted on the board until the winter of 1947. An increasingly eccentric and cantankerous Nuffield, now in his seventies and wearing Savile Row suits with the cheapest shirts he could buy, suddenly sacked nine directors, including his vice-chairman Miles Thomas, in a December boardroom purge.

Victor Riley, himself now in his seventies, was out after a lifetime dedicated to his family's business and its illustrious name. A Morris statement denied that there had been any disagreement. The reason was to increase centralization, reduce overheads and encourage younger staff. 'Lord Nuffield's objective is to produce cars as cheaply as possible to increase export sales to the utmost.'

The Morris Motors minutes of that meeting record that Victor Riley 'retired with the sum of £6,000' (£150,000 at 2004 prices) because of 'the premature determination (sic) of his contract of service with the company.'

The *Riley Record*, the factory motor club publication, saw it rather differently: 'After almost exactly 50 years, VR as he is affectionately known, has decided that the time has come to take things a little more easily.'

Victor had to wait a long time for his retirement presents, which suggests that he may well have continued to take some part in Riley matters. It was not until two years later, in 1949, that the staff got around to presenting him with a silver-plated model of an RMA, and his present from the factory, now Abingdon rather than Coventry, in 1952, was a real 1½-litre, MUC 250, that still survives, as does his wife's 1946 RMA, FHP 720.

It is thought that Nuffield got rid of the directors because he wanted to exert his authority over the business again as he believed they all had too much freedom, particularly Thomas. By that time the former William Morris, bicycle maker, was styling himself in the company's annual report as the Viscount Nuffield, GBE, FRS, MA, DCL, Ll.D.

However, rather than taking control he began losing his grip, which is why the so-called merger with Austin into BMC in 1952 was effectively an Austin takeover by the aggressive Len Lord, which began the demise of Riley as a distinctive force in the British motor industry.

---

*The frontal styling is even more reminiscent of the BMW 327 than the subsequent RMA in this picture given to the press. Apart from the changes to the lighting, there are no bonnet locks and no side jacking points. There's also nowhere to put the petrol and no rear-view mirror.*

first international show to be held since the end of the war. There were sixty-two entrants, twenty-five of them British, among them Riley who showed the 1½-litre and 2½-litre to wide acclaim.

In August 1947, Victor Riley went to a meeting with Government ministers at the Society of Motor Manufacturers and Traders' headquarters in London. The meeting was to try to define the shape of post-war car production. The Government tried to insist that each manufacturer produce only one model, but Victor was having none of it. He told them that the works at Foleshill was capable of producing 7,500 cars a year, but he could not get the steel to make them.

'When plans were being laid for post-war production', he told them, 'it was decided that the highest degree of efficiency would be obtained by producing two models but using the largest number of parts and components common to both.' And so it was.

Production began to build up again after the summer holidays of 1947 and in late September the Foleshill works produced 100 cars in a

week for the first time. 'Congratulations,' wrote Thomas to Victor Riley.

Production then was running at seventy-five 1½-litres to twenty-five 2½-litres a week and Foleshill continued to turn out whatever number of cars it could with the available steel. In the last week of October 1947, for instance, there were sixty 1½-litres and twenty-five 2½-litres produced.

It was not just steel that was in short supply; sometimes the leather for seating could not be found and some cars were built with Bedford Cord instead of hide on some upholstery panels.

A large demand had been created for the RMA by the excellent reviews it had received once the motoring magazines were able to do proper testing, though curiously the major tests did not appear until the autumn of 1947, while those for the 2½-litre had appeared in the spring.

Harold Hastings of *Light Car* tested the 1½-litre twice in 1947. One of the outstanding post-war designs, he noted, although not the smoothest or the most silent.

'It just asks to be driven hard, to be accelerated briskly in its gears, to be taken around corners in a way that would be foolish in some cars and downright suicidal on others, and to be allowed to cruise swiftly and effortlessly in all conditions.' His verdict was that this was a car that would delight the enthusiast.

Bill Boddy (RM Club honorary member) of *Motor Sport* was given one to test but returned it because a valve was sticking. He was not offered it again, something he was still complaining about in 1970.

Both *Autocar* and *Motor* also published full road tests in the autumn of 1947 (*see* table below). Considering that it was the same car, with the tests appearing within a week of each other, there were obvious discrepancies. The *Motor* test appears to give substantially higher acceleration and top speed figures, but if these are compared with a later test of an RMA by the same magazine in 1949, it seems that the first figures were an aberration. However, it has to be said that road testing in the 1940s was not the scientific discipline it is today, particularly in terms of metrology, and the quality of petrol available was highly inconsistent.

The last pre-war figures for the RMA's predecessor, the Nuffield 12hp, with essentially the same engine, are included as a comparison in the table; given that the weight of both cars was similar, there is not a great deal of difference between them.

Had the road testers been lavishly wined, dined and bribed, they could hardly have written more ecstatic reviews than those that appeared in October 1947. 'A very high opinion indeed has been formed of this car,' said *Autocar*, '...well-designed and honestly and soundly built, which should give an owner excellent service and which has such qualities as to lift motoring far above the plane of transport alone.' Whilst in these ethereal realms, it praised everything to do with the car – except the under-dash handbrake – and bemoaned the lack of a sunroof. A standard-type sunroof was to be offered later by Weathershields, while the coach-builders Tickford advertised a full-length sun roof rather like that of the Bedford Vega coach.

*Motor* didn't like the handbrake either, and while more down-to-earth than its rival, gave lavish praise to the car's tireless performance, excellent road-holding and didn't want to hand the keys back: 'There was a distinct feeling of parting with a friend.'

*Motor Sport* – again in GHP 179 – had problems with a sticking exhaust valve and thought the steering heavy and flabby, but again road-holding and performance were outstanding.

## In huge demand

The pent-up demand for the RMA vastly exceeded the supply available. Miles Thomas wished he had not so many friends and acquaintances. 'Every time I take my dog for a walk', he wrote to Victor, 'I am importuned by a Mr Harris who has an order for a 1½-litre from the Shire Motor Company of Banbury. Can you do anything about it?' This was 1947; Mr Harris would have to wait another four months at least.

The Thomas files are full of pleading letters from people desperate for Rileys – old acquaintances, wartime colleagues, serving officers and diplomatic staff who wanted to jump the queue.

|  | *Autocar* **Oct 1947** | *Motor* **Oct 1947** | *Motor* **June 1949** | *Motor* **12hp 1939** |
|---|---|---|---|---|
|  | GHP 179 | GHP 179 | HVC 16 | DKV 433 |
| 0–30 (sec) | 7.8 | 6.0 | 7.6 | 7 |
| 0–60 (sec) | 31.2 | 25.1 | 32.6 | 29.7 |
| Top speed | 74mph (119km/h) | 78mph (125km/h) | 80.4mph (129km/h) | 73.61mph (118km/h) |

ABOVE: *An early drawing of the driver's view in the RMA, substantially unchanged until the square instruments were introduced. Only the first forty or so cars had white knobs.*

LEFT: *Riley had a cavalier attitude to publicity pictures and brochures. This car displays features that did not make it into production, such as drilled wheels, faired-in sidelamps and small driving lamps. It was issued nearly a year after the car had been announced.*

## Horsepower

Rileys before the RMs had always been identified by their horsepower – as in the Nine, Twelve and Sixteen. In fact in 1946, the names Twelve and Sixteen were still being used in the factory to designate the RMs as they were built. Austin used such names until 1949.

These figures bore no relation to the real brake horsepower – the Riley Twelve hp or 1½ litre actually developed 54bhp at 4,500rpm. It was an entirely artificial construct known as the RAC or Treasury rating that the Government used to tax vehicles, for instance at a rate of £1 per horsepower per year.

The figure was arrived at by an arcane mathematical exercise of multiplying the diameter of the cylinder in millimetres squared by the total number of cylinders and then dividing by 1,613. This formula had been used since 1910; the French used a different calculation which is why the *traction avant*, from which the Riley borrowed its front suspension, was an 11 Light in France and a Light Fifteen in Britain.

The advantage of the system for British motorists was that it was much cheaper for tax purposes to use this rating than the real bhp rating and it encouraged the development of long-stroke engines, which meant high output from narrow cylinder bores and thus low tax.

For instance the Riley 1½-litre engine – a pre-war design – still had a stroke of 100mm while the Magnette engine of similar size, designed much later, had a stroke of 89mm.

Long-stroke engines are not very efficient compared with engines of the same capacity that have the short-stroke, large-bore configuration that is now universal.

The Treasury rating system was abandoned in 1948, though the use of horsepower figures in model names – this time in alleged real bhp figures – lingered on until the late 1960s in the Riley 4/72.

Except that although the 4 figure was correct for the number of cylinders, it was only 68bhp rather than 72 and the 4/68 that preceded it didn't even have 68 but only 66.5bhp. BMC could always win prizes for obfuscation.

They were nearly all to be disappointed, but some people got better treatment than others.

A son of the newspaper magnate Lord Kemsley wanted a Riley for his step-sister – she didn't even mind which model. 'As it is for a lady, I should say that the 1½-litre would be adequate', Thomas wrote to Victor, a sentiment that would find little favour today. It helped that Kemsley was a very good customer of Morris, from whom he ordered fleets of vans for newspaper deliveries.

Thomas, who had the pick of Nuffield production for his own car, chose a Riley 2½-litre and as a director of the company he was able to get 22½ per cent off the price.

'Over the weekend the Marquess of Blandford had a run in (it) and liked it very much', Thomas wrote in August 1947. One was ordered from Hartwells of Oxford.

But the marquess would have to wait as he had just taken delivery of a 1½-litre and under regulations introduced by the motor trade in 1946 to prevent a black market in new cars, owners had to sign a covenant that they would not sell within 12 months.

Breaking this covenant, that lasted with modifications until 1950, would lead to the marquess having to cough up liquidated damages of £410. However, there is a twist to the tale: Arnold Farrar recalled that Lord Blandford's RMA had been fitted with a 2½-litre badge. Who was he trying to impress?

This shortage of new cars lasted into the 1950s and pushed up second-hand prices to dizzy levels. For instance, a new 1½-litre in 1951 was £1,168 including tax. In June that year *Motor* advertised examples of the RMA car at £1,525, £1,495 and even a 1947 model at £1,100.

Miles Thomas's first 2½-litre was FHP 857, that was soon replaced by another, GHP 440; both had been passed on to him by Victor Riley, presumably factory cars, judging by their Coventry registration, that he had then bought.

### The works

William, father of the famous five Riley brothers, had, like many car makers, started by making bicycles in the nineteenth century before moving on to cars and then to patent detachable wheels, which were a big success. He decided that there was more money in wheels than cars, so the brothers Riley began their own car manufacturing business.

The factory from which the first Riley RMs emerged was in Durbar Avenue, Foleshill, Coventry. Riley chassis had been made there since 1916, when Stanley Riley, the chassis expert, established the Nero Engine Company to build a four-cylinder 10hp car that he had designed.

In Aldbourne Road were Percy's enterprise the Riley Engine Company and the Riley Motor Manufacturing Company run by Allan, which supplied bodywork for the cars; it was later renamed Midland Motor Bodies Ltd. In 1931, production was rationalized when both firms were taken over by Riley (Coventry) Ltd and the Foleshill works was expanded to cater for export production.

When Victor Riley sold out to Nuffield, Percy thought he had lost his engine business, but unknown to him it had been bought for £500 from the receiver by his friend the Coventry machine tool magnate Alfred Herbert, who presented it to him.

Percy renamed it P.R. Motors Ltd. He had intended to produce a small car, but died in 1941, by which time the firm was engaged in war work. Afterwards, the firm, now headed by his wife, Norah, began producing transmission systems, notably for dump trucks. The family connection ended in 1966 when it became part of Newage Engineers Ltd. The firm make a market-leading marine gearbox under the name of PRM Newage.

The works at Durbar Avenue was damaged during the war. Post-war Riley production there ended in 1949 with the move to Abingdon. The works then became Morris Motors Engines branch. It is now a Unipart warehouse.

After Pathfinder production stopped at Abingdon in 1957, the factory continued to turn out MGs and a few other BMC models until it was closed in 1980.

*The early side-exit exhaust was changed to a straight pipe exiting at the back. Body mounting points can be seen clearly in this shot.*
British Motor Industry Heritage Trust

BELOW: *The chassis line at Foleshill. Engines were dropped in by the hoist at the far end of the line.* British Motor Industry Heritage Trust

When he inherited GHP 440 it was a struggle to get the petrol coupons from Victor to run it – these being immensely valuable in this post-war period of shortages. Eventually they arrived – coupons for 174 gallons, that had to last six months. Given an average fuel consumption on the 2½-litre of around 20mpg (14ltr/100km), this would confine his travels to some 3,500 miles (5,630km). He complained of squeaking brakes and the factory replaced the Mintex linings with Ferodo.

Being unable to supply the home market was a constant source of worry for the sales manager, Victor Leverett. He knew that it was not only the management that was being badgered; Riley distributors were being besieged by desperate customers.

To provide answers for the sales staff, Victor wrote a series of specimen letters to himself, from a fictional John Smith of Old Bond Street, London, outlining the dilemmas that they might face. Writing back to Mr Smith on the vexed issue of who should get priority for the very few new cars available, Victor wrote:

> Some of the letters that come to my table are really pathetic, especially those from younger members of the medical fraternity just released from the forces, who in some cases, have no car at all. Some form of transport is absolutely essential to them to work up their practice and in my opinion they fully deserve priority.

There were of course some second-hand Rileys available as owners began re-commissioning them after a period propped up on blocks. But they sold at far beyond their original price. In 1939, the 16 horsepower Riley Touring Saloon, with twin SUs, retailed at £398. In February 1946, *Glass's Guide* put its second-hand price at £550. No wonder people wanted a new Riley.

By June 1948, Tom Sangster, who had taken over as sales manager after the death of Victor Leverett, was explaining to dealers that although a small proportion of cars had now been allotted to the home market, these would be built only when seasonal export demand had been satisfied.

However, this demand needs to be put into perspective. Motoring in the 1940s and early 1950s was largely an expensive middle-class pursuit. The working man and his family went by bus. Special trains took them to the seaside when factories closed for the summer holidays.

---

### Knickers, but no petrol

The Board of Trade added to the gaiety of the nation when the war ended by removing the ban on producing frilly knickers, though much more important was the restoration of a small petrol ration for the private motorist, who had not been able to get any since 1942.

Those who could prove the need for a car had always been able to get some petrol – dyed pink so that it would not be resold, though there were severe penalties for anyone using it for what was described by the government as 'pleasure motoring'.

There were no brands of petrol, only one-grade low-octane 'Pool', that could vary wildly in octane rating from 55 to 75. But the new ration soon came to an end. The vicious winter and dollar crisis of 1947 led to it being abolished in September of that year and it was not reinstated for another ten months and then at a ration of 90 miles a month. How frustrating for those very few lucky owners of the new Rileys, probably too upstanding to dabble in the black market where counterfeiting of ration coupons was rife and the price of a gallon was 12 shillings (equivalent to £18 today – £3.96/ltr).

Usual Riley club events were out of the question. 'Looking back on 1948,' wrote Arnold Farrar in the *Riley Record*, 'it has been a very difficult year from point of view (sic) of any motor club owing to the complete absence of any petrol for pleasure motoring in the first five months of the year.'

It was not until May 1950 that rationing was lifted – and there was then a steep rise in petrol tax.

# THE NEW  1½ LITRE SALOON

NEW body, new chassis embracing the lessons of the last five years. Built to Riley tradition, " as old as the industry . . . as modern as the hour," superb performance and road-holding, with inherent quality, blend to give *Magnificent Motoring.*

RILEY (COVENTRY) LIMITED, FOLESHILL, COVENTRY

*Bonnet locks and side jacking points are again missing in this 1946 advertisement.*

In 2003, government statistics showed that only 20 per cent of people lived in households without a car. In 1948, the proportion would have been reversed.

So of a small number of the population that could afford a car, the major demand was soaked up by the majors like Austin, Morris and Ford, leaving Riley and other makers to compete for business in a small market sector. That sector got even smaller when it was confined to the sporting saloon that was Riley's forte.

To assist new owners of the RMA, the *Sales and Service Bulletin* of May 1946 suggested that dealers should point out to them details that

'were not readily apparent'. These included: how to remove the small cap at the bottom of the radiator to insert the starting handle that was stowed under the rear seat; how to spring off the wheel discs; how to use the bonnet stay lock and where to find the chassis number (on the offside of the engine bulkhead) and the engine number (on the crankcase on the nearside of the engine just forward of the clutch housing).

It also showed how to use the jack and prefigured a very early change in the specification, the movement of the rear jacking points, from below the rear doors to a position under the overriders.

Some of the guidance to dealers from the *Sales and Service Bulletin* was as a result of experience. There were several accidents caused by owners not using the safety lock on the boot lid; those who failed to open both petrol caps when filling up were likely to get a faceful of petrol and there was some alarm in the service department when cars were brought in with tyre pressures of over 40lb per sq in (2.8kg/sq cm) rather than 22 front and 24 rear.

The RMA had had a very successful launch; demand was enormous as lovers of sporting cars clamoured for this exceptional car. The only problem was being able to get hold of one.

*The side jacking points, fully opening windscreen and side exhaust characterized the first few RMAs. This is Dave Thompson's beautifully kept EN 8601, which he has owned for decades.*

**Nuffield cars – specifications 1947**

| *Details* | *Riley* | *Morris* | *MG* | |
|---|---|---|---|---|
| | **1½-litre** | **8hp** | **10hp** | **TC** |
| BHP… | 55bhp | 29.6bhp | 37.2bhp | 54.4bhp |
| …at rpm | 4,500 | 4,400 | 4,600 | 5,200 |
| R.A.C. rating | 11.9hp | 8.057hp | 9.99hp | 10.97hp |
| Bore | 69mm | 57mm | 63.5mm | 66.5mm |
| Stroke | 100mm | 90mm | 90mm | 90mm |
| Cubic capacity | 1496cc | 918cc | 1140cc | 1250cc |
| Number of cylinders | 4 | 4 | 4 | 4 |
| Valves | OHV | SV | OHV | OHV |
| Number of main bearings | 3 | 3 | 3 | 3 |
| Pistons | Alloy | Alloy | Alloy | Alloy (Acrolite) |
| Piston rings | 4 | 3 | 4 | 4 |
| Connecting rods | Steel | Steel | Steel | Steel |
| Firing order | 1, 2, 4, 3 | 1, 3, 4, 2 | 1, 3, 4, 2 | 1, 3, 4, 2 |
| Sparking plugs | 14mm | 14mm | 14mm | 14mm |
| Carburettor | SU | SU | SU | Twin SU |
| Valve timing – | | | | |
| Inlet opens | 5deg early | 8deg early | 5deg early | 11deg early |
| Inlet closes | 55deg late | 50deg late | 45deg late | 57deg late |
| Exhaust opens | 60deg early | 52deg early | 45deg early | 52deg early |
| Exhaust closes | 20deg late | 20deg late | 5deg late | 24deg late |
| Tappet clearance – | | | | |
| Inlet (hot) | 0.003in (0.08mm) | 0.017in (0.43mm) | 0.019in (0.48mm) | 0.019in (0.48mm) |
| Exhaust (hot) | 0.004in (0.10mm) | 0.017in (0.43mm) | 0.019in (0.48mm) | 0.019in (0.48mm) |
| Clutch | Single dry | Single dry | Single dry | Single dry |
| Cooling | Pump/fan | Fan | Pump/fan | Pump/fan |
| Track (front) | 4ft 4¼in (1,327mm) | 3ft 8⅝in (1,133mm) | 4ft 2in (1,270mm) | 3ft 9in (1,143mm) |
| Track (rear) | 4ft 4¼in (1,327mm) | 3ft 10¼in (1,175mm) | 4ft 2in (1,270mm) | 3ft 9in (1,143mm) |
| Tyre size | 5.75 × 16 | 4.50 × 17 | 5.00 × 16 | 19 × 4.5 |
| Wheel size | 4.50 × 16 | 2.50 × 17 | 3.00 × 16 | 19 × 2.5 |
| Length | 14ft 11in (4,547mm) | 12ft 0in (3,658mm) | 13ft 2in (4,013mm) | 11ft 7½in (3,543mm) |
| Width | 5ft 3½in (1,613mm) | 4ft 8in (1,422mm) | 5ft 1in (1,549mm) | 4ft 8in (1,422mm) |
| Height | 4ft 11in (1,499mm) | 5ft 2in (1,575mm) | 5ft 5in (1,651mm) | 4ft 5in (1,346mm) |
| Ground clearance | 7½in (191mm) | 6⅜in (162mm) | 5¼in (133mm) | 6in (152mm) |
| Unladen weight | 24½cwt (1,245kg) | 15cwt (762kg) | 18cwt (914kg) | 15½cwt (787kg) |
| Petrol tank capacity | 12½gal (57ltr) | 5½gal (25ltr) | 7gal (32ltr) | 13½gal (61ltr) |
| Sump capacity | 8½pt (4.8ltr) | 5½pt (3.1ltr) | 5½pt (3.1ltr) | 10½pt (6ltr) |
| Gearbox capacity | 2pt (1.1ltr) | 1¼pt (0.7ltr) | 1¼pt (0.7ltr) | 1½pt (0.9ltr) |
| Rear axle capacity | 2¾pt (1.6ltr) | 1pt (0.6ltr) | 1½pt (0.9ltr) | 2pt (1.1ltr) |
| Cooling system capacity | 13pt (7.4ltr) | 15pt (8.5ltr) | 13pt (7.4ltr) | 14pt (8ltr) |
| Tyre pressure (front) | 22lb | 24lb | 23lb | 24lb |
| Tyre pressure (rear) | 24lb | 27lb | 25lb | 26lb |
| Battery voltage | 12V | 6V | 12V | 12V |
| Battery capacity | 59Ah | 51Ah | 50Ah | 51Ah |
| Turning circle LH | 30ft (9.1m) | 32ft 7in (9.9m) | 37ft 3in (11.4m) | 37ft (11.3m) |
| RH | 30ft (9.1m) | 35ft 1in (10.7m) | 39ft 1in (11.9m) | 37ft (11.3m) |
| Wheelbase | 9ft 4½in (2,858mm) | 7ft 5in (2,261mm) | 7ft 10in (2,388mm) | 7ft 10in (2,388mm) |

# 3 The 1½-litre RMA in detail

## The body

The genesis of the first RM body lay some ten years previous to its launch in the 1936 12/4 Touring Saloon, designed by Frank Hewitt. This was also referred to confusingly as the Close-coupled Saloon in official Riley parlance when it was mounted on a 16hp chassis in 1938. It was also unofficially known as the Continental, a name that would have been used had not Rolls-Royce registered the name 'Continental Touring Saloon', though Triumph seem not have been inhibited.

Nevertheless, in the works it was always known as the Continental, which has appeared scrawled on trim panels when the cars have been dismantled.

Close-coupled Saloon and Continental were generic pre-war coach-building terms that were used to describe cars whose occupants sat within the wheelbase, though when this became more usual when engines were moved forwards it came to mean a body shorter than usual.

It was a four-light saloon – that is, there were two windows each side – and it had a long

*The Continental body on which the RM coachbuilt bodies were based was first seen on the 1936 12/4. Imagine it with 1½in chopped off the height and with disc wheels, and the RM's lineage can clearly be seen. N. Trotman*

tail to give more luggage space, naturally, for touring. It also had considerably more luggage space compared to cars like the Kestrel, whose rear end came down at an angle of about 45 degrees directly behind the rear seat. However, because the spare wheel was in the boot, luggage room was still restricted compared with the RMA, which achieved much more space by putting the spare beneath the boot.

The body ran for one season on the 1½-litre 12 horsepower chassis but by the 1937 Motor Show it appeared on the 2½-litre Big Four, although it was not available to customers for some time afterwards.

The practice at Riley when a new model was being schemed was to overlay the new drawing over a previous model, so that the Riley ethos was maintained. In this case the RMA, drawn by stylist Bert Holmes, has many similarities to the pre-war car, particularly in the door shapes.

It was not just based on the Continental, it looked continental, with smooth sloping lines, a swooping tail, and headlights semi-recessed into the wings at a time when almost all British cars were square in shape with separate chromed headlamps mounted on the front wings.

The trend towards integrating headlamps had begun in Europe before the war with specialist coachbuilders like Letourneur et Marchand and Figoni et Falaschi building on chassis from makers like Delahaye and Delage. Britain's contribution to this movement was largely represented by the unhappy Singer Airflow of 1934–36 and the daring (for its time) Morris Eight Series E of 1938 with its fully integrated headlamps and waterfall grille.

The other similarity with the pre-war cars was the radiator – very like that of the last Kestrel, other than that the flutes were vertical in the Kestrel and bowed in the RMA.

*ABOVE: The bootlid was split, with the spare mounted inside the lower lid, which took up a lot of space. It also put some strain on the timbers and later it was relocated so that the load was taken by the chassis. N. Trotman*

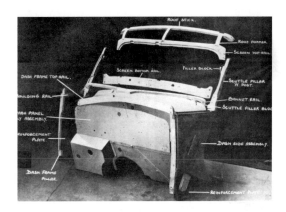

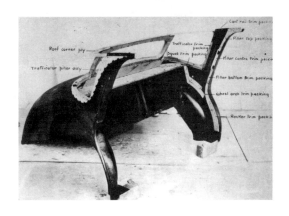

*RIGHT: Factory drawings showing the constituent parts of the wood framing, which was put together in a way that had not changed since the 1920s, or even before.*

ABOVE: *The body tub was then joined with the sills. The B-post on which the doors are hinged was steel rather than wood.*

*The BMW 327, announced in 1937, lent many frontal styling cues to the RM series, notably the headlight and sidelamp placings, quarter bumpers and the drilled wheels that appeared on the prototype RM but were not carried through into production. BMW Archiv*

## The prince of darkness

Riley suffered, as all car makers did at this time, from severe parts shortages as the component manufacturers were having to cope with the same difficulties as everyone else in obtaining material and keeping production going.

One of the major hold-ups to Riley production was caused by Joseph Lucas Ltd of Birmingham, suppliers of almost everything electrical on all British cars. The Riley's F700 headlamps, 1130A sidelamps, DKY4A distributors, RF 95 control box and all the other electrical bits and pieces – dynamos, starters, trafficators, windscreen wiper motors, batteries, horns – all came from a sole supplier, and if they had problems, production lines all over the Midlands came to a halt.

Though the Lucas emblem on its lighting boasted proudly of being 'King of the Road', a trademark established in 1878, the firm was often referred to by the sardonic as the 'Prince of Darkness', due to its unreliable products.

Miles Thomas, Nuffield's vice chairman, referred to the firm wryly in one memo: 'Mr Lucas's devices are not renowned for reliable working over long periods.'

On another occasion, obviously irate over some delays, Thomas wrote in a letter to Victor Riley: 'Keep after Lucas's (*sic*). It is only by making a nuisance of ourselves that we can get what we want from these people.' On personal terms however, the Riley management were very friendly with the scion of the dynasty, Oliver Lucas, who was to die young in 1948.

The Riley service department often had to give bad news to customers like Messrs Cripps of Nottingham, who wanted a headlamp and reflector lens for their 1946 1½-litre, chassis 36S 11240, the assembly being a slightly different fitting from the later version. The service department wrote on 3 December 1948: 'Lucas have been unable to fulfil our order…although we are pressing our suppliers it is regretted that we are as yet unable to indicate when these supplies will come to hand.'

In Lucas's defence it has to be said that they were victims of their own success – trying to supply a huge range of products demanded by different manufacturers. Short production runs of several different types of the same component for many different manufacturers were bound to lead to supply delays.

For instance in 1947 Lucas were making: 34 different models of dynamos; 45 starter motors; 68 distributors; 98 windscreen wipers and an astounding 133 different types of headlamps.

Because of the shortage of materials, the Government was desperate to try to reduce this sort of wasteful proliferation and some agreement was reached about rationalizing component production in the car industry. But a Government attempt to bully the car makers into producing only one model per manufacturer was less successful.

---

The car the 1½-litre most resembled from the front three-quarter view was the BMW 327, which was produced in fixed-head coupé and cabriolet form between 1937 and 1941. This was no coincidence; Victor Riley, as we have seen, liked the marque so much that he would have merged with it, and certainly a BMW 327 coupé, registered FXR 921, had found its way to the factory in Durbar Avenue where it was extensively examined.

There is a nice tale – perhaps apocryphal – that it had been seized from a German legation. However, given Victor's close links with BMW and the Aldington brothers, and the discussions about joint production, it might well have been acquired quite normally.

The similarities between the RMA and the BMW can be seen in the shape of the split windscreen – even the immediate pre-war Rileys had a single piece screen – and in the sweep of the front and rear wings, though the most notable resemblance is in the semi-recessed headlights. This was a BMW trademark in that era, although the lens of the BMW at 8.6in (22cm) without the chrome ring is much bigger than the Riley's at 7in (18cm).

A mock-up on a pre-war chassis was seen in the winter of 1944/45 and early publicity drawings from the summer of 1945 before the launch show the car with much larger BMW-type headlamps than appeared in the final production version, and also with BMW-type faired sidelights on top of the wings, rather than the standard Lucas torpedo sidelight that appeared on all production cars.

**1½-litre RMA technical data at launch**

*Engine*

| | |
|---|---|
| Number of cylinders | 4 |
| Treasury rating | 11.9hp |
| Capacity | 1496cc |
| BHP | 55bhp at 4,500rpm |
| Bore | 69mm |
| Stroke | 100mm |
| Compression ratio | 6.7 to 1 |
| System of cooling | Pump and thermo-syphon |

*Pistons*

| | | |
|---|---|---|
| Maximum rebore size | + 0.040in (1.01mm) | |
| Firing order | 1, 2, 4, 3 | |
| Piston clearance | top | 0.0026in to 0.0044in (0.06mm to 0.11mm) |
| | bottom | 0.0014in to 0.0032in (0.03mm to 0.08mm) |
| Ring gap | 0.008in (0.2mm) | |
| Number of compression rings | 3 | |
| Width of compression rings | 2mm | |
| Number of oil rings | 1 | |
| Width of oil rings | 5⁄32in (3.97mm) | |

*Oil pressure*

| | |
|---|---|
| | 19lb/sq in at 15mph |
| (minimum figures) | 35lb/sq in at 50mph |
| | 48lb/sq in at 70mph |

*Connecting rods and bearings*

| | |
|---|---|
| Gudgeon pin type | floating – secured by circlips |
| Fit in piston | light drive at room temperature |
| Fit in connecting rod | push fit |
| Crankpin diameter (standard) | 1.875in (47.49mm) |
| Minimum diameter for regrind crankpin | 1.825in (46.22mm) |
| Connecting rod – length between centres | 8in (20.32mm) |
| Type of bearing | White metal direct to rod |
| Side clearance | 0.002in to 0.004in (0.05mm to 0.10mm) |
| Diametrical clearance | 0.0015in (0.04mm) |
| Number of crankshaft bearings | 3 |
| Type of bearings – main | white metal |
| Standard main journal diameter | front and rear 1.75in (44.45mm) |
| | centre 2.75in (69.85mm) |
| Minimum diameter for regrind – main journals | 1.730in (43.94mm) front and rear; 2.730in (69.34mm) centre |
| Main bearings – length | front 2½in (63.50mm) |
| | centre 1⁷⁄₁₆in (36.32mm) |
| | rear 2⅜in (60.19mm) |
| End clearance – main bearing | 0.004in to 0.006in (0.10mm to 0.15mm) |
| Diametrical clearance – main bearing | 0.0025in (0.06mm) centre |
| | 0.0015in (0.04mm) front and rear |

| End thrust taken on crankshaft | rear bearing |
|---|---|

*Valvegear*

| | |
|---|---|
| Number of camshaft bearings | 3 |
| Type of bearing – camshaft | plain |
| Bearing clearance – camshaft | 0.0025in (0.06mm) |
| End thrust taken on camshaft | front bearings |
| Camshaft drive (type) | chain to both camshafts |
| Valve timing markings | crankshaft keyway vertical marks on chain wheels in line |
| Exhaust valve diameter | |
|    head and stem | 1⁷⁄₁₆in (36.32mm) head; 5⁵⁄₁₆in (128.59mm) stem |
| Inlet valve diameter | |
|    head and stem | 1⁷⁄₁₆in (36.32mm) head; 5⁵⁄₁₆in (128.59mm) stem |
| Valve seat angle | 45deg |
| Tappet type | mushroom |
| Inlet valve clearance for timing | 0.005in (0.12mm) |
| Inlet valve opens | 9deg or 2⅛ flywheel teeth B.T.D.C. |
| Inlet valve working clearance | 0.003in hot (0.07mm) |
| Exhaust valve working clearance | 0.004in hot (0.10mm) |
| Are guides removable? | Yes |
| Inlet opens | 9deg | before T.D.C. |
| Inlet closes | 45deg | after B.D.C. |
| Exhaust opens | 56deg | before B.D.C. |
| Exhaust closes | 20deg | after T.D.C. |

*Fuel system*

| | |
|---|---|
| Carburettor | SU horizontal H.2, fitted 90 jet, No. 3 needle |

*Clutch and gearbox*

| | |
|---|---|
| Clutch type | 8in diameter Borg & Beck |
| Type of facing | special Borg & Beck |
| Gear ratios | |
|    Top | 4.89 to 1 |
|    Third | 7.23 to 1 |
|    Second | 11.2 to 1 |
|    First | 19.42 to 1 |
|    Reverse | 19.42 to 1 |

*Front axle and steering*

| | |
|---|---|
| Camber | 1deg |
| Castor angle | 3deg |
| Toe-in | nil |
| Swivel pin inclination | 11deg |
| Track | 4ft 4¼in (1,327mm) front and rear |
| Turning circle | 30ft (9.1m) |
| Wheelbase | 9ft 4½in (2,858mm) |
| Tyre size and pressures | 5.75 × 16in (146 × 406.4mm) |
| | front 22lb/sq in (1.55kg/sq cm) |
| | rear 24lb/sq in (1.69kg/sq cm) |

*Rear axle*

| | |
|---|---|
| Type of axle | semi-floating |
| Type of drive | spiral bevel |
| Ratio | 4.89 to 1 |

*continued overleaf*

**1½-litre RMA technical data at launch** *continued*

| | |
|---|---|
| Adjustment | Vernier – no shims |
| End play | nil |
| Lash | 0.006in (0.15mm) |
| | |
| *Brakes* | |
| Type | Girling hydro-mechanical |
| Lining size | front:     9¾ × 1¾ × ³⁄₁₆in (247.65 × 44.45 × 4.76mm) |
| | rear:     9⅜ × 1½ × ³⁄₁₆in (238.13 × 38.10 × 4.76mm) |
| | |
| *Springs* | |
| Front | Riley Torsionic independent front suspension – two torsion bars parallel to the chassis |
| Rear | length 45½in (1,156mm) (eye centres) |
| | width 2in (51mm) |
| Number of leaves | 13 |
| Thickness of leaves | one to five, ³⁄₁₆in (4.8mm); others ⁵⁄₃₂in (4mm) |
| Camber – rear | 1⅞in (47.6mm), minus ⅛in (3.2mm) loaded (negative camber) |
| | |
| *Electrical* | |
| Distributor rotation | clockwise |
| Manual advance | yes |
| Automatic advance | yes |
| Breaker gap | 0.012in to 0.015in (0.3mm to 0.4mm) |
| Plug – make and type | Champion L.10.S |
| Plug gap | 0.030in (0.76mm) |
| Firing order | 1, 2, 4, 3 |
| Ignition timing degrees | 8deg B.T.D.C. full advance of manual control |
| Ignition timing – number of flywheel teeth | 2 teeth |
| Charging system | Lucas C.V.C. type special equipment |
| | dynamo C45YV |
| | control box R.F.91 |
| Battery | Lucas STWX9A – 12V 58amp/hour |
| Battery earth | positive |
| | |
| *Capacities* | |
| Sump | 10pt (5.7ltr) |
| Gearbox | 2pt (1.1ltr) |
| Rear axle | 2¾pt (1.6ltr) |
| Cooling system | 13pt (7.4ltr) |
| Radiator hose (top) | special pre-formed hose |
| Radiator hose (bott) | 2⅜ × 1in (60.19 × 25.4mm) diameter (2 off) |
| Petrol tank | 12½gal (57ltr) |
| | |
| *General dimensions* | |
| Overall length | 14ft 11in (4,547mm) |
| Overall height | 4ft 11in (1,499mm) |
| Overall width | 5ft 3½in (1,613mm) |
| Ground clearance | 7½in (191mm) |
| Total weight | 24¼cwt (dry), 2,716lb (1,232kg) |

Source: *Riley Sales and Service Bulletin October 1946*

One of the prototypes had just such lamps, CGU 936, a 1935 London registration, originally on a works Merlin 9.

The large headlamps were balanced by two small Butler driving lamps lower down on either side of the grille. In the final version the headlamps were made smaller and the driving lamps larger to maintain the proportionality.

Very early cars had side jacking points, another BMW (and pre-war Riley) feature, and another likeness in an early Riley advertisement shows the RMA with stylish perforated wheels, though the apertures are smaller than the BMW's telephone dial-type. They did not make it into production, being replaced with slotted disc wheels.

Another feature that went – for the better – was the horn grilles underneath the headlamps; Miles Thomas, Nuffield's vice chairman, took the credit for reducing the height of the production car by chopping down the prototype's pillars by 1½in (38mm). Other features that did not survive long were the placing of the rear number plate behind a glass panel, rather like the 1937 Monaco, a jack with a detachable ratchet handle, a round-topped dashboard and a taller radiator cap.

The bonnet was aluminium with steel sides – these being replaced by aluminium in 1949 then again with steel in the RME of 1952.

The RMA body was the template for the 2½-litre which was to follow soon afterwards and many of the features noted here are common to both models.

Like the pre-war Nuffield Rileys, and all the RM series, the wood-framed, steel-clad body was made at the Morris Motors' Bodies branch in Coventry, the former Hollick and Pratt factory bought by Nuffield in the 1920s that had extensive experience of ash framing, producing all the MG Midget bodies up until the TF in the mid-1950s and the Morris Minor Traveller, until it closed when production ended in the early 1970s.

A notable RM feature carried over from the previous decade was the leathercloth roof. The fabric was made by the Ioco Rubber and Waterproofing Co. of Glasgow, whose previous claim to fame was manufacturing the enormous gasbags for the airship R100. This fabric was later replaced with a top covering of a synthetic fabric called Melloroid and later still by Everflex. The roof fabric, with a hessian lining beneath, was stretched over a mild steel mesh base, supported by a wooden frame and packed with wadding.

It used up a lot of materials – 2½yd of hessian at 72in wide (2.29 × 1.83m); 6yd (5.50m) of wadding; one piece of leathercloth 84 × 40in (2.13 × 1.02m) for the centre panel and two pieces 78 × 22in (1.98 × 0.56m) for the sides.

At the time, it saved the use of scarce sheet steel, and in a *Sales and Service Bulletin* dealers were told that it was a sales point as it reduced drumming, which had caused complaints on some 1939 models.

It had other advantages, such as helping to reduce the weight and centre of gravity slightly. Nevertheless, it's been a cause of woe to restorers ever since, due to its propensity to let in water and rot the wooden frame beneath, but a sound, properly-fitted top makes the car look magnificent[1].

However, there have been many versions of a story that the RMs were originally to have had a steel roof. Bert Holmes, the body designer was said to have had two prototypes ready for inspection by Riley distributors, but was still lacking the roof panels. He was told to cover them in fabric so that the distributors could see the final shape of the car. According to Arnold Farrar, when they did set eyes on the cars they were so taken with the fabric roof that it was put into production. It would have reminded them of the successful Monacos of the early 1930s.

There is also a story that Bob Aves, the Riley development manager, had six cars made with steel roofs by a firm in Nuneaton; one of them may have been for Fred Green, manager of one of the Nuffield body plants.

There was leather of course on the well-padded seats; the front seats had neat leather pouches rather than door pockets on their backs, another throwback to the early 1930s.

On the rear seat, three could sit comfortably – the *Motor* called it a 'couch' on which a passenger could write a letter at 55mph (88km/h).

The driver had a large speedometer in front of him, marked British Jaeger, which was a posh name for the Smith's instruments used on cheaper cars. Smith's had taken over the English branch of the French/Swiss Jaeger company in 1927, the same year that they also acquired KLG plugs. There was also a comprehensive set of other instruments, as always expected in a Riley – ammeter, water temperature, oil pressure and fuel gauges.

The driver stared though one pane of the split windscreen which he was able to open partially for ventilation with a small crank. The front seat passenger did not have the option. The small rear window could be covered with a roller blind operated by the driver to block headlamp dazzle from cars behind, a common fitment in cars until dipping mirrors were introduced.

There were features that did not appear on cars of a similar class, such as twin petrol filler caps and a hand throttle.

Originally, all cars were finished in black cellulose, but duotone became available from late 1946 to order.

## The chassis

When the 1½-litre was launched in 1945, it contained tried and familiar features from pre-war cars, but also unorthodox and innovative fitments, such as rack and pinion steering, which set it apart from the general run of post-war offerings.

Many items were updated during the course of production, but the following were the main features at the time of launch. The 1½-litre's frame was based on the 1935 chassis of 4ft 3in (1,295mm) – known as the wide track to distinguish it from the other Nuffield chassis of 4ft (1,220mm) at the front. It was used first in late 1935 for the Adelphi and Kestrel, and the Continental Touring Saloon used it in 1937 with a wheelbase of 9ft 4in (2,845mm). For the RMA the dimensions were slightly stretched to a track of 4ft 4¼in (1,327mm) and a wheelbase of 9ft 4½in (2,858mm).

The chassis was extremely tough and designed to be so rigid that if one corner of the car were lifted, all the doors would still open and close properly. The deep box section pressed steel side members were 6in deep × 2in (150 × 50mm) wide. These were made of two U-sections of ⅛in-thick (3mm) steel, which were slipped inside each other so that the top and bottom were ¼in (6mm) thick. They were welded together on a jig with five substantial tubular cross-members. This was a technique that Riley had used for many years pre-war.

One of the early changes in 1946 was to make the jacking points stronger by moving them from the side, where they had been since 1936, to the front of the car.

## The Torsionic suspension

> It is increasingly obvious that, in their new independent front suspension, the Riley company has achieved a considerable technical triumph.
>
> Technical editor – the *Motor*

The independent front suspension of the RM Rileys was most effective – and it came in for wide praise for giving outstanding handling qualities. Independent front suspension was rare at that time; semi-elliptics were the rule, as they had been in pre-war Rileys. Singer was an exception in offering it before the war.

Riley had experimented with it in the mid-1930s in an Adelphi that had unequal wishbones and coil springs, but in the RM series it relied for its springing effect on two torsion bars – rods running parallel to the length of the chassis frame at the front that twist to absorb shock.

The idea was not new, it had been tried by Leyland in 1921, W.O. Bentley had fiddled about with a version for a Napier that was never built in 1930, and about the same time Ferdinand Porsche had patented a system of transversely-mounted torsion bars connected to trailing arms.

*The longitudinal torsion bars that gave the RMs their excellent suspension were adjusted at the rear of the bar housing from the nuts that point downwards.*

Despite the Riley factory giving their version a special name, Torsionic, that was used in publicity, it was not of their making. In fact it copied very closely another manufacturer's version of the suspension.

Its basis lay in the pre-war Citroën *Traction avant*, engineered by André Lefèbvre and introduced in France in March 1934. British versions were being built from knock-down parts in a Citroën factory at Slough that had been in operation since 1926 building right-hand drive cars for British and Commonwealth markets.

Two of the Slough Light Fifteen *Tractions* were sent to Foleshill or bought by Riley in 1936 or 1937. They came through the good offices of Bob Aves, who knew the competition staff at Riley from pre-war days. He worked at Slough and knew of Riley's interest in the suspension; whether Paris knew or approved of this scheme is not known. Riley were also familiar with the *Traction* as John Morris of SU carburettors, a frequent visitor to the factory, also drove one.

In Coventry, the front end was cut off a Riley chassis and the Citroën suspension was just bolted on. The result on the road was startlingly good compared with half-elliptic cart spring suspension that everyone else was using and the experiment, that seems to have taken place on two cars, but mainly on a Monaco driven by Allan Riley, determined the suspension configuration of the RM series before the war even started.

However, there had been some thought given to using independent front suspension in the 16 horsepower car of 1937 powered by the new Big Four engine, and the Citroën set-up was not the only one that had been considered. A Girling version that relied on coil springs was also tested extensively before the war, particularly in a 12/4 Adelphi, but was thought to be more suitable for racing. But as it was, development time and costs were against independent front suspension being adopted at that stage. The company was going broke, the upgrade was not vital and there was no chance of Riley indulging in a financial commitment that did not bring a large and quick return.

When the war was over, Riley recruited Bob Aves from Citroën in November 1945 to help with development of the new car, particularly the front suspension, perhaps realizing that it needed more development for the heavier RMA. Aves was rather dismissive of Riley's efforts so far. He told motoring journalist Jon Pressnell that he was not impressed by Riley's grasp of the technology involved. 'It was a new sort of thing for them. They didn't know anything about it, they just copied the front end of the Citroën and that was it. Consequently the torsion bars were too thick and heavy, they should have been thinner and longer.'

Apart from being much more sophisticated than leaf springs, the new front end had the considerable advantage of being assembled separately, so that the front suspension, steering and radiator mount were all carried in a cradle that was then attached to the chassis by ten high-tensile bolts.

The Coventry motor industry at that time must have had a close-knit relationship as Riley were not the only ones to pirate the Citroën technology. The same front suspension also appeared in another Coventry firm's offerings – the Armstrong Siddeley Lancaster and Hurricane. Then Lea Francis, whose chief designer Hugh Rose was a *traction* owner, put it into their 14 model of 1946. Rose, who had worked for Riley and had designed the original 1½-litre engine in 1933, was fairly adept at this sort of thing since the Lea Francis engine bore an amazing resemblance to Percy's double camshaft PR head. Rose had also tried unsuccessfully to borrow torsion bars from Riley to try them out on his own cars.

## How it worked – and still does

The front suspension's flexibility relies on a pair of double wishbones each side of the car linked to the stub axles. The bottom wishbone is splined into the longitudinal torsion bar – which is in effect an uncoiled spring. The spring action is produced by twisting the bar as one end is gripped, so as the wheels move up and down, the bars twist and untwist to dampen the motion. Further damping is done with a pair of tubular Luvax hydraulic shock absorbers mounted in the cradle at an angle of around 75 degrees, though the damping works only in one direction – when the wheel is rising.

The torsion bars are 2ft 6in (762mm) long and were pre-stressed on machines in the factory before being fitted. This meant that the initial elasticity of the bar was removed, otherwise it would have to be taken up after several hundred miles of driving. Any adjustments that were needed eventually were done at the rear end of the bar where it was attached to the chassis.

Riley were very proud, and rightly so, of this set-up, repeating many times the mantra that with Torsionic suspension 'all roads become good roads'. Uneven road surfaces, potholes and crevices were said to be smoothed out in a remarkable manner, something the magazine road testers were able to confirm.

## The rear suspension

This was a clever combination of semi-elliptic leaf springs in rubber bushes and an anti-roll bar running across the chassis between the rear dampers that were of lever arm 'door-closer' type. Later versions had telescopic shock absorbers and the anti-roll bar was deleted. The springs were rather longer than had been used in Riley chassis previously and these gave a greater range of movement. The only touch of exoticism came from the U-bolts holding the axle in place. To prevent squeaking as the axle moved these were lined with balata belting – cotton impregnated with an elastic gum from the milk-tree of Brazil.

It is interesting that Arnold Farrar, service manager at Coventry, and a few of his colleagues were unpopular with the designer Harry Rush because they removed the anti-roll bar from their cars, so there was some body roll before a skid developed. Farrar took the bars off both his RMAs GWK 300 and KRW 800, maintaining that with the bar in place there was no warning before a breakaway occurred and one would have to be very quick to correct it. He so advised Jim Fletcher, who still owns one of the drophead prototypes, who has still not fitted or needed it.

## The steering

Rack and pinion is one of the simplest and oldest forms of steering gear. It appeared on adult tricycles in the nineteenth century, but fell into disuse. The recirculating ball, the Bishop cam and peg (a Wolseley favourite used in the pre-war Nuffield Rileys) and the Marles cam and roller were the systems of choice for

*RIGHT AND BELOW: The front wishbone suspension and the rack and pinion steering were one of the few technical features not carried over from the pre-war years.*

*The frame combines minimum weight with maximum rigidity. Careful positioning of cross-members and deep, box-section members, downswept in the centre, give a low centre of gravity and consequent freedom from sway.*

British manufacturers, so there was some surprise when rack and pinion steering emerged on the RMA in 1945 – the first British car to employ it. Though it is now universal in car manufacturing, at that time it was so unusual that the *Autocar* described it as 'quite unorthodox' and the *Motor* as 'modernistic' and some reviews did not even use the phrase rack and pinion, preferring 'horizontal gear steering' or 'special Riley horizontal gear.' It was direct and efficient, with 2⅕ turns from lock to lock.

Neither made reference to the fact that it was common in France on pre-war Citroëns, and it was of course imported from the *traction avant* as part of the front end suspension package.

While rack and pinion is highly efficient in terms of precision and transmitting the driver's desires to the wheels, it suits smaller cars best, as at low speeds and without power assistance, heavier and larger cars require a great deal of effort to produce any movement – something RM drivers know only too well. 'Finger-light steering' boasted one advertisement of the 1½-litre. Up to a point, perhaps.

When RMs were being built, the adjustable steering column was the last thing to be assembled into the car, which made for easy mounting of the body as it did not have to be manoeuvred around the column.

## The transmission

One of the characteristics of Rileys up until the Nuffield take-over of 1938 was the use of torque tube transmission. It re-emerged in the RMA and continued until 1952 when it was replaced – probably for cost-saving reasons – by an open prop shaft.

It is basically a tube in which the propeller shaft runs. But to improve rear-end handling, the tube itself is anchored to the rear axle and to the chassis at the rear. In addition, in the 1½-litre there is a substantial bearing (or trunnion for those familiar with Meccano) anchoring it to one of the tubular cross members of the chassis. Originally, the bearings in this trunnion

needed lavish greasing to avoid grumbling noises in the transmission. From the tail of the gearbox came a short removable shaft that joined the propeller shaft at this bearing. This design of 1939, based on Victor's Autovia, enabled easy maintenance of the transmission.

The torque tube has advantages for a high-speed car that needs to hold the road well, as it locates the rear axle precisely and takes the load of resisting torque from the rear springing.

The rear axles in the early cars were of the Riley spiral bevel type; the torque tube disappeared when the spiral bevel was replaced by a BMC hypoid unit in the 1952 RME; the gearbox originated from a Morris Commercial design and has the peculiarity of some bolts having metric threads but Whitworth heads, a hangover from Morris's days of importing Hodgkiss components with metric heads.

At least two 1½-litre cars are known to have existed with pre-selector gearboxes, presumably built either for experimental purposes or to special order.

## Brakes

Pre-war, Riley had chosen rod brakes supplied by Girling and made by the motorcycle manufacturers New Hudson of Birmingham. 'The best brakes in the World' as Girling modestly advertised them. For the 1½-litre, Riley turned again to Girling, but progress had now led to a hydro-mechanical system – that is, while the rear used the traditional mechanical Girling rod linkages to brake the 16in wheels, the front worked under hydraulic pressure, providing 60 per cent of the braking effort. Total braking area of the 10in (25cm) front and rear drums was 126.48sq in (321.3sq cm). The 10in diameter hydraulic cylinder was linked to the brake pedal beneath the floorboards.

It was, however, rather surprising that full hydraulics were not introduced at this stage, given that Morris had been fitting them in the 1930s. They were not to be used until the introduction of the RME in 1952, though whether they were more efficient is a matter

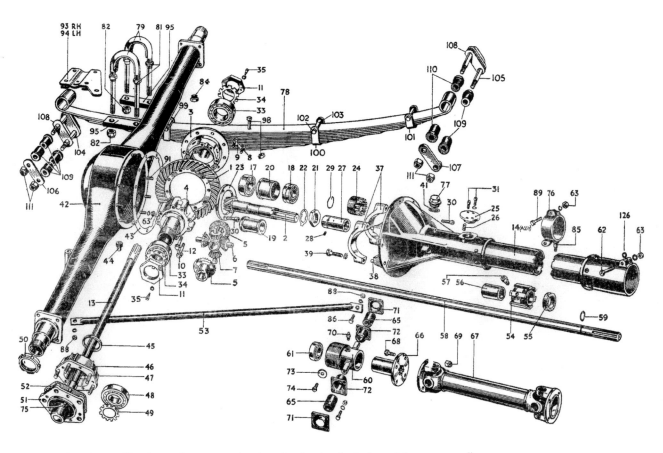

*The Riley spiral bevel rear axle was a complex piece of engineering that had served the company well. The later hypoid axle was much simpler and cheaper to make.* Workshop Manual

of debate, diehards maintaining that the rods to the rear gave a safety margin if there were a hydraulic leak, what Ford used to call 'the safety of steel from pedal to wheel.'

Although exact comparisons are difficult to find, tests showed that at 30mph (48km/h) a 1947 RMA needed 95lb (43kg) pedal pressure to stop in 33½ft (10.2m), whereas the RME needed 140lb (64kg) to stop in 32ft (9.8m). But this could be explained by how well the brakes were set up. The stopping power of the 1½-litre was most improved not by the full hydraulic system but by the introduction at the front of twin leading shoes instead of the original leading/trailing system.

## The engine and the PR head

The marvellous Riley engine that powered the 1½-litre RM series had its origins as far back as 1926, when Percy Riley designed an engine for the famous Nine, whose chassis with innovative torque tube transmission was drawn by his brother Stanley and gave outstanding handling for its time. The car was so good (60mph/97km/h and 40mpg/7.2ltr/100km from 1087cc) and so outside the normal run of British motor industry production of the time that it became known as the 'Wonder Car'.

The real wonder was the cylinder head – the PR head as it became known after its

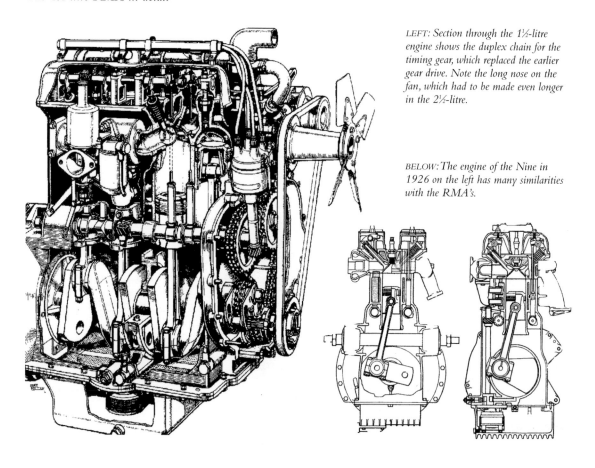

*LEFT: Section through the 1½-litre engine shows the duplex chain for the timing gear, which replaced the earlier gear drive. Note the long nose on the fan, which had to be made even longer in the 2½-litre.*

*BELOW: The engine of the Nine in 1926 on the left has many similarities with the RMA's.*

designer. It had hemispherical combustion chambers and inclined valves opposed at 90 degrees whose rockers were operated by light, short pushrods driven by two camshafts set high in the block. The camshafts themselves were driven in the original engines by two chains and later by a train of helical gears from the crankshaft.

The beauty of the design was that it combined the efficiency of an overhead cam engine, which it was not, with the simplicity of pushrod operation, so when the head had to come off, as it frequently did in those days for decarbonizing, there were none of the complications of timing that an overhead cam engine can bring. Valve adjustment was easy, so was access to the cylinder head nuts and the sparking plugs[2].

The use of overhead valves in a hemispherical head was common for competition and

racing engines, but for use in a family car it was revolutionary.

The bore was 60.3mm and the stroke 95.2, giving it an RAC rating of 9.01 horsepower. Although it put out some 34bhp at 4,000rpm (quoted figures vary widely) this was considered exceptional – 'an engine unusually powerful for its small size' commented the *Autocar*. A sports version developed 41bhp at 5,000 revolutions.

It was also very tunable; Reid Railton and Parry Thomas got 55bhp at 5,500rpm out of it for their Brooklands Nine, which took several records. On 17 September 1927 a Riley Nine racer driven by Railton completed a flying lap at Brooklands at 98.6mph (158.65km/h) and crossed the line at over 100mph (160km/h); 'when it comes to producing the best, England once again demonstrates its superiority', crowed the *Riley Record*.

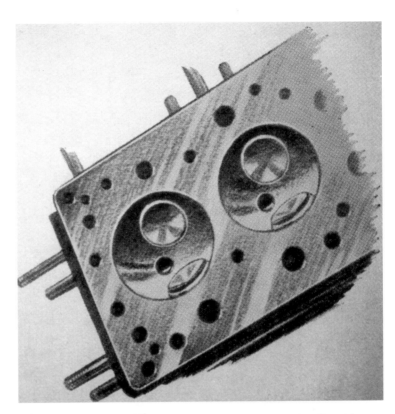

*Hemispherical combustion chambers with opposed valves were the most efficient set-up for a cylinder head but were very rare at the time.*

*Nuffield often used pictures of aircraft with cars to try to establish an association with wealth and speed. This RMA, with an unusual colour flash above the chrome waistline, has a 1946 Coventry registration.*

The PR head was a widely admired design that was to define Riley engine production for the next thirty years. The idea was also 'borrowed' by two motor-cycle makers. Edward Turner of Triumph, who had owned a Nine, used the layout to advantage when he designed his 500cc Speed Twin engine, which was in production for forty-five years, and Velocette adopted it for their singles.

The Riley Nine of 1927 made history for its advanced, rubber-mounted engine and other novel features such as four-wheel brakes that could be adjusted from the driver's seat. The steady development of this range of Monaco, Kestrel, Falcon saloons, Lincock coupés and Lynx tourers led in 1934 to the announcement of the famous 1½-litre engine that was to be destined for more than twenty years of production and that would power nearly 14,000 Riley RMs and some 8,500 pre-war cars.

It was the Nine engine writ large, though there were certain differences. The bore and stroke had gone up from the Nine's 60.3mm × 95.2 to 69 × 100 – dimensions it maintained until the end. The 1496cc engine had an RAC rating of 11.9 horsepower.

The original brief when it was designed on Victor's instructions by Hugh Rose and Ted Jones in 1933 was for a 1500cc racing engine that could be used to enhance Riley's sporting reputation. It was said that Percy did not want to develop it, since he would have preferred to exploit the company's existing six-cylinder engine range made in 1458cc and 1633cc capacities, though since the success of the Nine there had been some dissatisfaction with the 1458cc version.

Although from the outside the new four looked similar to the Nine's engine, with its trademark twin alloy rocker boxes it was larger and there were significant differences inside, notably three and not two main bearings. Between the two middle cylinder bores there was extra space to carry the centre bearing, and this was put to good effect by casting a passage through the block from the exhaust manifold on one side to the inlet manifold on the other to port through exhaust gases, thus creating a hot spot to aid combustion. Fine when the car was new, but very prone to corrosion.

There was also the problem caused by the hot gases eating away the aluminium inlet manifold, which was later changed to cast iron.

As to the head, hemispherical combustion chambers were retained, and four exhaust valves were arranged neatly along the near side of the block and the four inlet vales along the offside. The camshafts on either side of the block needed of course only four cams each since they were operating only four valves. The camshafts were chain-driven for the first 200 or so engines, then altered to be driven by gears, which was thought to be more reliable for racing. Initial power output was about 45bhp.

In the Victor of 1938, with a single Zenith carburettor, the engine produced 55bhp at 4,500rpm, which could propel it to 72mph (116km/h) according to *Light Car*. There were also two twin carburettor versions of it – the Special Series, usually with Zeniths, which produced 52bhp – and the highly successful Sprite with twin SUs. This also had larger inlet valves and advanced inlet cam timing that

could give 60 to 62bhp. In the six-light Kestrel it gave 80mph (128km/h) performance.

Vernon Barker's view is that this car was the benchmark for the RMs that followed and this was achieved by a reduction in performance, but with a refinement unavailable to pre-war Riley owners.

The unit was not without its problems. Oil leakage from the rear main bearing led to very large warranty claims until modifications in 1936 cured the leaks.

The highly efficient and sophisticated cylinder head layout was so much admired that it was often referred to in magazine road tests as the 'PR head' and from this first iteration there was little significant change in the basic block until it appeared in the first RMA.

Its last pre-war appearance was in the 1939 season 12hp six-light saloon, and in fact engine development for the RMA was largely completed before the war for this car when Harry Rush revised the 1½-litre engine for the 1939/40 season.

The most important change from earlier 1930s models was the improved 'cross-flow'

*The twin-carb factory conversion for the 1½-litre used the air cleaner from the 2½-litre engine and was said to give up to 15 per cent better acceleration.*

cooling in the cylinder head, first introduced in 1936 for the TT-winning Sprite engines, that directed water around each valve and close to the sparking plug. The water pump, first mounted on the timing case, was moved to the head and driven by a rubber belt from the crankshaft pulley that also turned the dynamo mounted high on the left-hand side. The gear drive to the camshafts was retained for the 1939 season and eventually replaced by a Renolds chain.

The crankshaft, a single piece forging, ran in three main bearings and was lubricated from an oil pump in the sump.

The engine mounting was substantially revised for better torque absorption; rather than being suspended at the front by a cross-member mounted in compressed rubber blocks, the engine was held steady by a much more efficient system of brackets set at 45

*A Riley advertisement.*

BELOW: *Deirdre is wearing a Pringle sweater ensemble and a styled skirt in Wilson and Glennie fabric in identical colours. 'Soon to be available in all good home stores' said the caption for the press. The car? An RMA factory demonstrator.*

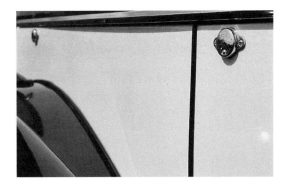

ABOVE: *External bonnet locks were soon discontinued when owners complained of thefts.*

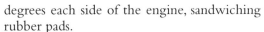

RIGHT: *There were several different headlamp lenses used; early cars had this 'owl's eye', which was replaced with the standard Lucas block lens.*

degrees each side of the engine, sandwiching rubber pads.

So the 1945 1½-litre engine in the RMA was virtually identical to the pre-war engines in both design and power output; the pre-war figure of 55bhp at 4,500rpm (50–52bhp in 1939) remained constant throughout the 1½-litre's ten-year post-war life.

The Riley trademark head of inclined valves with hemispherical combustion chambers was the most efficient of its type but still rare; even by 1947 only two other British manufacturers, Lagonda and Invicta, were using it.

Later on in the 1½-litre's life, a Sprite-like twin carburettor modification became available from the factory which claimed to 'increase acceleration up by 10–15 per cent',

with a fuel penalty of only two to three miles per gallon fewer. No power output figures were given. The kit used a new manifold modelled on the 2½-litre but slightly smaller to match the shorter inlet port spacings with the air cleaner from the 2½-litre, and the two SUs had 0.090in jets and AK needles. It cost £30.

All well and good – the kit meant that the RMA could hold its own to a degree with the 2½-litre – but hard-driven 1½-litres were very prone to run big ends if white-metalling had not been done well and sludge traps had not been cleaned.

Jimmy James offered his own go-faster conversion that consisted of skimming the cylinder head to improve the compression ratio and using a larger H4 carburettor.

---

1. The fabric covering on the A90 Atlantic saloon was just glued to the steel roof, as it was in the 1970s on cars like the Ford Granada. The fad made a return in Detroit in 2004, particularly on the Chrysler 300.

2. Overhead cam engines were not unknown: the M-type MG Midget of 1929 had a single overhead cam; Singer used them up until the war.

# 4 The 2½-litre saloon – RMB

A satisfactory blend of the best British and Continental styling without making the smallest concession to the vulgarity of transatlantic influence.

*Motor*

It was clear from the outset that Riley had produced an outstanding car in the 2½-litre RMB, launched in the middle of 1946. A 90bhp car – able to cruise at up to 90mph (145km/h) with outstanding roadholding – deserved the enormous praise that was lavished upon it. Almost as soon as the 1½-litre appeared, Riley announced that a more powerful version would follow.

There is a school of thought that says the 2½-litre was on the stocks before the 1½-litre, pointing out that if you take the last pre-war Kestrel with its Big Four engine and four-speed gearchange on the floor, it lacks only the independent front suspension to be the same mechanically as the RMB.

This is reinforced by the fact that seen from above, the RMB's bonnet sides are much neater than the RMA's and look much more fit for purpose. Whatever the intended order of events, the *Autocar's* editor, Montague Tombs, wrote on the announcement of the RMA: 'Later there will be a 16hp, four-cylinder Riley engine… this will be put into a car similar to the 1½-litre and should give a phenomenal performance'.

## The origins of the Big Four

The engine that was to power the post-war 2½-litre RMs began life in the summer of 1936 when Victor Riley and his great friend and chief designer Harry Rush, who had worked at Foleshill since before the First World War,

decided on the production of a high-performance, large-engined driver's car, that emulated the vintage big fours of the 1920s.

It was a bold gesture, undertaken in some secrecy from the rest of the Board, given the large investment that had been made in Briggs bodies, and the fact that one of their other engine developments, the V8 for the Eight-Ninety had a long and expensive gestation that took more than three years from 1933. Riley had not made an engine of more than two litres since the 17, a side-valve 2932cc unit which ended production in 1923. The new V8 of 2178cc, which was basically two Nine blocks mated together, appeared briefly in an Eight-Ninety Adelphi. It was a thing of beauty to regard, but was not a success.

Not only was the Big Four to outperform the V8, being faster from 0–60mph and having a higher top speed, the bizarre RAC road tax formula meant that while the Big Four was classified as 16hp, the smaller capacity V8 was 18hp – which meant it cost more to tax every year – and the list price was more expensive. It was not to last and was rapidly supplanted.

The Big Four chassis, designed by Stanley Riley, was again a development of the 1935 wide-track frame seen in the 1½-litre and had a wheelbase of 9ft 8½in (2,959mm), 4in (102mm) longer than the 12hp model.

Riley's unpublicized purpose for the Big Four was to produce a 2½-litre 100mph car, though financial troubles and the outbreak of war meant that this was never achieved on a production model. By the time it was ready, there was no competition application for it, as money was now in short supply.

*The New 90 H.P. 2½ Litre Riley Saloon*

*Early publicity for the 2½-litre emphasized the 90bhp engine. This soon changed, as a new cylinder head design in April 1948 pushed power up by 10bhp.*

*The New 90 H.P. 2½ Litre Riley Saloon*

The fastest road test, in an Adelphi saloon in January 1938, showed a top speed of 86mph (138km/h). There were, however, experiments – one on an unopened autobahn in Germany and another at Brooklands, when the magic figure was said to have been attained.

When the engine was announced in July 1937 in the short-lived 16hp Blue Streak, it produced 83.5bhp at 4,300rpm and had a single Zenith downdraught carburettor. The 'big' in Big Four came from the size of the cylinders, each more than 600cc. The bore was 80.5mm and the stroke 120mm, which was extremely long. It produced sufficient torque to pull at full throttle in top from as low as 8mph. It was based on the Bentley 3-litre engine of 80mm × 140mm that the factory had bought and stripped for development purposes.

The term '16hp Big Four' was used in catalogues and instruction books in 1937 and 1938 to describe the chassis, which were also known by their body style as Adelphis, Kestrels and so on, but the Big Four appellation was dropped after the Nuffield takeover in favour of plain 16hp.

The benefits of a large four, compared with a six or an eight, were cheaper production costs, easier maintenance and theoretically greater efficiency due to less friction; the drawbacks were vibration and harsh running, something that was very evident in the 1920s when engines of this configuration were common.

Although it was a brand new engine it followed the familiar Riley pattern of Percy's head with hemispherical combustion chambers, central spark plugs, valves opposed at 90 degrees and double camshafts set high in the block. It was fitted however with the notorious Hi-Charge induction system, an expensive and inefficient system of tuned inlet tracts that was not to last.

The *Autocar* said rather bafflingly of the engine in July 1939: 'It presents the type of performance which is dear to the heart of those who enjoy motoring as motoring', possibly meaning little gearchanging and long-legged performance. It added: 'It runs with a greater smoothness than might be expected by an optimist.'

This was a polite way of saying that this sort of engine, because of its high torque, was quite likely to thrash about in its frame. This was avoided to an extent by highly efficient engine damping – the front of the engine was suspended by a drilled cross-member whose ends were mounted in rubber blocks, while at the rear, rubber-loaded tie-rods or cables secured it to the firewall.

More than 220 Big Four chassis were erected before the receiver arrived in February 1938. In the few months until the Nuffield takeover, nearly ninety more were completed.

Subsequently under the Nuffield banner there were detailed modifications to the engine, including the adoption of a cross-flow head and the fitting of an SU carburettor instead of a Zenith. About one hundred cars were built before the war stopped production.

The last pre-war car to be sold by Riley was a 16hp Kestrel, EVC 880, which still exists and was registered in 1940. It has what is probably the prototype RMB engine numbered B1 and foundry-dated August 1939.

Victor Riley's gamble had proved a limited triumph. The car was a popular success by Riley standards and had the product line been rationalized into a 12hp and 16hp model much earlier the firm's crash may well have been avoided.

The pre-war Big Four was a landmark engine that was so well designed and fitted its purpose so completely that it dropped straight into the post-war RMB with only minor modifications.

It stayed in production until the last Pathfinders of 1957 and by that time the original 83.5bhp at 4,300rpm of twenty years previously had become 110bhp at 4,500rpm as more and more power was wrung out of this exemplary engineering achievement.

## The RMB in detail

Riley liked to say that the car was in the '100mph class', which is not quite the same as saying it would do 100mph, though this did stray into one or two advertisements, but there was little to touch it for speed and comfort at that time, other than the revived pre-war 2½-litre and 3½-litre Jaguars. It was displayed in public for the first time at the Motor Industry Golden Jubilee in the summer of 1946 and became available from November of that year, though mainly for export.

The RMA had paved the way as a development initiative for the 2½-litre and from a full-frontal view there was nothing to distinguish between them, other than a light-blue radiator badge, rather than the dark-blue badge of the RMA. The cars looked deceptively similar from many angles and were in fact the same from the windscreen pillar to the rear both internally and externally. Few would notice the larger tyres – 6 × 16in rather than 5¾ × 16in.

But it had a longer bonnet to accommodate the Big Four engine and a longer wheelbase, which was 9ft 11in (3,023mm) rather than 9ft 4¼ in (2,850mm). The overall length of the car was 15ft 6in (4,724mm) – 7in (178mm) longer than the RMA. Height and width were the same.

Many of the features noted in the earlier chapters on the 1½-litre, particularly in terms of the body and fitments, are of course common to the 2½-litre, though underneath, there were substantial differences compared with the RMA.

The chassis was effectively a 1939 16hp frame with the IFS cradle bolted on the front. It was obviously longer than the RMA's and made of heavier steel pressings. The Torsionic suspension was beefed up to cope with the extra weight of the Big Four.

The gearbox – that had its ancestry in the Morris Commercial side of Nuffield – and the clutch were larger, as were the propeller shaft and rear axle. The Girling hydraulic brake drum was 12in in diameter compared with the 1½-litre's 10in.

Luxuries like automatic chassis lubrication and four-wheel jacks which were on the pre-war Big Four chassis disappeared and the three-speed Warner gearbox with overdrive of the pre-war 16 was replaced with a conventional four-speed with synchromesh on the top three. The ratios were a good deal higher than the 1½-litre.

|        | 1½-litre | 2½-litre |
|--------|----------|----------|
| Top    | 4.88 to 1 | 4.11 to 1 |
| Third  | 7.22     | 5.83     |
| Second | 11.2     | 8.86     |
| First  | 19.4     | 15       |

This led to lower engine revs at high speeds – one of the many contributing factors that led to it being hailed as a relaxed high-speed cruiser.

*Engine speed at 60mph (96.5km/h)*
| | |
|--|--|
| 1½-litre | 3,740rpm |
| 2½-litre | 3,060rpm |

Other comparisons with the 1½-litre were the obvious power output differences – an increase of 35bhp to 90bhp at 4,000rpm from the smaller-engined car's 55bhp, which in real terms amounted to a 63.6 per cent power increase. There was however a penalty to be paid for the heavier duty chassis and components, an unladen weight increase of 448lb (203kg), an increase of some 16 per cent.

The compression ratio at the outset was 6.8:1.

Miles Thomas wrote to Victor Riley:
'Dear VR [sic]
I really do congratulate you on the feel of this new 2½-litre … the new front end is a vast improvement.' There is no further detail in this brief note of the 'new front end'. Does it refer to the look of the car compared with prototype versions, or was he talking about the Torsionic suspension?

Thomas also said that it had lost the 'austerity' look of the prototype because armrests had been put in and it was suggested to Victor that netting to hold maps should be put in the roof as it was on some pre-war cars. It seems that this was not acted upon.

What made the 2½-litre special was the engine, the smooth and powerful 2443cc Big Four that had been so successful in the pre-war 16hp cars and that was very little changed from its 1939 iteration, though the *Motor* described it as 'an engine of new design'. Certainly the cylinder head was better worked, as it was in the 1½-litre compared with its 1930s predecessor.

The engine appeared for the first time after the war *not* in a Riley, but in the record-breaking 2.4 Healey Elliott saloon announced in January 1946. It had two carburettors and a special exhaust manifold, producing 104bhp at 4,650rpm, considerably more than the RMB's 90bhp at 4,000rpm.

The RMB now had two SU carburettors on a cast aluminium inlet manifold and the engine damping was taken care of by the rubber-mounted cradle that carried the front Torsionic suspension that had been so widely acclaimed in the RMA.

There were two drive belts at the front of the engine: a large triangular belt from the crankshaft pulley to the dynamo and then upwards to the water pump at the top of the engine and back again.

But instead of turning the fan at the same time, the water pump spindle had an auxiliary pulley with a leather belt turning the fan at a slightly lower speed than the crankshaft. This rather clumsy arrangement, which was to be changed later in production, was said to have the advantage of enabling drivers to disconnect

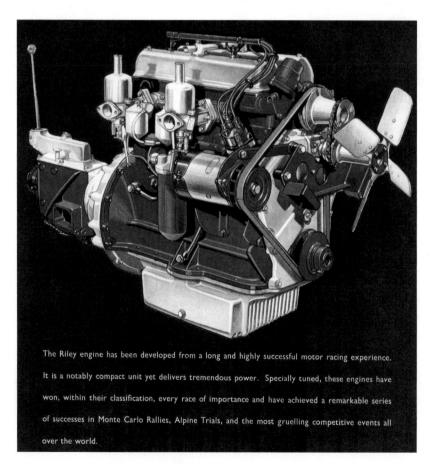

*The 2½-litre engine used twin SU H4 carburettors; early versions used a mechanical AC fuel pump before switching to an electric SU.*

The Riley engine has been developed from a long and highly successful motor racing experience. It is a notably compact unit yet delivers tremendous power. Specially tuned, these engines have won, within their classification, every race of importance and have achieved a remarkable series of successes in Monte Carlo Rallies, Alpine Trials, and the most gruelling competitive events all over the world.

*ABOVE: Big Four engines under test at the Durbar Avenue works. Note the water pipes and the bolted-on exhaust manifold.* British Motor Industry Heritage Trust

*To get effective cooling, the nose of the engine had to be extended to get the fan close to the radiator using an auxiliary pulley with a separate drive belt.*

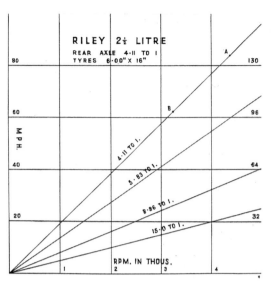

RILEY | 2¼ LITRE
REAR AXLE 4·11 TO 1
TYRES 6·00" X 16"

A = RPM AT MAX. BHP.
B = 2,500 FPM PISTON SPEED.

### Comparative performance data

|  | 1½-litre | 2½-litre |
|---|---|---|
| Engine cc | 1496 | 2443 |
| Acceleration: | | |
| 0–30 (sec) | 6.7 | 4.65 |
| 0–40 | 11.3 | 7.55 |
| 0–50 | 17.2 | 11.9 |
| 0–60 | 29.5 | 16.85 |
| Standing ¼ mile | 24.1 | 21.1 |
| Max speed (mph) | 74.8 | 90.1 |
| Fuel consumption: | | |
| overall (mpg) | 24.2 | 19.6 |

Source: Motor *1953*

Despite the fact that it had a 100mph speedometer in the 2½-litre and Riley claims in some advertisements 'a maximum of over 100mph', the saloon never seems to have exceeded 92mph in tests by *Autocar* and *Motor* in later years. Nothing came near the 96.28mph (154.91km/h) achieved by FDU 741 on the Milan–Como autostrada in 1946 and that with the 90bhp engine.

Nevertheless, there were few cars of the era that could beat the 2½-litre saloon's top speed – in the 90 plus club it was in elevated company with the Armstrong Siddeley Sapphire 346, Aston Martin DB2, Bentley Mark VI, Jaguars XK120 and Mark VII and the Healey.

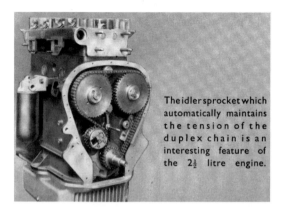

The idler sprocket which automatically maintains the tension of the duplex chain is an interesting feature of the 2½ litre engine.

the fan in cold weather without affecting components like the dynamo.

The real reason for the arrangement was to bring the fan closer to the radiator; had it been put on the nose of the pump, it would have been too far away to be effective in cooling. The radiator itself had four banks of tubes inside it rather than the three in the RMA, though they looked identical from the outside. So interchanging radiators between models can lead to an overcooled RMA or a very hot RMB – which runs very hot in traffic even with the correct radiator.

The substantial crankshaft, manufactured by Smith-Clayton in Lincoln, was made to EN19 specification in a very strong single-piece forging and ran, like all the engine bearings, in white metal cast onto a thick bronze shell. It's been known for this engine to run up to 6,000rpm without damage; the big end bolts are more likely to give than the bearings.

One of the first to get a Riley 2½-litre once production began was Christopher Jennings, editor of *Motor*, who took delivery of his car in August 1946. He was mightily impressed by what he called 'a most exceptional motorcar'.

Editors of *Motor* and *Autocar* enjoyed a privileged relationship with Riley, as they did with other car makers, not only being able to acquire models at that time which others could not, but also being frequently wined and dined in very expensive restaurants, attested to by the 'thank you' letters in the Miles Thomas archives.

**2½-litre chassis – technical data at launch**

*Engine*

| | |
|---|---|
| Number of cylinders | 4 |
| Tax per annum | £25 |
| Cubic capacity | 2443cc |
| BHP | 90 @ 4,000rpm |
| Bore | 80.5mm |
| Stroke | 120mm |
| Compression ratio | 6.8 to 1 |
| System of cooling | pump, thermo-syphon and fan |

*Pistons*

| | |
|---|---|
| Maximum o/size for boring | +0.040in (0.916mm) |
| Firing order | 1, 2, 4, 3 |
| Piston clearance (top) | 0.0175in (0.445mm) |
| Piston clearance (bottom) | 0.003in (0.076mm) |
| Ring gap | 0.008in to 0.012in (0.203mm to 0.305mm) |
| Compression rings | 2 |
| Width compression rings | ³⁄₃₂in (2.37mm) |
| Number of oil rings | 2 |
| Width oil rings | 0.158in (4mm) |
| Gudgeon pin type | floating, secured by circlips |
| Fit in piston | light drive at room temperature |
| Fit in connecting rod | push fit |
| Crankpin diameter | 2.3622in (60mm) |
| Minimum diameter regrind crankpin | 2.3122in (58.7mm) |

*Oil pressure*

| | |
|---|---|
| Oil pressure (lb/sq in) | 12lb at tick-over |
| | 40lb at 50mph |
| Oil pressure (kg/sq cm) | 0.844kg at tick-over |
| | 2.82kg at 50mph |

*Connecting rods and bearings*

| | |
|---|---|
| Length between centres | 8.625in (229mm) |
| Rod bearing | white metal direct to rod |
| Side clearance | 0.002in to 0.008in (0.051mm to 0.203mm) |
| Diametrical clearance | 0.0015in (0.381mm) |
| Crankshaft bearings | 3 |
| Type of bearing – main | split, white metal lined |
| Main journal diameter | 2.559in (65mm) |
| Minimum diameter for re-grind – main journals | 2.539in (64.5mm) |
| Main bearings – length | |
| – front and centre | 1.938in (49.23mm) |
| – rear | 2.7559in (70mm) |
| End clearance | 0in to 0.004in (0mm to 0.102mm) |

*continued overleaf*

**2½-litre chassis – technical data at launch** *continued*

| | |
|---|---|
| Diametrical clearance | 0.001in to 0.003in (0.0254mm to 0.076mm) |
| End thrust taken on | rear bearing |

*Valvegear*

| | |
|---|---|
| Camshaft bearings | 3 |
| Type of bearing | plain |
| Bearing clearance | 0.0015in to 0.004in (0.038mm to 0.102mm) |
| End thrust taken on | front bearings |
| Camshaft drive | duplex chain |
| Valve timing markings | chain wheels marked |
| Exhaust valve diameter | |
| – head and stem | 1.604in diam. (40.7mm) ⁵⁄₁₆ diam. (7.93mm) |
| Inlet valve diameter | |
| – head and stem | 1.604in diam. (40.7mm), ⁵⁄₁₆ diam. (7.93mm) |
| Valve seat angle | 45deg |
| Tappet type | mushroom |
| Inlet valve timing clearance | 0.005in (0.127mm) |
| Inlet valve opens | 17deg or 6.1 flywheel teeth B.T.D.C. |
| Inlet valve clearance | 0.003in (0.076mm) hot |
| Exhaust valve clearance | 0.004in (0.102mm) hot |
| Are guides removable? | Yes |

*Timing*

| | | |
|---|---|---|
| Inlet opens | 17deg | before T.D.C. |
| Inlet closes | 43deg | after B.D.C. |
| Exhaust opens | 45deg before B.D.C. | |
| Exhaust closes | 20deg | after T.D.C. |

*Fuel system*

| | |
|---|---|
| Carburettor | SU horizontal H.4 (two) Fitted No. EE needles |
| Fuel pump | AC mechanical |

*Clutch and gearbox*

| | | |
|---|---|---|
| Clutch type | Borg & Beck | |
| Type of facing | Special Borg & Beck | |
| Gear ratios | top | 4.11 |
| | third | 5.83 |
| | second | 8.86 |
| | first | 15.0 |
| | reverse | 15.0 |

*Front axle and steering*

| | |
|---|---|
| Steering type | Riley rack and pinion |
| Camber | 1deg |
| Castor angle | 3deg |
| Toe-in | nil |
| King pin inclination | 11deg |
| Track | 4ft 4¼in (1,327mm) front and rear |
| Turning circle | 37ft (11.28m) to left, 36ft (11m) to right |
| Wheelbase | 9ft 11in (3,023mm) |
| Tyre size and pressures | 6.00in × 16in |
| | 24lb/sq in (1.69kg/sq cm) front and rear |

*Rear axle*

| | |
|---|---|
| Type of axle | semi-floating |

| | |
|---|---|
| Type of drive | enclosed, spiral bevel. |
| Ratio or number of teeth | 4.11 |
| End play | nil |
| Lash | 0.006in (0.153mm) |

*Brakes*

| | |
|---|---|
| Type | Girling hydro-mechanical |
| Lining size (front) | 12in × 1.656in (305mm × 42mm) |
| Lining size (rear) | 12in × 1.656in (305mm × 42mm) |

*Springs*

| | |
|---|---|
| Front | Riley Torsionic independent front suspension – two torsion bars fitted parallel to chassis. Cam adjusters at rear ends of torsion bars |
| Rear | Length 45½in (1,156mm) |
| Width | 2in (51mm) |
| Number of leaves | 13 |
| Thickness of leaves | 1 to 5 (inclusive) 3⁄16in (4.76mm) remaining leaves 5⁄32in (3.97mm) |
| Camber | 1⅞in negative (47.6mm) |

*Electrical*

| | |
|---|---|
| Distributor rotation | clockwise |
| Manual advance | yes |
| Automatic advance | yes |
| Breaker gap | 0.012in to 0.015in (0.305mm to 0.381mm) |
| Plugs | Lodge HLNP |
| Plug gap | 0.025in to 0.030in (0.635mm to 0.762mm) |
| Firing order | 1, 2, 4, 3. |
| Ignition timing | 8 degree B.T.D.C. manual full advance |
| Ignition timing – number of flywheel teeth | 3, before T.D.C. |
| Charging system | Lucas C.V.C. special equipment |
| Battery | 72 amp/hours, Lucas STXW9A |
| Battery earth | positive |

*Capacities*

| | |
|---|---|
| Sump | 14pt (7.95ltr) |
| Gearbox | 2pt (1.13ltr) |
| Rear axle | 5pt (2.84ltr) |
| Cooling system | 21pt (11.9ltr) |
| Petrol | 12½gal (57ltr) |
| Radiator hose (top) | special pre-formed hose |
| Radiator hose (bottom) | 2¼in (57mm), 1¼in (32mm) inside diameter (2 off) |

*General dimensions*

| | |
|---|---|
| Overall length | 15ft 5½in (4,712mm) |
| Overall height | 4ft 11½in (1,511mm) |
| Overall width | 5ft 3½in (1,613mm) |
| Ground clearance | 7in (178mm) |
| Total dry weight | 28cwt, 3,136lb (1,422kg) |

*Top gear data*

| | |
|---|---|
| Road speed per 1,000rpm | 19.6mph |
| Piston speed per 10mph | 402ft/min |
| Litre per ton mile | 2,680 |

Main source: *Riley Sales and Service Bulletin April 1947*

## The Como adventure

Jennings was keen to test Donald Healey's new Riley-engined saloon at maximum speed, but there was nowhere in Britain where this could be done as Brooklands was now closed. He considered Belgium, where many post-war records were to be established, but finally decided on the Milan to Como autostrada, one of Mussolini's pre-war motorways.

Jennings's RMB, registered HXC 440 – that was later to be used in the magazine's British road test – would accompany the Healey across Europe to see just how fast the Westland would go. When Victor Leverett, Riley's sales manager heard of the trip, he joined too in the works demonstrator FDU 741, with mechanic Frank Millington. Before the war Riley had tested all their new models in the Alps so the expedition seemed ideal for factory testing.

It was a considerable adventure given the toll the war had taken; one of the *Motor*'s pictures shows FDU 741 in a bomb-shattered French village. The roads were bad to indifferent – the notorious pavé was in abundance and there was general rationing of petrol in most countries other than Switzerland, though in Italy the black market was thriving.

The three-car convoy set out at the end of October 1946. Leverett writing about it afterwards was proud to point out, as any sales manager would, that the Torsionic front suspension proved itself on French roads 'as we travelled down the Routes Nationale at a steady 80 with a comfortable ride and no driving strain.' Since the suspension had been developed in France by Citroën this was perhaps no surprise.

Jennings was equally enthusiastic about his car, calling the suspension a technical triumph.

*The famous RMB factory demonstrator FDU 741 reached more than 96mph on the Como autostrada in the autumn of 1946. It was a speed never officially bettered, which has led to questions as to how standard the engine was.* Temple Press

*A stop for adjustments on the expedition to Italy; one of the Rileys is by the garage doors in front of the record-breaking Healey that is still running on trade plates to avoid purchase tax. The tall figure in front of the centre garage doors is Victor Leverett, the Riley sales manager.* National Motor Museum

'Allied to the rack and pinion steering and the 9ft 6in wheelbase [it was of course 9ft 11in], the general results are something which many a racing car can not surpass.'

The three cars took a battering over hundreds of miles of French roads before entering smoother territory in Switzerland. In Italy, the Milan Automobile Club had set up the equipment to time the cars on the autostrada, which sounded a lot better than it actually was, since it had just been resurfaced and the top was loose. But it was no amateur event; there were professional timekeepers, white lines painted across the road and warning discs representing the standing quarter mile distance.

The journey was worth it. Healey's Elliott saloon became the fastest car in the world in series production when the Big Four powered it to 104.56mph. It was, of course, considerably lighter than the Riley saloon, weighing only 2,520lb (1,145kg) compared with the 2½-litre unladen at 3,192lb (1,450kg).

But the Riley too covered itself in glory. On a dry day, with a moderate wind, using Swiss petrol and real rubber tyres as opposed to the synthetic versions, which were often the only ones available, FDU 741 smoked away from a standing start to record some remarkable figures for a standard production car.

The standing quarter mile was achieved in 19.8 seconds, which as the *Motor* pointed out, was a time that before the war had been confined to a select few of the world's most powerful high-performance cars.

## The Healey connection

Donald Healey had known the Riley family for many years. During the 1920s he had campaigned a sporting Riley Red-winger, and in 1933, Victor Riley tempted him away from his garage in Cornwall to set up Riley's Alpine Trial team.

He was there only briefly before joining Triumph and then moving to Humber, where he met Achille Sampietro, a renowned chassis engineer. When he decided after the war to build his own sports cars at Warwick, he turned to Sampietro for its chassis and to his friend Victor Riley who agreed to let him have a supply of Riley engines, gearboxes and torque tube back axles. The axles had a final drive ratio of 3.5:1 instead of the RMB's standard 4.1:1, a reduction in engine speed of nearly 15 per cent.

Bodies for the early cars – aluminium over wood frames – came from Samuel Elliott of Reading, who were shopfitters rather than coachbuilders, and Westland Engineering of Hereford.

It was the start of a supply relationship that lasted several years. According to Brian Speirs, an expert on early Healeys, Victor Riley was very kind to Donald Healey and without him Healey sports cars would not have got started; part of that kindness was letting him have the engines and other parts on credit.

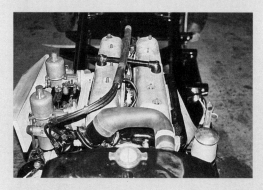

*The Big Four engine in a Healey Elliott saloon chassis.*

It's likely that many of the early engines and possibly other parts, were units left over from pre-war days, like those used in the prototype Westland roadster, a two-door four-seater.

The well-proven 2443cc Riley engine, while becoming known as the 2½-litre in Riley models, was described as a more modest 2.4 litre 'mounted on scientifically positioned rubber pads' in the early Healey.

Healey's Elliott saloon was launched in 1946. It became the fastest car in the world in series production when the Big Four powered it to 104.56mph (168.24km/h) in a test run on the Como–Milan autostrada, one of Mussolini's pre-war motorways. It was, of course, considerably lighter than the Riley saloon, weighing only 2,520lb (1,145kg) compared with the 2½-litre unladen at 3,192lb (1,450kg).

The Healey broke its own record in Belgium the July of the following year by doing 110.65mph (178.04km/h) in a flying mile on Jabbeke–Aeltre highway, and went on to score class wins in the Alpine Rallies of 1947 and 1948 and the Targa Florio. It is remarkable that Healey was still in business in the late 1940s, given that the huge purchase tax on his already-expensive cars pushed the cost of the saloon, for instance, up to £2,723, some £55,000 at 2004 prices.

Other Healey cars that used the same engine were: the Westland roadster (1946–50), the Duncan roadster and drophead (1947), the Tickford saloon (1950–54), the Abbot dhc (1950–54), the Sportsmobile dhc (1948–50) and the Silverstone roadster (1949–50). The Riley back axle was used with a variety of ratios – most of them very high.

The power output was increased; early engines produced 90bhp rather than Riley's 100bhp and later models generated 106bhp rather than 100bhp. Inlet valves were larger, but the exhausts were the same.

While Riley were more than happy to supply the Big Four engine and parts, the Nuffield management were less than enthusiastic, particularly after a visit to Coventry in 1946 disclosed that more effort was being put into supplying Healey than in getting their own 2½-litre into production. In fact, work on building the first Healey roadster body began in Riley's experimental department, but was later moved to Westland Engineering, officially because of a factory reorganization, but possibly as a result of the Oxford management's concerns.

These were high-level grumblings and one memo was sent to Riley saying that further co-operation with Donald Healey should be tapered off and then halted, but in the case of mechanical bits, this was patently ignored, as Riley continued to supply him with engines for another eight years, until 1954 when the Abbot drophead coupé and Tickford saloon – the last cars with Riley engines – were finally discontinued.

But by that time, Healey was no longer reliant on Riley, since his relationship with Len Lord of BMC had led to the production in 1953 of the first Austin-Healey 100 model, the BN1, which used the Austin four-cylinder 2660cc engine.

He had also realized that time was beginning to run out for the Big Four engine and even as early as 1950 and 1951 had sourced engines from Alvis and, for export models only, to the American Nash company.

Brian Speirs records the number of Riley Big Four engines sold to Donald Healey between 1946 and 1954 as 756.

*Autocar's editor took three other passengers across the Alps to the Geneva Motor Show in March 1947 and claimed to have reached an indicated speed of 105mph (168.9kph) on the return journey through France.*

In the maximum speed runs in the flying kilometre, the average of four opposite runs was 94.84mph (152.6km/h) and the best time was a sensational 96.28mph (154.91km/h). Not quite enough for Victor Leverett who thought that he could have squeezed an extra two or three miles an hour out of his car, had the road conditions been better. It would have put the Riley in the same elevated 100mph company as the pre-war Bentley eight-litre, Lagonda saloon de Ville, Hispano-Suiza 54/220 and Mercedes Benz Type 500 supercharged – and it would also have been much better for publicity purposes.

Apart from the effortless cruising speed of up to 90mph, the thing that impressed the *Motor* most was the front Torsionic suspension, which it called the most important feature of the whole car, a technical triumph resulting in performance that many a racing car could not surpass.

There were a few niggles; lights and horn were not powerful enough for the high speeds that were reached and brakes faded on the Alpine passes; these were changed as a result of this expedition.

Brake and cooling testing of the 2½-litre had been done at Gaydon, not at Chalgrove aerodrome where most Nuffield cars were tested, as the bends at Chalgrove were too sharp for sustained high speeds. Cooling testing in those days was a fairly rudimentary yet alarming occupation, where the test car towed behind it another car, or even a lorry, at various speeds up to the maximum, to stress the engine as much as possible.

The 2½-litre was launched on the Continent at the Geneva Motor Show in March 1947, the first post-war international motor show. A demonstration model was driven there by Victor Leverett and Jack Tatlow with Donald Healey as a passenger and with a cargo of petrol cans and an extra spare wheel. The cans were necessary because petrol was still rationed in France, though coupons for 33gal were issued at the French port of landing and more could be got in large towns. There was no petrol rationing in Switzerland.

After various adventures sliding in the snow on the Jura, they had a most successful show, demonstrating the car for their local distributor, Messrs J. & A. Waeny of the Grand Garage, Wabern.

The lure of Coventry in the winter was not strong enough to bring them back as soon as the show ended, so they headed for Monte Carlo and the casino – covering the 332 miles (534km) over the Alps at a remarkable average speed of 53mph (85km/h). The following day returning to Calais, a trip of 824 miles (1,326km), they averaged 51½mph (83km/h) – and that included getting lost in Lyons. As Victor put it: 'for high-speed Continental motoring, the 2½-litre Riley is unsurpassed'.

Also returning to the Alps on the road to the Geneva Show that March was FDU 741, this time with the *Autocar*'s editor at the wheel and three other passengers aboard. Again they achieved high average speeds, particularly on the return journey through France, which excited them beyond measure:

> We watched the needle climb quickly around the dial to 90 and continue more slowly to the 100. Still it went on, 101, 102, the engine pulling strongly and the car riding as steadily as at half the speed. Up to 105 it went, the maximum reading and, with the crew urging it on excitedly, hard up against the stop, where we kept it for between two and three miles.

It has to be said that this was not a proper road test and that there was no attempt to distinguish

---

**The RM toolkit**

New cars today are not expected to be maintained by their owners, so they come with either no toolkit at all or the type of vanity toolkit of useless metric spanners found inside a BMW bootlid.

RM owners were expected to take maintenance seriously – to be able to do a lot themselves and get themselves out of trouble. In the 1950s, few keen drivers would dream of making a long journey without a toolkit like this, taken from the Riley service parts list.

| | |
|---|---|
| Double-ended spanner | ⁵⁄₁₆in × ¼in Whitworth |
| | ³⁄₁₆in × ³⁄₈in |
| | ⁷⁄₁₆in × ½in |
| Single spanner | ⅛in |
| Box spanner | ⁵⁄₁₆in × ¼in Whitworth |
| | ³⁄₁₆in × ³⁄₈in |
| | ⁷⁄₁₆in × ½in |
| Adjustable spanner | |
| Spark plug spanner | 14mm |
| Tommy bar | 2 off |
| Pliers | |
| Hammer | ¾lb |
| Screwdriver | |
| Jack | |
| Starting handle | |
| Wheel brace and hubcap remover | |
| Tyre pump | |
| Grease gun | |
| Brake bleeder tube and container assembly | |

---

between the indicated speedometer reading and true speed. In addition, there has also always been the slight suspicion that works cars like FDU 741 and indeed the 1½-litre road test cars had benefited from a little extra tweaking at the factory that did not find its way on to the production models. After all Riley was making a version of the Big Four engine for Healey with 14bhp more available than in the standard car. Could this have found its way into FDU 741? These figures were never bettered in official tests, even when the power output in later saloons was boosted to 100bhp.

The practice of tweaking test cars was not unknown although manufacturers always denied it officially. Jaguar's first 3.8 E-type road test cars reached the important 150mph mark, which E-types were never to achieve again, even with bigger engines.

FDU 741 had a hard life; in 1948 it was one of the four Rileys opening and closing the Isle of Man TT course for the motorcycle races.

## Pushing up the power

By the time the first post-war London Motor Show opened in October 1948, there had been several changes to the RMB, notably a large increase in power in April 1948 from 90bhp to 100bhp, achieved through the use of larger inlet valves and other cylinder head modifications, such as solid tappets and modified pushrods. There is some disagreement as to whether these began from chassis 58S/2976 or 58S/2959.

There were heavier rear springs, the steering wheel was larger at 18in (460mm) rather than 17in (430mm), and other internal changes were a lower floor, a narrower gearbox tunnel and bonnet fasteners that opened from inside the car – most of these body features, of course, common to the RMA. There was a dashboard-mounted dip-switch to counter long-standing criticism of the floor-mounted version.

'Behind the scenes', trumpeted the Riley publicity, 'there has been unremitting labour in

*The RMB was more than 30 per cent more expensive than the RMA in 1947, which might have been thought to be a high premium to pay for the extra engine power.*

*This unusual woodcut appeared in the* Geographical Magazine *in 1952. It is one of the few advertisements that claims a maximum of more than 100mph, even though this was never validated.*

design, research and experiments, enabling us to announce … improvements to both engines, particularly the 2½-litre which has astonished auto engineers throughout the world.'

Not that there were many 2½-litres for the home market, though the show was a huge success. 'If Britain cannot buy cars, at least it likes to see them' remarked the *Autocar*, which, like its fierce competitor the *Motor*, had been producing a 'motor show on paper' in 1946 and 1947 to keep readers up with developments.

Although a few cars were produced in 1946, it was 1947 before series output really began and then only 600 or so RMBs left the Coventry works. By 1948 this had more than doubled and production rose steadily.

*Autocar* had revisited the RMB at the start of 1949 and was even more impressed. 'No car in existence feels more solid or safer, or is under better control than this Riley right through the speed range up to and over an honest 90mph.'

Capt. Raymond Flower, whose family owned the Cairo Motor Company, once drove the 50 miles (80km) between Port Said and Ismailia on the west bank of the Suez canal in 34 minutes in an RMB. When his passenger and others refused to believe such an average had been reached, he turned around and did it again.

In 1951 *Autosport* used a factory 2½-litre, FMO 165, to cover the Monte Carlo rally, and with three up gave it 'a real tousing'. The conclusions were that it was well-built, handsome and one of the finest high-speed touring cars on the market. There was one curiosity in the report:

> Luggage accommodation can best be described as vast. So much stuff can be accommodated in the rear that it encourages people to take far more baggage than is strictly necessary.

RM owners might care to disagree. Some of the brochure drawings showing cases crammed in the RM boot were often the subject of much artistic licence. To answer complaints of lack of room, a device was available that enabled the boot lid to be left fully open by filling the space with a curious box that acted as a boot extension.

*LEFT: Chris Watkiss drew a lot of the Riley advertising material, but although he was a fine draughtsman, he had to adhere to the convention of the 1940s and 1950s of elongating the cars and shrinking the passengers.*

*BELOW: Though Riley boasted about boot space in their advertisements, it was often inadequate and proprietary boot extensions similar to this could be bought.*

# 5 Major improvements and Abingdon

The design of all Riley models has been so satisfactory that little other than detail alterations have been necessary since their original introduction.

*Autosport* 1950

In 1948 the motor industry was still diverting large proportions of its output to export markets, but cars were getting less scarce on the home market and the London Motor Show was revived for the first time since the 1930s.

So what was the competition for Riley's two sporting saloons at the London Motor Show of 1948? The 1½-litre sold for a basic price of £675, not including purchase tax; this basic price was often the only one quoted in lists due to constant changes in purchase tax. It was never a cheap car as this sort of money would buy the best part of three Ford Anglias or two Austin A40s.

One puny contender was MG's YA saloon, another pre-war design, with the Midget's XPAG 1250cc engine, rack and pinion steering and independent front suspension. It was much cheaper at £525, but considered staid and underpowered.

There were very few cars in the 1½-litre category in 1948, let alone sporting versions. One contender was Gerald Palmer's revolutionary Jowett Javelin. It was £35 cheaper, had 80mph (130km/h) performance, all-torsion-bar springing and rack and pinion steering. It sold far more than the RMs, but the marque was more likely to be associated with its plodding flat-twin Bradford van than sporting success, at least until the 1950s when Jupiter versions began running at Le Mans. Curiously, Jowett was brought down by the very firm that was

partially responsible for the collapse of Victor Riley's company. Briggs, who made Jowett's bodies, were taken over by Ford, who refused to negotiate a contract.

Just about in the same class was Jaguar's 1½-litre saloon, though it was nearer to 1800cc being powered by a 1776cc Standard engine. It was essentially the pre-war model, with upright looks and separate chrome headlamps.

The RMB, at £880 before tax, was almost in a category of its own for engine capacity. Austin's A90 Atlantic with the 2660cc engine that was later to appear in the Healey, was aimed at the American market and might have been considered rather brash by a Riley customer. A more serious competitor was Jaguar, who offered a 2½-litre six-cylinder engine, again in a pre-war body, at £50 more than the RMB.

So both the RMA and RMB had little competition in the market targeting the sophisticated sporting driver. Both cars fitted neatly into the gaps between family cars and the highly reputable but much more expensive offerings from Alvis, Lea-Francis and Armstrong Siddeley, who kept prices a whisker below £1,000 to avoid double purchase tax.

## Changes for the better

In the autumn of 1948, ready for the Motor Show, a series of substantial improvements were made to both saloons.

Externally, there was little to be seen other than that the plated covers on the bonnet sides that covered the carriage locks – or budget locks as they were also known – disappeared, as the bonnet was now released by knobs each side of the glove tray. This was said to be in response to demands from owners for better security. There was still a post–war crime wave. The *Sales and Service Bulletins* frequently carried numbers of stolen RMs – HXK 729 in January of 1948 and GDU 229 in May for example.

The 2½-litre now had detachable bonnet sides, undone by bolts at either end.

The observer, looking at the back of the two models, might have detected that the exhaust tail pipe of the 1½-litre now pointed straight backwards, like the 2½-litre, rather than being angled to the side as in the early models. Probably no-one noticed that the Ioco leathercloth roof covering had been replaced with a new plastic called Melloroid, that was said to have a high resistance to blemish and wear.

Internally, there were improvements in both cars to rubber sealing, around the windscreen, doors and pedals particularly – areas where dust and damp had been identified as a problem by export markets.

The gearbox tunnel was narrowed to provide more legroom and the floor was lowered slightly, to make the seats 1in (25mm) lower as there had been complaints about the headroom. This was cleverly achieved since the overall height of the cars and their ground clearance was unchanged.

There were now front armrests, folding armrests on the rear seats, an extra ashtray on the facia and a new hand dip switch, again on the facia, to replace the previous foot-operated dipper. The headlamps were changed from the 'owl eye' pattern to standard Lucas block lenses on both models.

There was one very welcome addition – given the memories of the winter of 1947, one of the coldest on record. What the *Autocar* called 'an air heating plant', an optional extra costing £25, operated by a knob on the facia, could deliver heat to either the driver or passenger, or demist the windscreen. In factory parlance this was the 'Riley Patent Air Conditioning System' that had a huge blower motor in front of the radiator, though most owners seem to have chosen the two options available from Delaney Gallay or Smiths.

Mechanical changes to the 1½-litre were small; in the engine bay the air intake elbow and air cleaner were moved to give better access to the carburettor and to enable the inlet valve cover to be taken off more easily.

The front hydro-mechanical Girling brakes were now of the HNS1 type, with the upper pull-off spring of the single leading shoe attached to the back plate rather than the trailing shoe.

From chassis 38S 15001 there was a new crown wheel and pinion and in left-hand drive cars the starter motor was transferred to the right-hand side, the main oil feed moved from the left to the right-hand side of the block, and the throttle changed from rod to cable operation.

The 2½-litre's front brakes now had twin leading shoes, but the most important refinement was a big increase in power from 90bhp to 100bhp at 4,500rpm. This was achieved by fitting larger inlet valves, that were no heavier than the previous valves as they were more concave.

All steering wheels had originally been 17in Bluemels sprung spoke, with a cast alloy rim and round spokes. They were to be changed to a mild steel rim with square section spokes and rims were pearl and later brown.

## The move away from Coventry

Soon after these changes were announced came rumblings of a major reorganization of the Nuffield organization and in December 1948, the board minutes of Morris Motors recorded a decision to move MG production from Abingdon and combine it with the Riley lines in Coventry.

The directors said confidently: 'This will create a tidy bloc comprising our two "specialist" cars with Bodies Branch on their doorstep.' All three companies would be under one management and the moves would be made in March 1949.

It appeared to make sense as Bodies Branch specialized in the wood-framed coachwork that was used both by Riley and the MG TC and later the TD. However, the proposal caused outrage at Abingdon, whose MG management were deeply attached to their home in the old Pavlova works in the Oxfordshire town. They immediately began furious lobbying against the idea, pointing out that it made more sense to move Riley production to Abingdon.

George (Pop) Propert, general manager at Abingdon for some twenty years, impressed on the Morris management the alternative proposal that if Riley production were moved, the Durbar Avenue factory in Coventry could then be used to expand the Morris Engines Branch – a definite plus.

Further intensive lobbying on behalf of Abingdon was done by Cecil Cousins and John Thornley at MG, particularly of Morris' chief planning engineer, Tom Richardson, who was to make the final recommendation to the board.

On the other hand, there was no strong body of opinion at Riley agitating for MG to join them in Coventry – it was a different culture in a different county.

By the following month, January 1949, the Morris board's plan had suddenly gone into reverse. MG's move to Coventry, that was such a good idea a few weeks before, was now abandoned due to 'inexpediency' as the board minutes recall it. The reason given was lack of space at the Foleshill factory.

There was some truth in this. Riley had the capacity to produce about 7,500 cars a year, though actual figures were nowhere near this level; in 1948 there were fewer than 3,500 cars produced at Foleshill.

Abingdon could produce 12,000 vehicles a year, though both works were tiny compared with Cowley, 7 miles away, that could produce 168,000.

*Cheerful chaos on the body line at Foleshill in 1948. Note the wings piled up on the left and the rear seat cushions on the car roofs.*
British Motor Industry Heritage Trust

**Abingdon tales**

***Brian Moylan*** *spent many years at Abingdon, where he still lives, 24 of them in BMC's competitions department, where he helped to prepare cars for international rallies.*

'I started working in the MG Factory in 1950 as a fitter in the service department where customers could bring their cars for servicing or repair. Riley production had been transferred from Coventry the previous year, so much of our work was on Rileys.

The Riley was undergoing subtle changes that had not been notified to our department. i.e. the torque tube which runs from a short propshaft from the gearbox to the back axle often required replacing. The replacement had to be bolted to the rear axle and put into the car as a complete assembly; it was entered into the tunnel and then moved forward with a jack under the differential.

For the first part of its movement the boot floor stopped the axle from being jacked up to its correct position causing the nose of the torque tube to foul the top of the tunnel. I overcame this by putting a short plank under the floor and jacking it up just far enough for the tube to clear.

Another fitter attempted to solve the problem by having a mate on the other side and between them they attempted to wriggle the axle forward. Unfortunately they had placed the axle stands under the rear jacking brackets and their wriggling caused the car to move forward off the stands allowing the car to crash down far enough to land on the fitter's head. On returning to work after recovering from the effects of the accident he sued for damages. I don't know the outcome but he left shortly after.

There was an epidemic of cars coming in suffering from a 'grunt'. This occurred when hitting a bump and several cars were sent out again with a promise that when a remedy was found they would be recalled. Eventually the cause was detected when testing a car without the gearbox cover in place. It was realized that in the static position the gearbox was perfectly in line with the short propshaft that went between the gearbox and the torque tube. But if accelerating at the same time as hitting a bump, the torque of the engine plus the differing angle of the torque tube caused the Hardy-Spicer universal joints on the short prop to 'knuckle out'. It was remedied by redrilling the fixing holes in the gearbox mounting bracket to realign the gearbox/propshaft.

During the winter of 1952 there was a mild flu epidemic in the factory causing a shortage of operatives on the production lines, so one or two of us fitters from service were drafted in temporarily to fill the gaps on the lines. My task was fitting the left-hand front wing which is supported by a large bracket. The operative fitting the right-hand wing gave his bracket a couple of thumps with a hammer, which brought the fixing holes into line. I asked him to show me where he hit it, but he replied: 'I've only ever fitted this side wing, I don't know what goes on over your side!'

By 1954 1 was looking for a change of scenery in the factory and I asked the shop foreman what other opportunities there were. He told me that the Racing Department would be opening soon and he would put my name forward as one of those fitters to man the new department. But meanwhile there was a vacancy on production in the rectification department, which paid on piece-work and offered the chance of earning more money.

When a car came off the end of the line it was taken out on the road for testing and a report was made on any faults found. It was the job of the rectification department to cure those faults. The system of payment was eight minutes' pay for any job taking less than 40 minutes; any others e.g. gearbox, engine and rear axle changes had fixed times. These times were quite tight. The best cars were those that had half a dozen jobs that could be put right in a couple of minutes.

One job that entailed removing the Riley gearbox was called 'Clutch Fingers'. These fingers, there are three of them, are what the release bearing pushes against to operate the clutch. If they are not adjusted accurately a pulsing can be felt through the clutch pedal. Sometimes the pulsing may be so minimal that it was not considered to be worth fixing. The shop foreman was the arbiter of the need or otherwise. It was possible that by carefully working the clutch for a couple of minutes the fitter could find a level spot, at which time he would call on the foreman to come and try it. If he agreed then the time-consuming task of removing the gearbox and adjusting the clutch was avoided. But the foreman knew the trick as well so it wasn't often that you could get away with it.

Early Rileys had split front bumpers i.e. a separate left and right bumper blade. Very often one of these stuck forward. The rate-fix time allowed for the bumper blade to be removed, the holes filed out and re-assembled correctly. But it was not unknown for a fitter who needed to make up his time to slacken off the bolts, drive the car against the steel roof-support, put a piece of wood in front of the bumper to protect the chrome and tighten up the bolts when the bumper straightened up.

These are some of the dodges that were practised but the foreman had his eagle eyes everywhere and anybody that committed any act that harmed the efficiency or appearance of the car was soon looking for another job.'

*Geoff Allan began work at Abingdon on 1 February 1954.*

'All the cars coming off the line at Abingdon were road-tested and the Riley had a longer route than the MGs. The cars that needed rectification were put out in the yard to be picked up and driven in to the bay.

I'd been there a fortnight when I picked up a 1½-litre which had 'no brakes' written in six-inch letters on the windscreen. The footbrake didn't work, but the handbrake did, so I drove in very gently into the bay, but when I tried to stop it, the pistol-grip and 18in of cable came off in my hand. I ran over a Pathfinder bonnet and then hit a stack of 48 Magnette bonnets that went down like dominoes, one after the other, with a huge crashing sound that seemed to go on forever.

I saw my life passing before my eyes; I'd only been there a fortnight, but the foreman, George Morris said: 'Don't let it worry you'. They were very good like that at Abingdon.

Another thing we had to do quite often with the 1½-litre was to take off the rear axle and grind about ⅛in off the front gearbox mountings because the chassis was being fouled at the rear end. One chap, Jack Smith, spent his time rectifying bonnet lids, which seemed to need up to half an inch filed off both edges to make them fit.

I also worked on Pathfinders. When we had all that trouble with the servos, we used to take them apart and lubricate the diaphragm with castor oil.

We also had difficulties with the half-horn ring on the Pathfinder steering wheel that was also used for the direction indicators. It was a crude device and used to cut through the wires. Getting the trim to fit along the bottom sills was difficult, so was getting the die casting strips above the lights; we used to hit those with a mallet to get them to fit.

The Pathfinder had an excellent bench seat which moved on ball bearings, operated by two cable-operated catches, one on each side under the seat. But because the driver's cable was 18in long and the passenger's 36in, the cables stretched at different rates, so quite often the passenger side stuck.'

*Derek Slingsby worked in the service department at Abingdon from 1951 as deputy to Arnold Farrar – whom he recalled as a well-respected man who did not suffer fools gladly. He also has fond memories of the RM series:*

'They were a very good, solid motor car – if I'd had enough money at the time I would have bought one. In those days owners could ring up the factory for an appointment and take their cars in to the service department. There were few major service problems with the RMA and RMB, unlike the Pathfinder that was to come later.'

**1949 Riley production year**

|  | 1½-litre | 2½-litre | Totals |
|---|---|---|---|
| Coventry | 408 | 315 | 723 |
| Abingdon | 1,090 | 1,202 | 2,292 |
|  |  | **Total** | **3,015** |

**1950 Abingdon production year**

| Riley 1½-litre | 1,356 |
|---|---|
| Riley 2½-litre | 2,232 |
| **Total Riley** | **3,588** |
| MG TD Midget | 4,767 |
| MG Y-type saloons and tourers | 2,075 |
| **Total Abingdon** | **10,430** |

Nuffield car production was being consolidated and not only Riley was moving; the assembly of Wolseley cars that had been based since the early 1920s at the Ward End Works in the Washwood Heath area of Birmingham, was moved to Morris's headquarters at Cowley. Sales departments were also merged – Riley, Wolseley and MG were now under the same management at Morris's Cowley works. Riley engineering responsibility was also moved there.

'It must be emphasised' said Lord Nuffield in Morris Motors' annual report for 1948, published in June 1949, 'that these transfers will not result in any abandonment of individuality as the products of the Wolseley and Riley Companies will retain their identities to the full, as well as their many special features.'

Fine words, and Nuffield no doubt meant them, but the merger with Austin into BMC some three years ahead would begin to put paid to his promises.

So in 1949, Riley car production at Durbar Avenue ended after more than half a century and the move to Oxfordshire began. The service department began operating from Abingdon on 1 April 1949 with deliveries from there starting in July.

The move to Abingdon took between six and twelve weeks and naturally disrupted production, though not substantially in volume terms, since the previous year the 1948 total from the Foleshill works was 3,232, only some 200 or so cars fewer. However, all figures at this time tended to be erratic due to materials shortages, which gradually lessened at the end of the 1940s.

The disruption would have been far worse had Rileys been produced on powered tracks with conveyor feeds, which would have had to be torn up and relaid, rather than being pushed by hand around the factory, a tradition that continued at Abingdon, where there was no diminution of the quality that had been produced at Coventry, even though several other Nuffield models were being produced there at the same time. In fact the production process was a lot less haphazard than it had been at Foleshill.

Some Riley employees moved permanently to Oxfordshire, but many of the management, like the general manager Jack Tatlow and

*One of the last pictures taken on the finishing line at the Coventry works that Riley had occupied since 1916, which they were to leave in 1949. Despite the fact that Maroon, Green and Ivory were being offered as colour options for the saloon from December 1948, the majority are in Black.*
British Motor Industry
Heritage Trust

the chief designer Harry Rush, having the benefit of factory cars, commuted some 60 miles each way every day on the A34 to Abingdon or Cowley. It was on this road that Rush met his death.

Some anecdotes suggest that there was friction between the Abingdon workers and those brought down from Coventry but certainly by 1951, according to those who worked there, the two cultures were integrated, leading to a happy working relationship.

The production methods were the same as at Coventry. The chassis from John Thompson of Wolverhampton had the engine installed and was pushed down the line until the body that had come from Bodies Branch at Coventry, was lowered onto it.

Although the production tables in the Appendix give chassis points at which production switched from one factory to the other, it is quite likely, given the time involved, that RM production was taking place in Coventry and Abingdon simultaneously until the change-over was completed.

As production of RMs built up at Abingdon, further improvements were announced in the autumn of 1949, for the 1950 model year, that were largely internal and cosmetic.

The defining feature was the new facia in walnut with two round and four square bronze-faced instruments. Square water temperature, oil pressure, ammeter and fuel gauges were neatly placed between the round speedometer and clock. Sporty drivers could specify a rev counter that was incorporated with the clock and the lighting level could be controlled with a rheostat.

Underneath was a row of switches, all now logically grouped together for the first time. Headlamps, side lights and the pass lamps were operated by push-pull action and the driver could select one or two of the pass lamps at a time. These began at chassis 39S 17210 on the 1½-litre and 59S 5218 on the 2½-litre.

Seating was improved with double-sprung seats, map pockets were moved to the doorsides and front armrests could be folded flush

into the doors. There were now two interior lights rather than one, a plastic steering wheel, Bakelite ashtrays, deeper door fillets, recessed sun visors and a new headlining.

All the cars were well equipped, but only the coupé had a heater as standard and radios were extra on all models.

After the years of austerity when almost everything was black, there was suddenly an outburst of colour in 1949. In addition to the bronze instruments, the steering wheel had a gold pearl rim and the new ICI wonder paint Metallichrome, forerunner of today's metallic finishes, was offered for the first time.

In June 1949, *Motor* tested the 1½-litre again. It described it as being at the high-water mark of development as a reliable and economical vehicle for fast long-distance travel, though there were some caveats. Silence and smoothness had fallen rather below standards set by modern cars of lower performance. The engine produced appreciable vibration when idling and some mechanical noise at town speeds, though it was pointed out that thanks to Riley's racing heritage, it operated safely at substantially higher sustained piston speeds than was often thought desirable.

| Standard finishes October 1949 | |
|---|---|
| BODY | TRIM |
| *Saloon and coupé* | |
| Black | Beige, maroon, green, brown |
| Autumn Red | Beige, maroon |
| Almond Green | Beige, maroon |
| Sun Bronze | Maroon |
| *Roadster* | |
| Black | Beige, red, green |
| Almond Green | Beige |
| Clipper Blue | Beige |
| Red | Beige, red |
| Ivory | Red, green |

It also complained that passengers were thrown about a bit in the rear seats, saying they 'do not travel in such tranquillity as the driver', and also that slamming the rear door from inside could give one an unexpected blow on the hip; door pockets and the shelf below the facia were disappointingly small.

However, there was praise for roadholding, steering and an engine outstandingly willing to pull well, showing that despite its essentially pre-war design, the RMA was wearing well.

For the 1952 model year there were cosmetic changes to bumpers, to give a more modern look. New full-width front bumpers and twin-rail rear bumpers were added in August 1951 from chassis 41S 19635 for the 1½-litre and 61S 8338 for the 2½-litre.

The twin-rail was designed by Gerald Palmer, the architect of the Pathfinder. It was seen as a necessity if full-width rear bumpers were to be fitted, otherwise the spare wheel could not pass into its housing beneath the boot.

Bill Boddy in *Motor Sport* complained that the elegant Rileys had been 'desecrated by a towel rail'; whatever the aesthetics of the design, it has led to chipped chrome and broken

*The styling turntable at Cowley was used to preview changes in the body style in 1951. This Almond Green RMA with Woodland Green wings is seen with and without the full bumper.*

D-lights as the door is released from two locking pegs at the base then lifted by the lights and hooked into the lip at the leading edge of the boot floor.

There was a more elegant solution available that had been adopted by Armstrong-Siddeley, which was to hinge the bumper, so that it folded down after two knurled nuts had been unscrewed.

These changes were to be carried over into the 1½-litre's final incarnation, the RME.

## The RMB2 engine

The first major mechanical change in the 1950s was another update of the original Big Four, with what was known as the RMB2 engine with 6.7:1 compression ratio, revised cams and valve gear and modified front suspension cradle. Engine number RMB 2/1 began in the spring of 1952 at chassis 62S 9332 – or 9353 depending on which Riley publication you happen to believe.

The front of the engine was cleaned up so that there was only one drive belt instead of two – the separate belt that had driven the water pump disappeared after engine B8175, as the nose of the pump carrying the fan was now longer and close enough to the radiator.

This also meant that the front suspension cradle had to be redesigned to allow for the path of the single belt. The change to the camshaft and valve timing was to provide quieter running, and there were various small alterations such as a change in the distributor rotation to anti-clockwise in 1953. From engine RMB2/945, shell bearings were used in the big ends instead of the old white metal type.

*Gerald Palmer's 'towel rail' rear bumper replaced the original quarter bumpers from August 1951 to try to update the styling, though many owners think the original spare wheel cover boot lid was better designed for opening and closing.*

*Possibly the ugliest Riley ever conceived, this was an attempt to update the basic RM body by moving the headlamps out to the wings that were probably modelled on those of the Morris Six, recessing the driving lamps and putting chrome flashes on the wing curvature to try to break up the vast expanse left behind. The wings at the side were faired into the driver and passenger doors in a sweep that ended at the bottom of the rear wheel arch. It looked marginally better from the side view.*
British Motor Industry Heritage Trust

## The RMF

In the autumn of 1952 came what was to be called the RMF – a change almost indistinguishable to the outsider because again it was nearly all mechanical. It was essentially a minor updating to carry on the Riley line until the BMC-inspired Pathfinder was ready.

The RMF began at chassis 62S 9911 late in 1952 with the adoption of a full hydraulic brake system that, it seems, did not alter the stopping power of the car, but made the brakes easier to maintain. The chassis numbers were now prefaced with RMF.

The other major change was the disappearance of the traditional Riley transmission by torque tube and spiral drive rear axle to an open propeller shaft with a hypoid axle – changes that were mirrored in the RMA. The hypoid axle was quieter, cheaper and enabled the floor to be lowered.

Another 1952 change was a larger rear window from 62S 10107.

So the progression of the changes to the 2½-litre was: the RMB, the RMB2 from the time of the modifications to the front of the engine, then finally the RMF with the introduction of all-hydraulic brakes.

Despite the *Autocar*'s encomium, and many others like it, the 2½-litre reached its production peak in 1950 with the RMB when 2,232 2½-litre cars were produced, though this figure now included the roadster and drophead, which were coming to the end of their production runs.

It has been suggested that the RMB saloon and its successor the RMF went into rapid decline in 1951 with plunging sales that panicked the management at Cowley. This is not quite the case.

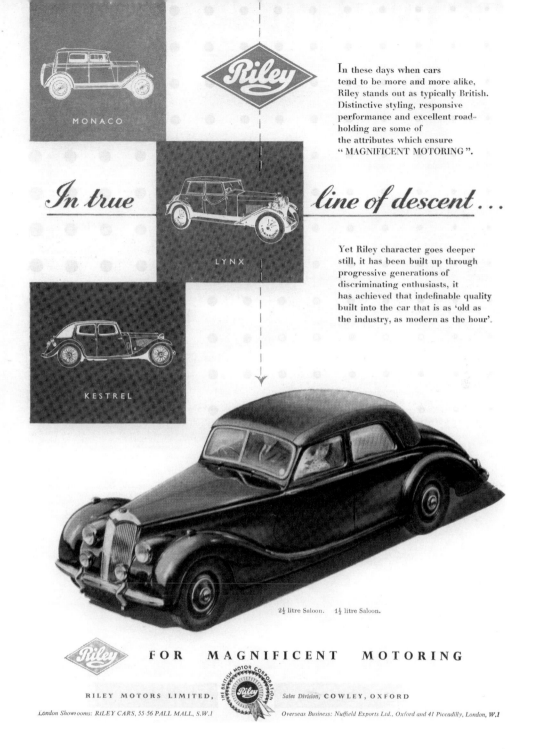

MONACO

*In true*

LYNX

*line of descent...*

KESTREL

In these days when cars tend to be more and more alike, Riley stands out as typically British. Distinctive styling, responsive performance and excellent road-holding are some of the attributes which ensure " MAGNIFICENT MOTORING ".

Yet Riley character goes deeper still, it has been built up through progressive generations of discriminating enthusiasts, it has achieved that indefinable quality built into the car that is as 'old as the industry, as modern as the hour'.

2½ litre Saloon.   1½ litre Saloon.

FOR   MAGNIFICENT   MOTORING

RILEY MOTORS LIMITED,   *Sales Division,* COWLEY, OXFORD

*London Showrooms: RILEY CARS, 55 56 PALL MALL, S.W.1*   *Overseas Business: Nuffield Exports Ltd., Oxford and 41 Piccadilly, London,* **W.1**

The output figure of 2,232 in 1950 was indeed followed by a decline to 1,457 in 1951. However, this does not take into account the fact that the chassis numbers for the roadster and drophead are included in the 1950 figure.

If these are stripped out – 241 in the case of the roadster and 375 in the case of the drop-head – the 1950 saloon production figure was 1,616, and the 1951 figure 1,345. By 1952, there were no more roadsters or dropheads and the 2½-litre sold 1,059.

So the decline was quite gentle until the final year of production, 1953, when 699 were made, but by this time plans were well advanced for the Pathfinder that was to be shown at the London Motor Show in the autumn. There are anecdotal tales of many lying around in dealer's showrooms well after production ended, though this was common when new models were being introduced.

The RMF was not in production for long and only just over a thousand were built between 1952 and 1953. There was not to be a 'spatted' version like the 1½-litre RME; the car had a clearly defined end as the new Pathfinder was already well advanced, so there was no attempt to give it a facelift to extend its life.

So how did it stand up against the competition of its day? There are several sporting saloons with which it could be compared, such as the Sunbeam-Talbot 90, but perhaps the closest in concept to what has been called, perhaps unkindly, a 'gentleman's toy' was the Alvis TC21/100, the Grey Lady.

In December 1982, *Classic and Sportscar* did a back-to-back test of an RMF with an Alvis – both similar hand-built cars with sporting drivers in mind. The Alvis was a 3-litre and cost about £200 more in 1953. The TC21/100, that was a bit of a marketing con trick, was really a standard TC21, but Stanley Horsfield, Alvis' sales manager, had persuaded the factory to install a higher rear axle ratio to enable him to claim 100mph from 100bhp and had added go-faster goodies such as bonnet air scoops.

In the magazine test, the Alvis was praised for its smooth, torquey engine and excellent ride, but lost points for ponderous steering and gearchanging. The Riley, on the other hand, LTR 176, was 'raring to go'. Cornering could be done surprisingly quickly and with the better gearchange and 'an engine that cries out to be used to the full', the Riley won the day. Incidentally, the same magazine analysed average asking prices for all RMs between April and August 1982 and came up with the pointless figure of £1,833.

Some dozen 2½-litre chassis were not fitted with factory bodies; these could have included some estate car versions like the RMAs, but also prototype bodies for cars like the six-light saloon. Some of these are detailed in the chapter on specials.

# 6 The roadster and the drophead coupé

## The roadster – RMC

The decision to go ahead with the RMC was taken by the board of Morris Motors on 25 March 1948. They had seen a prototype but decided it should go into production only if the bumpers and back end were restyled. No numbers for production were specified by the board, though at the same meeting they agreed to construct 5,000 Morris Minor tourers, of which 75,000 were eventually built.

The genesis of the RMC roadster, announced in March 1948 as the Sports 3-Seater, was a response to the 'export or die' philosophy that gripped British industry after the war. It was intended as an export-only car whose

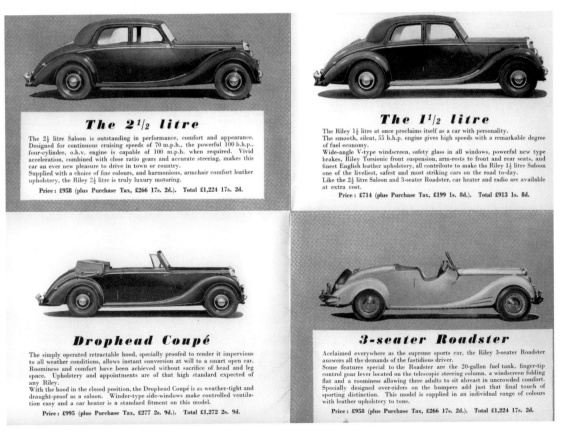

**The 2½ litre**

The 2½ litre Saloon is outstanding in performance, comfort and appearance. Designed for continuous cruising speeds of 70 m.p.h., the powerful 100 b.h.p., four-cylinder, o.h.v. engine is capable of 100 m.p.h. when required. Vivid acceleration, combined with close ratio gears and accurate steering, makes this car an ever new pleasure to drive in town or country.
Supplied with a choice of fine colours, and harmonious, armchair comfort leather upholstery, the Riley 2½ litre is truly luxury motoring.

Price: £958 (plus Purchase Tax, £266 17s. 2d.). Total £1,224 17s. 2d.

**The 1½ litre**

The Riley 1½ litre at once proclaims itself as a car with personality. The smooth, silent, 55 b.h.p. engine gives high speeds with a remarkable degree of fuel economy.
Wide-angle V-type windscreen, safety glass in all windows, powerful new type brakes, Riley Torsionic front suspension, arm-rests to front and rear seats, and finest English leather upholstery, all contribute to make the Riley 1½ litre Saloon one of the liveliest, safest and most striking cars on the road to-day.
Like the 2½ litre Saloon and 3-seater Roadster, car heater and radio are available at extra cost.

Price: £714 (plus Purchase Tax, £199 1s. 8d.). Total £913 1s. 8d.

**Drophead Coupé**

The simply operated retractable hood, specially proofed to render it impervious to all weather conditions, allows instant conversion at will to a smart open car. Roominess and comfort have been achieved without sacrifice of head and leg space. Upholstery and appointments are of that high standard expected of any Riley.
With the hood in the closed position, the Drophead Coupé is weather-tight and draught-proof as a saloon. Winder-type side-windows make controlled ventilation easy and a car heater is a standard fitment on this model.

Price: £995 (plus Purchase Tax, £277 2s. 9d.). Total £1,272 2s. 9d.

**3-seater Roadster**

Acclaimed everywhere as the supreme sports car, the Riley 3-seater Roadster answers all the demands of the fastidious driver.
Some features special to the Roadster are the 20-gallon fuel tank, finger-tip control gear lever located on the telescopic steering column, a windscreen folding flat and a roominess allowing three adults to sit abreast in uncrowded comfort. Specially designed over-riders on the bumpers add just that final touch of sporting distinction. This model is supplied in an individual range of colours with leather upholstery to tone.

Price: £958 (plus Purchase Tax, £266 17s. 2d.). Total £1,224 17s. 2d.

*Riley called these cars its Four Aces.*

main market would be the United States. After all, MG was highly successful in the market for small, uncomfortable sports cars there – why couldn't Riley do the same in the larger luxury sports car market, especially as some US manufacturers did not sell convertible models?

The design was said to have originated from a trip to America by one of the sales staff who had talked to distributors there and come back with a notion of what the Americans wanted. The result was certainly flamboyant by British standards and different from front to back compared with the 2½-litre saloon. Cut-away doors, a huge tail, three-abreast seating and four chrome overriders on large front and back bumpers made it look florid, some might say vulgar, in comparison with the elegant and restrained saloons.

In fact not a single panel was the same, other than perhaps the strip that divided the two bonnet halves – even the bonnet was wider as were the wings. It meant that not only the metalwork but also the ash frame were different from the RMB.

While the publicity maintained that it was built by 'men of creative genius who have always designed cars around an ideal rather than a price', this hand-built extravaganza would be a huge money-loser unless it sold in very large numbers, as there was no commonality of parts. Even the front shock

absorbers were different; the brake hoses were ½in shorter than the saloon's and there was a fundamental difference in the distance between the bulkhead and the dashboard, which affected the placing of the controls so the driver and passengers sat further back than in the saloon.

Underneath the fancy body was the 2½-litre chassis, though the two original prototypes were built on the 1½-litre chassis with left-hand drive. It was certainly a striking prototype that Riley's general manager Jack Tatlow took to the Geneva show in March of 1948 to investigate 'continental reactions', as the *Motor* put it, though he did not arrive until after the show had started, and nothing survives of any reaction. The ivory car, registered FVC 386, had scarlet upholstery, hood and wheels. Like Alvis's whale-shaped TB 14 roadster of the same year, it was a minor and short-lived sensation.

The roadster chassis was not identical to the 2½-litre; the rear springs had nine leaves rather than eleven, there were different outriggers to carry the open body and the frame was strengthened front and rear to carry the huge one-piece bumpers. They wrapped around the rear wings so that 'no dire results would arise when they are subjected to American-style use!' as the *Motor*'s man put it, he obviously having little faith in driving skills across the Atlantic.

*The profile of the roadster looks better with the hood down.*

*Rear bumpers are massive; two quarter bumpers welded to a chromed steel beam.*

*BELOW RIGHT: American-style rear lights have a certain elegance compared to the rest of the styling.*

Neither did Riley it seems, having set the bumper height at the US standard of 18in (457mm) and bolting onto the top of the eight very large overriders some horn-shaped stops to prevent other cars riding over them and hooking on. According to Riley publicity, these overriders added 'sporting distinction', but were more popularly described as 'cow horns'. There was more chrome on the hubcaps that were fully-chromed as standard; the 1½-litre and 2½-litre and drophead coupés were fitted with part-painted hubcaps.

The major mechanical changes were to the steering and gear change. The steering was lower-geared with three turns from lock-to-lock rather than two and a half and the gear change in the first models was on the steering column. This was of course to accommodate the three-abreast seating, which Riley thought would be a major selling point, but it required a lot of fiddling about.

To fit in three people, the steering wheel had to be moved 3in (75mm) nearer the driver's door; this meant that it did not line up with the steering box in the 2½-litre chassis, so to make it work, an intermediate gearbox was used to transfer the motion laterally. Then, with the steering wheel so near the door, the standard 18in (460mm) diameter wheel would not fit,

so the size was reduced to 17in (430mm).

The striking lines were different in almost every particular from the saloon's, though the family resemblance was maintained in the headlamps and front grille. The bonnet line was dropped by 1½in (38mm) – which meant that the radiator was smaller – and a fold-flat windscreen hinted at sporting performance. The doors were cut away to allow American elbows to droop nonchalantly and the huge boot could carry masses of their luggage. Also concealed in the boot were the twin filler caps which fed a petrol tank of 20gal (90ltr) compared with the saloon's 12½gal (56ltr) – as the car was expected to do long freeway trips in America.

The caps had fume-tight lids and there were tubes to drain away any fuel that was carelessly splashed about. Because the tank was so big, there was a curious bodged-up system for measuring the fuel level, using two senders. When the ignition was switched on, the contents up to the first 12gal were indicated, then there was an instruction marked on the gauge 'Push switch for top half' – as a dashboard switch measured the extra contents.

The dash, wider than the saloon's, had a special wax finish to prevent it being bleached by the harsh sun of California and Australia. The hood folded away and was stored with the detachable side screens behind the seat neatly beneath a cover.

## Effortless power and speed

There was to be a two-seater version later in production, but in early versions instead of the saloon's two front seats each with a width of 23in (585mm), the roadster's bench seat was 54in (1,370mm) wide and had a 5in (127mm) adjustment. There are archive pictures of the time showing three large men sitting in the car looking notably glum, as if they had a premonition of the roadster's lack of success.

This was a shame, because despite its raffish looks, it really is a very good car, possessing the Big Four virtues of effortless power and speed with fresh-air motoring. The lower centre of gravity means that it handles even better than the saloon.

The *Autocar* tested FVC 386 in September of 1948 and loved it, calling it a car for the connoisseur, a 75mph cruiser capable of covering big distances fast and tirelessly, its large tank giving it a 450-mile (725km) range. With the hood down 'a beautifully quiet, swift form of travel is experienced, a sensation in motoring that could hardly be bettered in fine weather'. It visualized it flying across France or on 500-mile (800km) hops between cities in South Africa or Australia. Small criticisms were made in the road test of heavy steering and a flapping hood, but overall from the pleasingly British

front-end to the fishtail exhaust, not a standard fitment, there was only approbation.

The point was made that the roadster was not tuned for higher speed, but although it was 120lb (54kg) lighter than the saloon, its acceleration times were similar. The data in the September 1948 test of the roadster, which now had the 100bhp engine rather than the 90bhp at launch, can be compared with the *Autocar* test a few months later of the 2½-litre saloon with the same uprated engine (*see* below).

|            | Roadster    | Saloon      |
| ---------- | ----------- | ----------- |
| 0–30 (mph) | 5.9 (secs)  | 5.9 (secs)  |
| 0–50       | 14.0        | 13.0        |
| 0–60       | 19.0        | 18.4        |
| 0–70       | 28.0        | 27.1        |
| 0–80       | 38.3        | 38.8        |

Though acceleration times were similar, the roadster had the edge on top speed as tests showed it to be about 6mph faster than the RMB.

In August 1948, Major Goldie Gardner's EX 135 streamliner had hit 175mph (282km/h) on the Jabbeke highway in Belgium using the prototype four-cylinder Jaguar XK engine. The roadster was given an opportunity on the same 6-mile stretch the following month. Driven by the Riley sales manager, Tom Sangster, with the hood down and the windscreen flat, it averaged 97.98mph (157.68km/h) over two electrically timed kilometre runs; it must have been a disappointment to Riley that another 2.02mph could not be squeezed out of it – what a publicity gift it would have been.

The XK engine, now six cylinders, appeared in the Jaguar 'Open Two Seater Super Sports', later renamed the XK 120, at the 1948 London Motor Show and was hailed as 'the most beautiful production sports car in the world'. In high-speed testing in 1949, Jaguar's test driver achieved a speed of 133mph (214km/h) during a press preview.

The XK 120 probably put paid to Riley's ambitions for the roadster, which suffered from

*Riley sales manager Tom Sangster, who succeeded Victor Leverett, had started his career with the Swift motor company. Here he is at the wheel of the prototype roadster, GVC 705, that reached 97.98mph (157.64kph) on two timed kilometre runs in Belgium on 1 September 1948. Note the windscreen tied down with string and the buttons on top of the overriders that disappeared on later models. It's not clear what 'international record' was broken.*

a fatal confusion about what sort of car it was meant to be largely due to Riley's failure to understand the American market. Perhaps it would have done better had it been faster, to meet Jaguar's challenge. Riley's sales manager certainly thought so as the minutes of Morris Motors for June 1950 record him making a plea to the board to be allowed to market a 'high-performance two-seater'. The board probably decided that far too much had been spent on the roadster project already, since no such car ever appeared.

When the roadster was first announced, there were no UK prices quoted as there was no intention to sell it in Britain at that stage. 'Acclaimed everywhere as the supreme sports car' said the sales brochure hopefully.

The *Motor* shared this misplaced optimism describing it as 'a car which should have a strong appeal the world over and particularly in America, where it will provide the room to which users in that continent are accustomed …and a performance which will enable it to show off the excellent lines of its tail even to the high-powered cars of the States'.

The reality was different; only seventy-seven went to America, the market for which it was designed, another 130 or so went to Australia. Given the distances that are covered in Australia, the 20gal (91ltr) tank has proved its worth. There are stories, that may be true, that Riley were so desperate to get rid of unsold cars in the USA that they brought them back to Britain and re-exported them to Australia,

*Nuffield were fond of posing cars in front of old buildings to give an 'English' tone to their advertising.*

presumably after swapping around the steering wheel. It has to be said that Riley sources in Australia treat these tales with some scepticism.

As the American magazine *Special Interest Autos* put it in 1984: 'Here was a car, roughly the size of a Chevrolet, powered by a four-cylinder engine that was 25 per cent smaller than a Model A Ford, selling in this country for at least as much money as a Buick Roadmaster.' No wonder it would not sell.

Cliff Baker, who worked for Nuffield exports in the USA, recalled some years ago that when a consignment of roadsters arrived from England it was discovered that the wings had been painted in synthetic enamel and the bodies in cellulose, which meant that the shades did not match. After an initial panic and a decision to respray the wings to match the bodies, someone had the idea of marketing

them as duotones – and charging more for them. It even led to compliments on the subtle British use of colour, but to no avail.

About 60 per cent of production of this initially export-only model went abroad, far fewer than Riley had planned and by the London Motor Show of 1949 it was available in the UK at £1,224, the same price as the saloon.

## The two-seater

However, the 'fingertip control' of the steering column change was much disliked by British drivers, due to its inherent sloppiness in the linkage, and a two-seater version with floor change was introduced to meet the complaints. Some owners got Riley dealers to convert their cars to floor change from a kit that had a curved lever, but there was a factory conversion kit that may have been available with a straight lever – which would have meant a considerable stretch to select first gear.

It has to be noted here that there were never two individual seats in the roadster; it was available only with a bench seat that either seated three or two, depending on the position of the steering column.

*The floor change in the roadster was much preferred to the three-seater's column change.*

Another benefit of the two-seater model was that the steering wheel could now be made larger, moved back to its logical position, without the transfer gearbox as it no longer needed offsetting.

Arnold Farrar, the Riley service manager, remembered that the reason for moving the wheel more towards the centre was so that the driver could reach the floor gearchange.

All the three-seaters were made in Coventry, though after the move to Abingdon, both two- and three-seaters were being produced at the same time. They can be distinguished – apart from the seating – by the chassis prefix; three-seaters begin at 58SS 2802 and two-seaters at 60 2S 4731 – the 2S signifying two-seater. Note that the chassis numbers for the roadster, apart from the prefixes, are not in a series of their own but form part of the 2½-litre sequence. The first production car, a left-hand-drive version, GVC 705, still exists.

There is also a four-seater roadster (which could have been a factory special) that has the unique distinction of never having had a hood frame.

Body numbers of roadsters ran from A34500 to A35000, making a total of 501 cars, but two roadster chassis were bodied as drop-

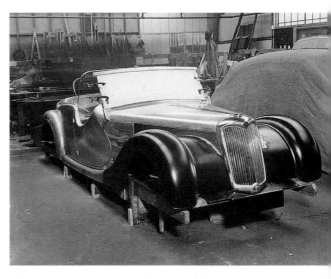

*The roadster body was hand-made in an expensive and laborious process, since there was no part of the wood framework or the panel structure that was the same as the saloon – other than the strip between the two bonnet halves.* British Motor Industry Heritage Trust

*Two-seater roadsters are identified by the '2S' on the chassis plate.*

head coupés by the Dutch coachbuilders Verheul (*see* Chapter 7) and the two 1½-litre left-hand-drive prototypes are unlikely to have had body numbers, leading thus to the conclusion that there were 505 built, rather than the 507 which is often quoted.

Roadster production was in small batches, as it was common in those days for the management to sanction a certain number of cars to be built – in the case of the roadster and the drophead it seems to have been 500, though had the roadster been a success, this number would certainly have been increased with a further sanction. As it was, the early production was of single cars, then as orders came in, small batches, then after the move to Abingdon, batches of twenty-five at a time.

Building the body was a time-consuming affair, given the amount of bespoke woodwork and there are tales that after the front and back were assembled a craftsman made the doors to fit the space between them – which is why it is said no pairs of roadster doors are identical.

It's certainly notable that most roadster drivers seem to have a considerable amount of ironmongery installed to keep the doors closed when they are pressing on.

There were several minor changes in production – removable bonnet sides beginning at chassis 4875, modified left- and right-hand doors at 4731 and revised wiring harness to accommodate a separate solenoid from 5235.

There was competition at the time from not only the Jaguar XK120 Roadster, at only £40 more, but also from the Triumph Roadster, £200 less, and from 1950 an excellent and rare car that also had two occasional seats, the Lea-Francis 2½-litre Sports. It had, of course, a very similar engine to the RMB and torsion bar front suspension – two things that Hugh Rose took with him when he left Riley to join Lea-Francis.

| Roadster colours | |
| --- | --- |
| BODY | TRIM |
| Ivory | Red |
| Black | Red |
| Scarlet | Beige |
| Light Green | Beige |
| Ming Blue | Beige |
| *From April 1949* | |
| Black | Beige, red or green |
| Autumn Red | Beige |
| Clipper Blue | Beige (1949 Motor Show car) |
| Red | Beige or red |
| Ivory | Beige or red |
| Almond Green | Beige |
| Sun Bronze | Beige |

It was plain by 1950 that there was no future for the roadster; Jaguar's version had stolen the market at home and abroad, selling 7,612 up until it was replaced in 1954. The Riley version had been a hugely expensive mistake with body panels that fitted no other car in the range.

Nevertheless, the roadster has a large survival rate in percentage terms compared with other RMs and has a much higher value. The total number built was 505 or 507, depending on whether prototype cars are included; production trickled to a halt in early 1951. As to survivors, the Riley RM Club estimates that there are sixty-five roadworthy cars in the UK. Phil Soden of the Riley Motor Club of Australia, whose own roadster has now done more than 700,000 miles, has counted twenty-six roadworthy cars there and there are said to be nine in America with a handful elsewhere. There are also numbers of unroadworthy cars still awaiting renovation.

## The factory drophead coupé – RMD

Throughout the war years, when new cars were not available and most existing cars laid

*Roadster owners require some ironmongery to stop the doors flying open as the body flexes.*

up, car manufacturers would run magazine advertisements to promise great things when the hostilities were over.

When the war finally ended, the motor industry organized a Jubilee Cavalcade in London to celebrate the fiftieth anniversary of car manufacture, to remind everyone of what they had been missing and to stoke up interest in new models – though there were almost none of those available for the home market. There were similar cavalcades in Cardiff, Birmingham, Coventry and other cities.

*The first drophead prototypes took part in the Cavalcade of the British Motor Industry in 1946. They are seen here in Regent's Park, London, with Victor Leverett, the Riley sales manager at the wheel. Though both proclaim on the windscreen 'This car is being exported', it is highly unlikely that they were since the drophead did not go into production until 1949.*

The 100 H.P. 2½ LITRE **Riley** DROP-HEAD COUPÉ

**H**ERE is another thoroughbred Riley of grace and power . . . swift and smooth-running. Built by men of creative genius who have always designed cars around an ideal rather than a price ; it combines acceleration and high speed with a sureness of road-holding which is quite outstanding.

PUBLICATION No. NEL 113

# *Drophead Coupé*

The simply operated retractable hood, specially proofed to render it impervious to all weather conditions, allows instant conversion at will to a smart open car. Roominess and comfort have been achieved without sacrifice of head and leg space. Upholstery and appointments are of that high standard expected of any Riley.

With the hood in the closed position, the Drophead Coupé is as weather-tight and draught-proof as a saloon. Winder-type side-windows make controlled ventilation easy and a car heater is a standard fitment on this model.

**Price : £995 (plus Purchase Tax, £277 2s. 9d.). Total £1,272 2s. 9d.**

*This is one of the surviving 1½-litre prototype dropheads that has the narrow header rail and saloon-type sills.*

The London event was huge; on 27 July 1946, more than 150 pre-war cars from an 1898 Benz to a 1939 Railton, and including a Riley Nine Special Series Kestrel, processed slowly down Park Lane, along Piccadilly and Oxford Street to Regent's Park where they were reviewed by the King and Queen. The motor industry's faltering post-war start was represented by 107 new cars that came from all the manufacturers, among them new proto-type Rileys – two drophead coupés.

If there were ever a classic British two-door four-seater convertible, this was it. In side view there are few similarities to the 1939 12hp Sprite drophead Touring Saloon – apart from the door handles and the pram irons that keep the hood rigid. The Nuffield car was bulky – the RM version was lower, sleeker and more elegant, though the post-war car is longer and lower – but the wide doors, sloping tail and the chrome pram irons that keep the hood rigid are reminiscent of the pre-war model.

Several prototype bodies were made, three on the 2½-litre chassis – two built at Coventry and one, NFC 400, made at Abingdon. These early cars had running boards the same length as the 1½-litre, external bonnet locks and sharp-cornered quarter lights. They also had a very narrow header rail.

## Changes to doors

The first versions also had heavy steel doors, with a tensioning rod to give support to the door pillar. Later cars had aluminium doors. Jim Fletcher, the owner of LYX 92, one of the 1½-litre prototypes, has noted that although the chassis number 39D16122 is a 1949 number, the glass in the doors is dated 1946, so the RMD drophead was a car that took an age to get into production, because of the need for development and the concentration on the saloons.

Having first appeared in 1946, the next sighting was two years later on the Riley stand at the London Motor Show in the autumn of 1948 when an ivory right-hand-drive drophead made its debut, at a total price, including tax, of £1,214, which was £49 more than the RMB saloon.

Not until the following year did it go on sale properly and by then the 1½-litre chassis had been replaced with the 2½-litre. There were substantial modifications to parts of the body.

The thin header rail was made much broader to give more stability to the structure and to combat severe scuttle shake. The battery was moved from the bulkhead to beneath the floor on the passenger side (rhd) for the same reason.

There was further stiffening by the addition of a plate about 6in (15cm) behind the rear seat, and the sills, which were the same as the saloon originally, were strengthened by the addition of substantial timber members each side. Nevertheless, many of the body panels, particularly at the front, were identical to the RMB saloon.

The hood originally had a heavy wooden frame to contain the rear window, but difficulties in clipping in the lining and stowing the hood led to it being replaced with a chromed brass frame with a Plexiglass light.

The car was much easier to produce than the roadster, as the chassis needed little alteration from the saloon version, requiring only different additional body mounting brackets and a battery box support.

'Built by men of creative genius who have always designed cars around an ideal rather than a price', burbled the Motor Show publicity in 1949, though not forgetting to mention the price, which was £995, neatly keeping it under the double-purchase tax barrier of £1,000.

As it was, the £277 purchase tax that was applied made it £1,272, which meant the differential between it and the RMB had stretched to £145. It had the luxury of a heater as standard, something for which buyers of the saloons had to pay extra.

Naturally much was made of the folding hood – 'simply operated, specially proofed to render it impervious to all weather conditions'.

These claims were to be tested by *Motor Sport*, whose former managing editor T.G. Moore, ran into heavy thunderstorms in Denmark during a 2,000 mile (3,200km) continental tour in his own drophead. He reported that the hood remained water-tight under all conditions and proved 'a great joy' as it could be folded down and stowed in the well behind the rear seat in less than a minute.

With the hood down, there was no more impression of speed at 80mph (130km/h) than at 40mph (65km/h), though with the hood up he reported a fair amount of wind noise at 70mph (110km/h), probably from the hood irons that project from the side of the car.

Riley suggested a maximum of 4,700rpm but our intrepid tester pushed it to 5,000rpm without any valve bounce; at those revs he was doing an indicated 94mph, not a true speed, since he had earlier noted that the speedometer was 6mph fast at 80mph.

Hard to beat as a dual-purpose car and distinctly good value for money, was his conclusion.

Despite his praise of the hood, it was still troublesome even with modification. Further changes, in a works drawing dated July 1950, show changes to the roof lining to avoid friction wear.

Alternate batches of left- and right-hand-drive cars were produced fifty at a time initially, with production rates tailing off as the sanction of 500 cars was reached in 1950. A total of 503 bodies were produced.

*Mittel-European peasants gasp in amazement as the Riley drophead coupé – somewhat larger than life – sweeps by.*

At least one of the spare three bodies languished for some years in a corner of Jimmy James's service depot at Kentish Town in London. A Professor Berry noticed it when he took his RME there for a service in 1958 and asked if the bodies could be exchanged. It was then a dull metallic brown with red upholstery. NXM 866 was acquired by Allan Fuller in 1971, restored and painted ivory in the 1980s and in 2005 was still in his ownership.

Compared with the roadster, the drophead was an export success, with 417, more than 80 per cent of the total, going overseas.

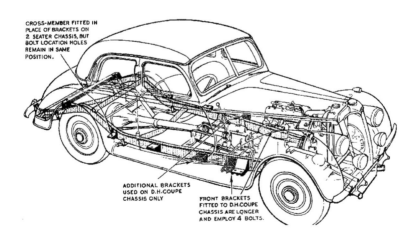

CROSS-MEMBER FITTED IN PLACE OF BRACKETS ON 2 SEATER CHASSIS, BUT BOLT LOCATION HOLES REMAIN IN SAME POSITION.

ADDITIONAL BRACKETS USED ON D.H.COUPE CHASSIS ONLY

FRONT BRACKETS FITTED TO D.H.COUPE CHASSIS ARE LONGER AND EMPLOY 4 BOLTS.

# 7 Woodies, dropheads, specials and other curiosities

## The woodie

The heyday of the British woodie, described variously as a wooden-bodied shooting brake, estate car or station wagon, falls directly into the period of the RMA and RMB.

Though British coachbuilders had been using the woodie style in small-scale production since the 1920s, the years between 1946 and 1954 saw a huge increase in the production of these vehicles – driven entirely in the early years by the post-war shortage of steel.

Car manufacturers could barely get steel to make chassis, and often lacked the raw materials to construct sufficient bodies, so firms like Riley, Austin, Alvis and Lea-Francis supplied chassis to anyone who could put a wooden top on them, from professional firms like Riverlee Motor Bodies of Birmingham and Jennings of Sandbach to the village carpenter commissioned by a local, for there was no shortage of wood or of aluminium left over from the aircraft industry's wartime production. Some results were excellent, others less aesthetically happy.

DCX 887, for instance is known in Riley club circles as the Pigeon Loft, while EVN 808 is the Flying Greenhouse.

The original shooting brakes of the 1920s and 1930s had been conceived as luxury vehicles to carry landowners on hunting parties on their private estates, but post-war woodies were more utilitarian. Construction, design and materials were not always to the highest specification and the high maintenance required to keep the exposed woodwork in good condition meant that most woodies did not last more ten years.

*One of the most elegant of the woodies was this HBH made in Hillingdon, West London, by a firm that also made caravan bodies. The son of one of the firm's founders has been trying to track it down. Colin Peck*

In the days when everyone wore hats, the low and sleek RM was a most unlikely candidate as a utility, but the severe shortage of new vehicles meant that bodybuilders would adapt whatever chassis they could get their hands on.

An additional attraction in those straitened times was that the woodie qualified as a commercial or utility vehicle and thus avoided the punitive purchase tax – much as a Minivan did in the 1960s – though top speed in the 1940s was not meant to exceed 30mph.

Riley's Coventry neighbour, Lea-Francis, were prolific in their sales of woodies – around a thousand of them up until the early 1950s – but Riley had far fewer woodie-bodied cars and only in the years 1947 to 1949.

Some 227 1½-litre and eleven 2½-litre bare chassis left the Coventry works and it is believed that many of them ended up as woodies.

By the late 1940s, steel was becoming more plentiful and Riley were able to return to producing everything in their own works.

*RIGHT: The constructors of woodies were of varying ability from the professional to the ungifted amateur. This was constructed in the Portsmouth area and is known as 'Harvey's hearse' for the good reason that it was once owned by a man called Harvey and it looks like a hearse. Alec Gatherer*

*BELOW: A 1947 RMA chassis 37S 14093 is beneath this traditional shooting brake body that was originally in Maroon and Light Oak. GWF 84 was sold on 2 December 1949 for £1,175, which was very expensive considering that a new RMA that year was £913. But continuing shortages of new cars drove up second-hand prices. Gwyn Morris*

*This woodie is in Australia and could be a home-grown product.* Phil Soden

*BELOW LEFT: A sad woodie awaits restoration in Essex.* Colin Peck

There are now only a handful of Riley woodies left, due to the ravages of decay. Those which have been recorded include bodies by:

**Bonallack:** built at least two woodies, CAN 832 (*see* picture opposite), which is notable for its fastback styling and has been restored, and CAN 102. There was also a hearse-like contraption in black with no apparent woodwork that was attributed to them.

**Clifford Dibben of Southampton:** made caravan bodies and were responsible for a curious version, FCR 339, furnished in mahogany, that had two doors on the nearside and one on the offside. It may well have been used by a children's home.

**Frank Grounds of Birmingham:** a high-roofline woodie, HOX 926, with single-piece top-hinged tailgate, probably the only woodie on an RME chassis, but that was previously on a 1947 RMA. Frank Grounds' name appears in the list of Monte Carlo entrants.

**Heywood, Biggs and Hill,** of Hillingdon, West London: bodied an unknown quantity of Riley RMs and Citröens into stylish woodies. The Woodie Car Club (www.sitegarden.co.uk/woodied/news8.htm) has been trying to find out on behalf of the son of coachbuilder Alfred Hill if any survive. HB&H also used to build caravans.

The founders also worked for Park Royal Vehicles, on the Routemaster bus.

**Jensen of West Bromwich:** a body that may well have come from another car – an Alvis - now resides on chassis 37S 13975, though it is registered in Jensen's home town as DEA 593. It has a single windscreen and like the Dibben car has two doors on the nearside and one on the offside.

*A recently restored Bonallack shooting brake. At least two of these survive.* Allan Fuller

**Massey of Market Weighton, Yorkshire:** at least three examples, GWF 322, FWF 999, HWF 993. May also have bodied a van.

**J. Urquart and Son Ltd of Petersfield, Hampshire:** This 1½-litre offering was noted in the motor magazines of the time. It was 66lbs (30kg) heavier than the saloon, with oak frame work and timber panelling. It was upholstered in plastic and had fixed back panelling and permanent seats, so did not qualify as a utility vehicle.

**Vincents of Yeovil:** made in their body shop at East Coker from a bought-in pattern, EVA 626, one of a pair. It had a cream rexine roof, plywood panels, oak frame. The tailgate hinges were from a household door. Vincents bodied a 2½-litre estate car chassis 58S 3536, registration AKS 763.

There were probably scores more woodies that have never been recorded as they were built by firms that have long disappeared.

Other commercial vehicles on Riley chassis included two or three high-roofed Luton vans built for a London dress manufacturer, an ice cream van and at least one pickup.

## The six-light and other saloons

The six-light Riley saloon, built on the 2½-litre chassis, was created for Herbert Clarke, a director of Morris Engines' branch in Coventry, who had been in charge of Nuffield's Spitfire engine plant at Castle Bromwich during the war.

It is said to have been the last car to be built at Coventry before the move to Abingdon and though several standard panels were used in its construction, it had a steel roof and a Jaguar Mk V-style bootlid. There were also different internal features to the RMB such as a revised instrument panel and chrome grab handles.

There has been much speculation as to whether this was a prototype for a Riley limousine, but given the owner's standing at Nuffield, it is more likely that it was a one-off to his own specification.

Other non-standard saloons included a conversion by Tickford the coachbuilders, who offered to install a full-length sunroof on standard 2½-litre saloons. One peculiar saloon, KGF 10, built for a doctor, had a pre-war Nuffield 12 body on an RMA chassis, but with post-war front wings and bonnet.

Another oddity was the powder-blue EVN 808, which had Perspex panels in the roof and windows let down by leather straps as in old railway carriages. There were also some pre-war Kestrel bodies put on post-war chassis; these were retrofitted rather than being factory constructions.

In Switzerland, Adolf Ditting produced in 1949 a steel-roofed saloon that had long swooping front wings faired into the doors; another Swiss coachbuilder confined his efforts to remodelling the radiator shell to make it more pointed.

*The six-light saloon was sometimes thought to be a prototype for a Riley limousine, but it was much more likely to have been built to special order for a Nuffield executive.*

*Interiors changed little over the years, but became more luxurious. The square-topped seats were the later versions.*

LUXURIOUS INTERIOR. Interior of the new 1½ litre Riley is wide and roomy, styling is distinctive. Seat backs and cushions are covered with fine quality pleated leather. A central arm-rest forms part of the rear seat and an arm-rest is fitted on each rear door. Both front seats are adjustable. In territories where it will be required, a car heater is a standard fitting.

The oldest surviving RMB, 56S 2014, constructed in August 1946. It is now under restoration.

The Reinbolt and Christe replicas make hood stowage a lot more elegant than the standard factory versions. But with hood up, visibility from the rear seats was dismal. Colin Readey

*The rakish lines of the roadster failed to impress the Americans, the target market.*

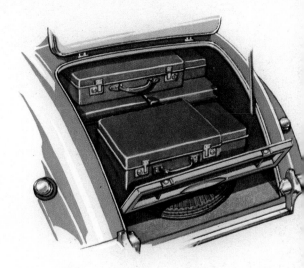

The wide V-type windscreen affords splendid all round road vision, and both wings are visible from the driver's seat. A full range of instruments, including a water temperature gauge, is well grouped in a handsome walnut panel. The spring spoked steering wheel is adjustable

Without giving any appearance of bulkiness in the tail, luggage locker is of exceptional capacity. All the lugg necessary for an extended tour can be stored without diffic The spare wheel is housed in a separate compartment

# THESE FINE FEATURES BRING

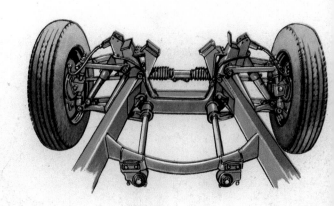

A view showing the extra long swivel pins, tubular struts and dampers. The rack and pinion steering gear can also be seen. Steering is always accurate and positive even under really rough conditions.

Riley " Torsionic " independent front suspension forms a complete unit which incorporates the steering mechanism, forming an extremely rigid front end. The lower struts are attached to short parallel torsions bars with cam adjustments at the rear ends. Very little maintenance is required.

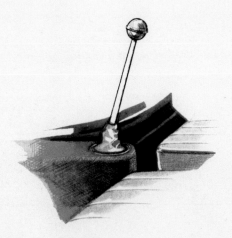

A gear change lever of the short remote control type is fitted. It is correctly sited and synchromesh on second, third and fourth gears, aids rapid, silent gear changes in dense traffic or when overtaking.

Operated by concealed locks, and opening on each side, the distinctive Riley bonnet is uncompromisingly British in appearance. Twin pass lamps are standard and jacking points are located under the quarter bumpers.

 **MAGNIFICENT MOTORING**

Like the Riley engine, the chassis frame has been developed from the experience of many years of racing. It combines minimum weight with maximum rigidity and is downswept at the centre to give a low centre of gravity. This allows fast, safe cornering and ensures complete freedom from sway and roll at all times

# Riley

# 1½ LITRE 2½ LITRE

2½ LITRE SALOON (in Metallichrome Grey)

—and here's the secret of  super performance

Among those motorists who study engine details the Riley has always held a high position of esteem because enthusiasm for the niceties of engine design is often the first step towards Riley ownership. The world-famous Riley is available in a 2½ litre model, capable of 100 miles an hour, and a 1½ litre model which also provides the thrill of sports car performance. Proved leadership in design makes permanent a Riley owner's enthusiasm for his car.

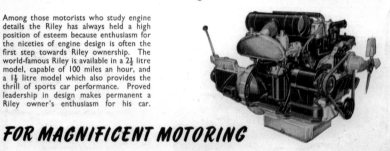

## FOR MAGNIFICENT MOTORING

*PREVIOUS PAGE: This brochure was prepared for the 1951 London Motor Show and shows how Riley publicity continued to emphasize advances in steering and suspension still not found on many other makes.*

*BELOW: The Flowing Well pub near Abingdon was used in Nuffield publicity pictures. This is not one, but a re-creation using a 1949 RMA. It has been fitted with a 2½-litre back axle.*

*ABOVE AND LEFT:*
*This drophead body*
*was left over when the*
*factory stopped making*
*the car. It was found*
*many years later and*
*put onto an RME*
*chassis.* Allan Fuller

*Ivory became a popular colour*
*from 1948, particularly for the*
*Roadster, which often had*
*white-wall tyres as well. Ivory*
*was not listed for a while in the*
*early fifties due to an explosion*
*of Metallichrome finishes, but*
*returned with the RME.*
*However, the factory was usually*
*flexible enough to provide any*
*colour to special order.*
Allan Fuller

Just like new…a meticulously restored RMA engine bay in chassis 36S 10177, one of the earliest RMAs known to survive. EN 8601 has been with the same owner for more than forty years.

ABOVE AND ABOVE RIGHT: Many owners prefer the classic pre-war round dials to the later panel with some square instruments.

BELOW: The 1½-litre drophead prototype seen here did not make it into series production, being replaced on launch in 1949 with the engine from the RMB.

*Good try, pity about the back end.*

*A very neat conversion of RMA chassis 39S 16402 into a two-door coupé. The roof retracts into a* coupé de ville *position just behind the driver's seat. The running gear comprises an MG 1789cc engine and gearbox. The wheels, too, look like MG.*

**Police RMs**

Riley RMs were popular with police forces, most using 2½-litre cars for their speed and power, though even more popular were big Austins like the 105 Westminster, which in 1956 was £300 cheaper than a Pathfinder.

Gloucestershire police acquired a large RM fleet – twenty-six at least – of both 1½-litre and 2½-litre saloons between 1946 and 1949. In June 1948, they announced that they were enlarging their fleet with more 2½-litres 'to combat the crime wave' that had got steadily worse since the end of the war.

*Gloucestershire police were one of the main users of RMs. They bought ten RMBs in 1946 and lined them up for this picture in front of the Pittville Gate at Cheltenham.*

The Gloucestershire constabulary allocated a two-man crew to each car, some of which were fitted with grab rails on the exterior, so that the passenger could ride on the running board during hot pursuits. On one occasion, a car ploughed into a brewery lorry at high speed when a tyre burst. The car was cut in half and one of the policemen seriously injured. After that the cars were fitted with double-skinned inner tubes.

The Gloucestershire Rileys were sold off when they had done well over 100,000 miles (161,000km) and replaced with Pathfinders and Wolseleys. The total post-war figure was forty-five Rileys according to *Motoring*.

*Collecting one of the first Gloucestershire cars from the works at Foleshill.*

The force was probably Riley's largest police customer other than Essex, which did a lot of driver training on RMs for other home counties forces. Other constabularies that used RMs included Portsmouth, Devon, Brighton, Norfolk, Sussex, Buckinghamshire, Oxford and Cambridge. They were also popular among Scottish forces – among them Aberdeen, Berwick, Dunbarton, Lanarkshire, West Lothian and Roxborough and Selkirk.

Factory analysis of the service records of the fleets of the Gloucestershire, Portsmouth and Stirling forces showed that the only serious engine rebuilds were the replacement of big ends at huge mileages; pistons, bores and rings were not touched.

Buckinghamshire bought a fleet of nine Pathfinders in 1955 and the City of London police ran at least two Pathfinders.

Abroad, three Pathfinders were delivered to the Rhodesian police and one drophead was reportedly used by police in Victoria, Australia.

*Police two-way radios were very bulky and needed extra power. This is a Gloucestershire car of 1951.*

*continued overleaf*

**Police RMs** *continued*

*The Brighton force had just taken delivery of these cars. The driving lamps have been moved to the sides and brackets put on ready for the installation of the Police signs.* Peter Roberts Collection

*An original Portsmouth police car with all the special items intact. It is owned by Steve Kinch.*

The police radios of the time were in their infancy – Devon constabulary, for instance, did not use wireless patrols until 1948 when they were introduced in the 'H' Division covering Plympton & Roborough.

Adaptations had to be made for police equipment; the Butler driving lamps were often moved outwards from the centre to make room for Police signs and for loud-hailers.

The radios were cumbersome and quick to drain batteries, so forces often fitted heavy-duty dynamos and batteries and additional ammeters to monitor the current.

The Riley RM Club database has traced eighty-six former police RMs, of which some twelve may be roadworthy.

*A Sheffield-registered police Pathfinder heads a royal procession in Stirling in 1955.*

## Specials

A well-known special is 42 EPB, a 1947 1½-litre, which judging by the registration mark was probably rebodied about 10 years later. There has been much speculation that it was done by a London firm FLM Panelcraft, or even Bertone, as it bears a resemblance to his Alfa Giulietta coupé. Neither coachbuilder has any claim to it. It was first offered for sale in 1973 when it was red with no interior trim, had full-width bumpers and RM wheels. Later it may have been worked on by a coachbuilder in the Ashford area of Kent.

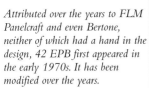
*Attributed over the years to FLM Panelcraft and even Bertone, neither of which had a hand in the design, 42 EPB first appeared in the early 1970s. It has been modified over the years.*

The bodywork was assembled on chassis 37S 12701, shortened by about 14in (35.5cm) and, according to records, the car might have been painted yellow or silver originally, but has been racing green for a number of years. There are bucket seats to the front and small single rear seats. The car was advertised for sale in 1990 for £22,000.

A much-used special on the Isle of Man was JMN 194, built by Crosbie and Cowley of

Douglas for Captain P. Kissack on an RMB chassis. It had a two-door, four-seater aluminium body over a steel-tube frame with louvred bonnet, held firm by straps and with cycle wings. It was used in 1948 as a course car during the Isle of Man TT races.

## The Köng coupé

Possibly the most flamboyant Riley ever built is the Köng coupé – a two-door RMB that appeared at the 1949 Geneva Motor Show, offered by coachbuilder Walter Köng of Basel at the enormous price of 80,000 Swiss francs, enough for several luxury cars. It is still owned by a Swiss and draws crowds whererever it goes.

The front is reminiscent of the Jaguar XK 120, with a narrow radiator, and similar bumpers, the sides show the influence of early Healeys and the roof has glass panels that can be taken out and stored in a special compartment in the boot. Interior trim is brown leather but the steering wheel and the dash housing the standard RM instruments are a startling red.

*The Köng coupé is possibly the most flamboyant Riley every built. Introduced at the 1949 Geneva Motor Show on the 2½-litre chassis it was priced at 80,000 Swiss francs, an enormous amount which ensured that Herr Köng was able to build only one. The car is still in Switzerland. Both the dashboard and steering wheel are a startling scarlet.*

## The 'rare prototype'

In 1990, a dealer's advertisement appeared in the classic car press for what was described as a 'rare prototype' of the RMA, registered HG 9295, a Burnley number – unlikely for a Coventry factory car. It turned out to be no such thing, as the Riley cognoscenti were quick to point out.

It was a combination of the chassis of a 1947 saloon, 37S 12618 and a Kestrel body from a 1937 1½-litre whose chassis had rotted away. The RMA had been hit up the backside in an accident and registered as an insurance loss. It was bought from the insurance company and divested of its body that was then replaced with the Kestrel's by Albon Crofts, the Croydon coachbuilders. The restoration was well documented and the car was sold on with all the restoration details, which perhaps went astray some time later.

Another car on a post-war chassis with a 1937 Kestrel body is BDK 547, that Colin Ready fitted with very little modification.

## Other dropheads

Several firms, apart from the Riley factory, produced drophead bodies on both 1½-litre and 2½-litre bare chassis.

These are the best known:

## Bonallack

The firm better known for truck bodies put dropheads on six RMA chassis between 1948 and 1949, according to Sir Richard Bonallack. They were known as Rapid Coupés and have a wider flash on the doors than the standard coupé. DAN 93 survives as does CJD 257, which has a three-position hood and mainly aluminium body panels. Some of the cars are said to have had one-piece windscreens.

## Epps

The *garagistes* Epps Brothers of Croydon Road, Penge, in south London, were notable for building ten two-door dropheads on bare 1½-litre RMA chassis. There were apparently two styles, one rather conventional, the other not so, but the common factor was the V windscreen with thick pillars, said to have been modelled on the American Cord 812 Phaeton of 1937. Apart from the thickness, the distinguishing feature was that the surround was painted rather than being chromed. Arnold Farrar disliked the style and criticized the pillars for their reduction of driver vision.

One of the cars that survives in the conventional style is MPF 423 – once one of Mr Epps' personal transport vehicles, which has the usual RMA wings and running boards, but the doors

*An Epps coupé taking part in the* Daily Express *Rally. The original Riley wings were below that bulbous bodywork. Note the Epps trademark of the Cord-type windscreen.* National Motor Museum

are much deeper than usual so the window glass is smaller – again a visibility issue.

The car was restored from a bare chassis in eighty days by John Kirby, the Riley RM Club spares secretary, in time for his daughter's wedding. He discovered that the car was oak-framed – even the boot floor – and that it was probably the prototype, as the nearside sill was built up of laminations as the shape was being determined, whereas the offside sill was solid, presumably a copy of the other. But neither side of the car matches the other completely. The original chassis number dates it to 1947, but the 7 has been overstamped with an 8.

The other style of car was completely different, with American-influenced bulbous front wings that were swept into the doors, no running boards and rear wings that covered much more of the wheels. These wings were actually fitted on top of the existing Riley wings, so the implication is that when the chassis arrived at Epps on a lorry, the wings were already in place on the otherwise bare chassis.

According to correspondence with one of the Mr Epps, reported in the Riley RM Club magazine some years ago, all the panel work was rolled by hand, the timber cut from ash logs and the trimming done in the body shop. These were expensive cars, costing £2,000 when an RMA saloon could be had for £863, because they fell foul of the double purchase tax regulations.

It is said that five of each type were made, with two or three being exported. Mr Epps, who also bodied two Rolls-Royces, said he would have created more Riley dropheads, but the supply of chassis was uncertain.

The Epps' garage was demolished and the firm was bought by Saunders and Abbott of Croydon, which is now part of a company holding Skoda and Kia franchises in the south of England.

## Mead

Typical of the small coachbuilders who would put a drophead on anyone's chassis was Richard Mead, of Dorridge in the West Midlands. Alvis, Jowett and Bristol chassis went through his works near Solihull and emerged as drop tops as did a single Riley chassis that was originally a saloon. It became GOM 875, a drophead looking remarkably like the Rover Marauder, for which Mead had a supply contract.

Mead had been apprenticed to the Corsica coachworks in London, but was dismissed when they found he was under-age. He then worked for his father, also a coachbuilder, and during the war was at Jensen.

He told the author that after he advertised his coachbuilding services in the *Autocar*, the chassis arrived by train, then he and his staff of ten set about clothing them with aluminium alloy panelling on wooden frames that were created from scratch each time. Fortunately he was able to call for help on his father, who worked in the sawmill next door making laminated sections for the new razor-edge Triumph.

In those post-war days of shortages, there were restrictions on the use of fabric to make the hoods and trim – a Cotton Permit had to be obtained and any fabric used reported to Customs and Excise. 'They made life unbearable', he said, 'always breathing down your neck, particularly before a Budget.'

In the 1950s, when the major manufacturers were no longer plagued with shortages, small businesses like Mead's began to struggle. He emigrated to what is now Zimbabwe and spent many years working in the copper mining industry. In his latter years he lived in Northern Ireland and still kept an interest in renovating cars, still using the wheeling machine he had used at Dorridge.

His only Riley has disappeared.

## Reinbolt & Christe

For some reason there was at that time a large market for drophead coupés in Switzerland. Riley's own drophead was not to appear until the autumn of 1948 and not to enter serious production until 1950, so J.H. Keller, the Riley dealer in Zurich, seizing the opportunity, commissioned a drophead coupé from the small but famous coachbuilding firm of Reinbolt & Christe in Basel. They are best known for their striking two-seater Horch 710 Spezial of 1934, which continues to win prizes at major concours.

The Swiss Riley prototype drophead appeared first in the summer of 1948. Reinbolt & Christe had taken a standard RMB saloon and converted it into a two-door car. The original wings, running boards, front seats and instrument panel were retained, the windscreen was strengthened and the chassis stiffened at the hinge points of the wide, heavy doors.

Though it maintained the original lines, albeit with longer chrome waist strips, it looked a lot cleaner than the Riley factory version that was to follow, because the hood folded away flat at the rear. The disadvantage was that when it was up, the back seat passengers had no side visibility at all. A version appeared at the Geneva show in March 1949 with grey leather upholstery.

Apparently the RMBs were shipped to Basel CKD, which avoided too much disassembly of the saloon bodies. A small series of the dropheads was made before Reinbolt & Christe went into liquidation at the start of the 1950s. The Keller records have disappeared and the practice in Switzerland of allocating a registration number to the owner of the car not the vehicle makes it difficult to trace the history of the cars. However, one survives, owned by a member of the Riley-Club

Switzerland, as does a series of excellent Reinbolt & Christe replicas made in Britain on 1½-litre and 2½-litre chassis in 1991 and 1992, that are now officially recognized by the RM Club.

Their maker was Colin Readey, a naval surveyor and a prolific collector, who once had twenty-six Rileys of various ages – and whose ventures have included converting a roadster to a drophead and putting a 1937 Kestrel body on an RME chassis.

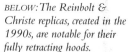

*A 1937 Kestrel body on an RME chassis.* Colin Readey

BELOW: *The Reinbolt & Christe replicas, created in the 1990s, are notable for their fully retracting hoods.*

*ABOVE AND BELOW: The Verheul drophead, designed and bodied in the Netherlands, made its debut at the 1950 Amsterdam Motor Show.*

He had owned three factory dropheads and decided to build the first Reinbolt & Christe replica for himself. He was able to get the body measurements and picture details of features like the fully retractable hood from the owner of the surviving Swiss car. Others then wanted similar replicas and his business, Anglesey Marine Charter, had the woodworking skills to make up the bodies and put them onto chassis whose bodies were beyond recovery. One of the cars, REH 198, had huge holes in the wheel arches covered with brown paper coated with underseal.

At one time there were ten people working on the project in Plymouth – there are four on 1½-litre chassis and four on 2½-litre. Colin Readey said he found the factory drophead to be rather lightly built; his cars are still ash-framed, but have more steel bracing which makes them heavier, and, he says, makes the 1½-litre somewhat underpowered.

The replica cars are listed in the box.

**Verheul**

A remarkable drophead was shown on the Riley stand at the 1950 Amsterdam Motor Show. Designed by Dirk van der Mark, the Riley distributor in Amsterdam, and bodied by the Dutch firm of Verheul, whose works near Rotterdam was better known for coach and bus bodies.

| Replica Rileys | | |
|---|---|---|
| RME 20988 | JCY 367 | 1½-litre prototype |
| 37S 12711 | MJO 438 | |
| 42S 20263 | MXN 950 | 1½-litre |
| RME 21743 | ODU 571 | |
| 61S 8476 | not known | 2½-litre car returned to Norway |
| 61S 9139 | NTF 659 | 2½-litre |
| 62S 9786 | REH 198 | 2½-litre |
| 60S 6695 | LLB 195 | last car |

The two-door car appeared on the stand with Riley's own drophead, but looked much more modern as it owed nothing to the standard styling for British dropheads. The lines were long and sweeping, reminiscent of American automobiles, with spats, white-wall tyres and a hood that folded away completely.

It is thought that three might have been made; however, no trace remains. The Verheul works was taken over by British Leyland in the 1960s and burned down in 1971.

There are also two surviving dropheads made by Trent Coachworks, and the Victoria Carriage Company. What appear to be lost are two dropheads known as the Rose and the Princess, their provenance unknown.

*The attempt to market the Verheul drophead was made by Riley's Amsterdam distributor. His advertisement for the car says it is in stock, with no wait for delivery. He also offered what he called a four-seater sports sedan with open top, which is taken to mean a saloon with sunroof 'in stock very soon'. K. de Kock*

# 8   Improvements to the RMA – and the new RME

A car which above the ordinary inspires confidence and affection.

*Autocar* March 1953

Bewilderment in matters Riley, particularly in regard to chassis numbering and cross-over dates, is far from unknown and many have lain in darkened rooms pondering the mysteries.

Confusion is easily understandable in the case of the RME, the last version of the 1½-litre, because the factory introduced it with unseen mechanical changes, then some 1,350 cars later produced the revised body styling, by which most people recognize the RME – most notably the spats in the rear wheel arches.

In addition, chassis change points are not immutable, and there was a period when chassis were marked with both the 42S of the last RMA sanction and the new letters RME that from then on prefaced chassis numbers. It was well known at Abingdon that left-over parts lying about on the line at the time of the changeover could easily lead to odd bits and pieces being fitted in revised models.

The RME appeared in 1952, at chassis 42S or RME 20505, which marked the first substantial mechanical changes since 1945. Brakes were now all-hydraulic and an open prop shaft driving a hypoid rear axle replaced the long-serving Riley torque-tube system. The axle ratio was higher overall at 5.125:1 compared with the RMA's 4.89:1, which, matched to a previous RMA test, showed a 3sec improvement in the 0–50mph figure, though the mean top speed was the same at 74.25mph (119.5km/h).

*Riley* 1½ LITRE

*The new hypoid rear axle was much simpler than the traditional spiral bevel type.*

*The Delaney Gallay heater became standard for the first time on the 1½-litre saloon in May 1953. The 2½-litre had a Smiths heater as standard from chassis 10494.*

The rear axle changes were in addition to suspension alterations made at the end of 1951; the old semi-elliptics with recuperating lever-arm dampers were replaced with telescopics, which meant that the anti-roll bar could be deleted.

These unseen mechanical changes seem to have been largely cost-cutting in their effect, though the hydraulics seemed to pull the car up better; one set of tests showed that at 30mph they stopped the car in 32ft (9.8m) with 140lb (63.5kg) pedal pressure, compared with 40ft (12.2m) at 150lb (68kg) in the previous hydro-mechanical system, though this could have been affected by the state of the brake adjustment at the time.

*Autocar*, which tested the RME in early 1953 over some 2,000 miles (3,200km), found that the brakes needed adjustment after 1,000 miles (1,600km) to reduce free travel and that fairly heavy pressure was needed for maximum stopping power. They were 73 per cent efficient with a pedal pressure of 130lb (59kg). The 0–60 time was 25.1sec, prompting the magazine to note tactfully: 'This is a car to swing along at high speed on the open road, compensating its owner by its solidity and good furnishings for any short-comings in split-second acceleration.'

The underbody mechanical changes were also carried through on the 2½-litre. One of the last tests before it disappeared was carried out by the *Autocar* in the winter of 1952 that hinted politely that, compared with modern suspensions, the Riley had a somewhat refined vintage ride and that the gear change was 'a little more masculine than it is usual to find today.' Nevertheless, there was the usual praise for a quality car that had sports car performance. Mean top speed was 94mph (151.2km/h) and 0–60 was achieved in 16.4sec.

A small development in comfort from 4 May 1953 was the heater becoming standard, in the chassis RME 21644. Until then the Delaney Gallay heater had to be specified at the time the car was built, as fitting the heat exchanger and the distribution system after the body was built was very difficult.

Then there was the larger rear window, from chassis 42S 20778; the roller blind that was used to avoid headlamp dazzle from the rear was discontinued in favour of a dipping mirror.

**1½-litre RME – final specification 1955 model year**

ENGINE: Exclusive Riley design: four cylinders, bore 69mm (2.72in), stroke 100mm (3.94in), capacity 1496cc (91.25cu. in). Brake horse power 55 at 4,500rpm. Machined hemispherical combustion chambers; inclined valves actuated by short push-rods and rockers from twin camshafts mounted each side of engine and chain driven from crankshaft; sparking plugs centrally situated; gear-type oil pump; full-flow renewable filter sump capacity 10pt (5.6ltr); sturdy three-bearing crankshaft of special design; aluminium alloy pistons with four rings; large diameter gudgeon pins, with burnished finish.

IGNITION: By 12-volt battery and heavy-duty coil. Distributor with centrifugal and manual advance control. Suppressor equipment. Champion 14mm sparking plugs.

COOLING SYSTEM: The cooling system is of the pressurized type; water circulation is by centrifugal pump and controlled by thermostat. Temperature indicator on instrument panel. Cooling system capacity 13pt (7.5ltr).

FUEL SYSTEM: A 12½gal (56ltr) fuel tank with twin filler caps, one each side of the car, ensures a long range. The fuel is fed to the SU automatic, adjustable jet carburettor by an A.C. mechanical fuel pump. Mixture control for cold running on control panel.

CLUTCH AND GEARBOX: Single-plate Borg and Beck dry clutch and four-speed gearbox with synchromesh engagement on second, third and fourth gears; conveniently placed central gear change with remote control. Gear ratios: first 20.372, second 11.736, third 7.585, fourth 5.125, reverse 20.372,

TRANSMISSION: By tubular intermediate shaft to Hardy Spicer tubular propeller shaft with needle-bearing universal joints.

REAR AXLE: Semi-floating, extremely rigid in construction. Final drive by hypoid gears, giving long life and silent operation.

SUSPENSION: Front suspension is by Riley Torsionic independent units with torsion bar springs and sturdy, tubular suspension arms, controlled by telescopic hydraulic dampers. Rear suspension is by long semi-elliptic springs with flexing rubber mounting bushes, controlled by telescopic hydraulic dampers with anti-sway mounting.

BRAKES: Girling hydraulic fully compensated brakes operate on all four wheels from a master cylinder and foot pedal. The hand brake operates on the rear wheel shoes from a pistol-grip handle located under the facia board, through cable and rod mechanism. Individual adjustment for the brake shoes is provided on the brake back-plates, which simultaneously adjusts the hand brake.

FRAME: The Riley frame is light in construction yet possesses exceptional rigidity. Scientifically placed crossmembers provide maximum strength with minimum weight.

STEERING GEAR: Transverse rack-and-pinion steering gear with tie rods directly connected to steering arms on swivel pins giving accurate steering. Large diameter steering wheel is adjustable for position and carries a central horn switch and self-cancelling direction indicator control. Left-hand or right-hand steering is available.

ELECTRICAL EQUIPMENT: 12-volt positive-earth system, incorporating heavy duty belt-driven dynamo with constant voltage control and 51 amp/hr battery with correct acid level device; double dipping headlamps with pre-focused twin-filament bulbs and block lenses. Headlamp dipping switch on facia and headlamp main beam warning light; sidelamps; twin tail-lamps with stop light and reverse light; two roof lamps with individual switches; twin Windtone horns; dash control starter switch; twin-blade windshield wiper with concealed electric drive motor;

*continued overleaf*

---

**1½-litre RME – final specification 1955 model year** *continued*

two fog-lamps; ignition warning light; heater warning light; instrument panel illumination; ignition switch direction indicators; automatic reverse light switch.

INSTRUMENTS Speedometer with total and trip recorders; clock; ammeter; radiator temperature gauge; fuel gauge; oil pressure gauge. Revolution indicator available as extra.

CONTROLS: All controls are conveniently placed and positioned to give maximum driving comfort and safety; the manual throttle, mixture and ignition setting controls are accessibly placed on the control panel with the ignition switch, lamp switch, starter switch, heater switch and panel light switch. The windshield wiper switch is centrally situated on the screen rail, and the headlamp dipping switch on the end of the facia close to the driver's hand.

BODY: The greatly improved body is fitted with adjustable bucket-type front seats and a comfortable rear seat with folding centre arm-rest. All seats are within the wheelbase for maximum riding comfort. Seat cushions and squabs are covered with leather; a heater with in-built demisting ducts to the windshield is fitted as standard for territories where required. Safety glass throughout; winding door windows; large parcel shelf behind rear seats; improved front wings; twin sun visors; two-position anti-glare rear mirror. Ventilating air scoops to front windows and badge bar optional extras.

Special jacking points are provided under the bumper overriders front and rear. Provision has been made for fitting HMV car radio.

WHEELS: Steel disc wheels with five-stud fixing and Dunlop 5.75-16 tyres.

COLOURS: Finished in:

| | |
|---|---|
| Black | with Maroon, Green or Biscuit upholstery |
| Maroon | with Maroon or Biscuit upholstery |
| Green | with Green or Biscuit upholstery |
| Blue | with Grey upholstery |
| Grey | with Rust, Maroon or Green upholstery |
| Ivory | with Rust or Maroon upholstery |

DIMENSIONS:

| | | |
|---|---|---|
| Wheelbase | 9ft 4⅝in | (2,860mm) |
| Track | 4ft 4½in | (1,334mm) |
| Ground Clearance | 7½in | (190mm) |
| Overall Height | 5ft 1in | (1,550mm) |
| Overall Width | 5ft 3½in | (1,613mm) |
| Overall Length | 14ft 11in | (4,547mm) |

Source: *Riley brochure*

---

## The 'spatted' RME

The external distinguishing characteristics of the RME did not appear until the London Motor Show in October 1953 and they were in production from chassis RME 21855. Chassis 21877 won the bronze medal for coachwork at the show. The prototype, RME 43S 21379, registered JBL 353, still survives.

The 'spatted' RME was to be the last revision before the end of the 1½-litre and the links with the old Riley works in Coventry. It was aimed at one last lease of life, since sales had been falling sharply since 1950 and by 1952 they were down to 1,050 cars – a long way from the post-war boom of 2,720 cars in 1947.

*Faired-in sidelamps were on the original RM specification but were dropped in favour of Lucas torpedo lights. They made a come-back on the RME but proved a rust-trap.*

*The RME's roofline was raised by the simple expedient of inserting this small wooden block.*

The body revision was forced upon BMC after it became obvious that a suggested RMA replacement, a 1½-litre engine in the heavy all-steel Pathfinder body, was a hopeless cause; the prototype had aroused widespread derision in the factory (*see* Chapter 9).

So the face-lifted 1954 model-year car was described in Riley publicity as 'the New Look 1½-litre', and went on, 'the long low lines of the luxurious body proclaim to all that this is one of England's outstanding cars', though *Autocar* complained: 'at first glance it is difficult to see what has been altered', then went on to say this was because the changes had blended in so well.

The running boards had disappeared and the door bottoms were now flush with the sills. The front wings now had a helmet shape with faired-in sidelights, similar to the first prototypes though more angular, and there were built-in foglamps and sidelamps. A proposal to blend the front wings into the doors was fortunately abandoned.

In the rear wheel arches were rather natty coverings, usually the preserve of much more expensive cars of the past, which has led to these models being dubbed 'spatted RMEs'. The spats were not to everyone's taste, though others saw in the restyled bodywork references to the Park Ward Bentley Foursome coupé of 1949. Curiously, spats had also appeared on the BMW 327 in 1937, the car that was said to have provided some of the inspiration for the RMs.

There were small subtle changes to make the car look larger; the window apertures in the doors were ½in (1.3cm) deeper, the windscreen wider and deeper. There was a very slight change to the height of the body, which was some 1½in (3.8cm) higher at the rear – achieved by inserting small wooden blocks in the rear of the framework supporting the roof to elevate it slightly. It also had the effect of providing more headroom in the rear seats. This became known in the trade as the ranger roof, for no reason that is obvious now.

The front seats were redesigned to make them squarer rather than the traditional bucket shape and they were piped in contrasting colours, which had been common in the RMA and RMB range since 1949.

Other minor alterations during production included slimmer windscreen surrounds, a chromed-section roof gutter with rubber inserts, the lengthening of the rear waist strips and different petrol filler caps. These were now stainless steel replacing the chromed brass versions of the earlier models. From late 1954 the old D-lamps at the rear were replaced with wing-mounted lights and a centrally placed reversing light that was the same Lucas unit as used on the roadster as a rear number plate/reversing light.

In addition to the external alterations there were various options offered, some new, some old, such as a scoop to direct air into the car; there were also two types of wind deflectors available as after-market accessories, a rimless version made by Weathershields, the other a much more expensive heavily chromed version by Auster, who made fold-flat windscreens for racing cars.

Other factory options were a rev counter, badge bar and HMV radio. It was also possible to specify twin carburettors.

In standard mode, *Motor*'s road test figures of May 1954 showed a top speed of 76.3mph (123km/h) and a 0–60 time of 31.8sec that was much the same as the previous year's test, but remarkably slow compared with the same magazine's test in October 1947, when top speed was 78mph (125km/h) and the 0–60

time 25.1sec. Granted that the 1½-litre had put on weight – 196lb (88.9kg) – over the years, but the RMA in 1947 had been running on poor pool petrol, leading again to the suspicion that those early road test cars had been tweaked.

The RME's price was now £1,205, which, thanks to tax changes, was now £134 cheaper than in 1952 and very competitive since even a boring Lea-Francis 14bhp was more expensive, though the sporting driver might have been tempted by a Sunbeam-Talbot 90 convertible at only £7 more.

The facelift worked, and sales bounded up again to 1,747 in 1954, the highest sales figures since 1948, but it was a short respite.

The 1½-litre had been in production for nearly ten years; it still looked sleek, dignified, and even better than it did in 1945 – 'very pleasing, up-to-date, but not ultra-modern' – as *Motor* politely put it, implying that it was perhaps a shade old-fashioned compared to the plethora of American-influenced models available elsewhere and certainly against the new Pathfinder alongside which it was appearing in dealers' showrooms.

*Autocar* was more pointed: 'The 1½-litre Riley begins, incredibly enough, to look a little high alongside its bigger brother, the Pathfinder. For a car that has had a noticeably low roof line for years, this is a quaint effect.'

---

**Rileys in the small ads**

In 1970, Bill Boddy of *Motor Sport* tested a rather rough 1½-litre RME, MTR 999 chassis 22750, that seems to exist no longer. He got it from the famous Riley garagiste E.T. Lundegaard of Gloucester, who had twenty-one Rileys in stock at the time.

The engine was 'positively filthy', the boot smelled of damp and the interior of rubber. The tyres were all different, many things did not work, but it ran well. It was for sale at £275.

Boddy analysed the asking price for thirteen RMs that were for sale in the small ads in *Motor Sport* in September 1970 and discovered that the average price for the five 1½-litres was £185; the five 2½-litres averaged £275 and the three 2½-litre roadsters, £301. Trade ads had a 1949 2½-litre for £75 and a 1946 1½-litre for £95.

He concluded that by shopping around, a worthy RM specimen could be had for £100 and a good one for £200. The three-year MoT test had begun in 1967, so it is assumed that they were all roadworthy at that stage.

He seems not to have been tempted by the 1½-litre offered in a trade ad by a Ken Dodd fan who advertised it, with spare engine, a 'trifle tattiludinous but a glorious runner' at £45.

*The London Motor Show of 1952: on the stand are a 2½-litre engine and chassis, a 2½-litre saloon in Woodland Green and Beige and a 1½-litre in Silver Streak Grey and Maroon. The chassis exhibit was seen for the first time the previous year.*

It was also very expensive to produce, with a hand-built body and a costly engine that was not used in any other car in the British Motor Corporation that had rationalized 1500cc production on the B-series engine.

The last London Motor Show at which it appeared – in metallic Peacock blue and grey – was in the autumn of 1954. It was a strange decision to exhibit it since production was winding down and only twenty-nine were sold in the following year. The last RME, chassis 23950, left the works in March 1955.

Many RMEs hung around in showrooms for quite a while and the factory was desperate to be rid of them. It is said that dealers were given two each and told to sell them at list price, but the buyers could have whatever modification they wanted at no extra cost, colours included.

The London dealer Jimmy James, for example, had a cream 1955 spatted RME, but with old-fashioned front wings and running boards, a metal steering wheel and Lucas Flamethrowers as built-in driving lamps. Morris of Conduit Street in the West End had a 1½-litre in red and black 'with many extras'.

There had been no proper strategic planning to replace the RME with another Riley. BMC had fiddled about unsuccessfully with an over-bodied, under-engined prototype 1½-litre version of the Pathfinder, which might have been called the RMG, but essentially, due to poor product planning, they left a gap in the Riley medium sporting car market from 1955 to 1957.

It was taken over with astonishing speed by the RME's Abingdon stablemate, the MG Magnette, of which eight were made in 1953, 3,819 in 1954 and 8,927 in 1955.

The Riley gap was eventually filled by a car Morris rejected as a replacement for the Minor, which went on to sell more than any other model in Riley history, the 1.5.

LEFT *and* BELOW: *The lever arm dampers at the rear were replaced by telescopics that gave better handling and enabled the anti-roll bar to be removed.*

## Famous owners

Riley RMs seem to have been owned by an inordinate number of comedians and other showbiz folk, but retrospective lists like these tend to favour this typecasting, because the people are well-known, or at least were some decades ago.

According to Derek Slingsby who worked in the service department at Abingdon in the 1950s, Princess Mary, the Princess Royal of the time, also owned a Riley.

Rileys in general tended to be bought by upper-middle-class professionals such as diplomats, senior officers in the services, doctors and dentists, whose names have not lingered; fortunately, some of their cars have.

Many motoring editors and correspondents also drove Rileys, probably on long-term 'loan' from the factory, a practice that continues today in some quarters.

*1½-litre*

ENID BLYTON
Children's author, drove PXT 565, which still survives and has just been restored. It was owned by her publishing company between 1955 and 1960.

SIR CHARLES GRANT
Chairman of Grant's Whisky – SC 9109 survives.

MAX MILLAR
Artist who drew intricate cut-aways for *Autocar* – LLB 200.

HARRY MORTIMER
Brass band conductor.

FRANK MUIR
Broadcaster and wit.

REG PARNELL
Racing driver. KNU 556 and later a 2½-litre roadster. His best Grand Prix placing was third at Silverstone in 1950 in an Alfa Romeo 158.

A.E. RUSSELL
Chief engineer, Bristol Aeroplane Company. His ill-fated Brabazon airliner had the project number GDU 167, the same as his Coventry-registered Riley that lasted much longer as it still survives in Essex.

PRINCE TOMISLAV OF YUGOSLAVIA
A member of the Serbian royal family who became a stateless person after the war because he was banned by the communists from living in Yugoslavia. Came to Britain and became a Sussex apple farmer. Returned in 1991 after the regime changed. Owned JUG 1, that was said to have glass-topped picnic tables and concealed petrol filler caps. It had a roof incorporating a wind-down rear window from an Austin A90 Atlantic. Later became OBP 511.

CHARLES VICTOR
British actor, who appeared in more than 120 films, such as *Calling Bulldog Drummond*, between 1938 and 1963. He called his car Traveller's Joy, after a play in which he was appearing in the West End of London at the time he bought it. At one time it had an ivory roof.

*2½-litre*

SIR ANTHONY EDEN
Later Lord Avon; as Prime Minister, he led Britain into a foolhardy war in the Middle East. Doubts have since been cast on his mental state at the time, though this was after he had bought his Riley.

*continued overleaf*

**Famous owners** *continued*

LORD BIRKETT
Judge at the Nuremberg trials and later British Director of Public Prosecutions. He represented Wallis Simpson in her divorce from Mr Simpson which allowed her to become Duchess of Windsor. 'I do not object to people looking at their watches when I am speaking. But I strongly object when they start shaking them to make certain they are still going.'

BILLY COTTON
Brass band leader, catchphrase 'Wakey, wakey'. NRW 798 is in regular use in Yorkshire.

GEORGE EYSTON
Broke the land speed record three times and set hundreds of other records at Brooklands, Montlhéry, Pendine Sands and the Bonneville flats driving a variety of cars, a great number of MGs but also including a pre-war Riley. He became a director of Castrol and was often seen at Abingdon, because of his close connection with the MG competitions department.

CLARK GABLE
Hollywood superstar. Fond of convertibles like his 2½-litre drophead and Duesenberg Model JN.

TOMMY HANLEY
Comedian, star of wartime BBC radio show *ITMA* (*It's That Man Again*). Drophead coupé.

EARL HOWE
Racing driver, won at Le Mans in an Alfa Romeo in 1931 and triumphed in many other races; president of the BRDC.

CYRIL LORD (2)
Millionaire carpet magnate; remembered by the irritating TV ad: 'Here's luxury you can afford by Cyril Lord'.

LORD MOUNTBATTEN (2)
Fresh from a chequered naval career and then Viceroy of India, he designed in 1946 his own duotone colour scheme, the 'Mountbatten split' of black and light blue. Unlike the factory duotone the bonnet and scuttle were in the second colour which extended higher up the doors and more towards the rear. 'My 2½-litre is really lovely-looking', he says in the *Riley Record* of March 1947. 'It holds the road beautifully and has very fine performance.' True, but it sounds as if somebody made it up in Coventry. His first 2½-litre, HXM 1, had special door trims.

Other Riley peers included the Lords Blandford, Brabourne, Napier and Redesdale (RJO 2).

JACK SOLOMONS
Boxing promoter – NPA 892.

BILLY TERNENT
Bandleader – KLM 1 still survives.

*Pathfinders*

SIR ANTHONY EDEN
*See* above.

SYD ENEVER
Chief engineer at Abingdon.

GEORGE EYSTON
*See* previous entry.
In July 1954, he took delivery of Pathfinder chassis number MA/891 with 'special engine'. He specified bucket seats and had it painted in an unusual shade of Bristol Red.

IAN FLEMING (almost)
James Bond's creator owned an RMF and ordered a Pathfinder, but before it was delivered he sold the film rights to *Casino Royale* – and bought a Ford Thunderbird instead.

*The* Riley Record *rounded up some stars of the time and pictured them with their Rileys.*

*continued overleaf*

---

**Famous owners** *continued*

MANTOVANI
Sugary bandleader – regarded by his fans as the king of the light orchestra; much loved by listeners to the BBC Light Programme.

LORD MOUNTBATTEN
Had a duotone Pathfinder in the 'Mountbatten split' of black and blue a year before duotones were officially introduced. He specified that the steering column should be moved as high as possible and that the dip-switch should be foot-operated, which was a reversion to what had appeared on early cars.

LARRY PARNES
The first (of many) 'Svengali' of British pop – managed Marty Wilde and Billy Fury.

SULTAN OF PERAK
Monarch of one of the thirteen states of Malaysia.

DICKIE VALENTINE
Crooner, died in a car crash in 1971.

DAVID WHITFIELD
Ballad singer; Hull-born version of Mario Lanza; won the first British golden disc for *Cara Mia, Why? (Must we say Goodbye)*.

A 1949 cover of the *Riley Record* (*see* page 119) showed eight showbusiness personalities standing by various RMs. Some did actually own their own cars.

They were:
ARTHUR ASKEY
Comedian, stalwart of music hall and radio shows; notable pantomime dame.

JIMMY EDWARDS
Actor and comedian with handlebar moustache – 1½-litre MPK 960.

DICK BENTLEY and JOY NICHOLS
More comedians, who appeared with Jimmy Edwards in the BBC radio show *Take it From Here*. Bentley owned 1½-litre KUL 300.

LESLIE HENSON
Comedian – RMB JYF 70.

JOHN McCALLUM
Forgettable 1950s film actor who became a TV producer. Drove a 1½-litre drophead, GRW 114, in the film *The Calendar*. The car has survived, the film has not.

VALERIE HOBSON
Actress, married to the disgraced politician John Profumo. Two 2½-litres and possibly an RME, JGU 720.

EDWIGE FEUILLÈRE
Obscure French actress.

# 9   The Pathfinder

Riley had wanted to call a car the Pathfinder since the end of the war – perhaps as a tribute to the Pathfinder Force, elite night-bombing squadrons whose pilots dropped flares to light the German targets for the heavy bombers that followed them.

The firm had, of course, been heavily involved in war-work, including the manufacture of parts for the Rolls-Royce Merlin engine.

Riley registered the name in June 1945 with the Society of Motor Manufacturers and

Traders – thus ensuring that no-one else could use it on a car, but it was not until 1953 that it appeared on a car that was large, handsome, fast – and flawed.

It is without doubt that the Pathfinder has had a bad press and has come in for some totally undeserved abuse – even half a century later on the internet. The *Auto Lemon* website, for instance, calls it 'the unfortunate Gerald Palmer-designed Pathfinder, which had nothing but the traditional four-cylinder Riley engine to recommend it'.

*One of the first mock-ups of the Pathfinder shows significant differences from the final production version. This has a two-piece chrome-surround v-shaped windscreen, thin bumpers and long overriders. There are no pass lamps and the gaping holes at the front were filled in. Other prototype pictures show a centre gear change that was eventually moved to the side of the car.*
British Motor Industry Heritage Trust

It had a great deal more, but there has always been a debate as to whether the Pathfinder was a real Riley, or just another version of a Wolseley 6/90 introduced as part of the Nuffield group's rationalization of production. This had been put in hand well before the merger of Austin and the Nuffield companies into the British Motor Corporation in April 1952.

Part of the problem is that it is rarely called by its RM series designation – in this case RMH. The RM designation for Rileys, as we have seen, was not introduced until after the BMC merger and was for internal purposes only; it was not used in publicity or mentioned in road tests of the time.

The new car could obviously not be called a 2½-litre since it needed to distance itself from the Riley that had been in production since 1946. It could have been called a 4/110 if it followed the Wolseley style of naming cars by cylinders/bhp, but that would have sounded boring for a Riley, so Pathfinder must have sounded a great idea to Nuffield's marketing men when they introduced it at the London Motor Show in 1953.

True, there were similarities with the Wolseley as there would naturally be, given that the body shell was commonized and built on the same body track, but there were also important differences. The Wolseley body was higher on the chassis to make it look more imposing – Gerald Palmer's idea.

The Riley was also the first to be schemed by his office. Although there is a popular misconception that the Wolseley came first, it was in fact produced many months later. The Pathfinder still had the legendary Big Four engine, whereas the Wolseley used the new BMC six-cylinder C-series 2639cc engine.

The 6/90 Wolseley used a column shift for the four-speed Morris 'box that persisted with the failure to employ synchromesh on first gear.

## The side gear-change

The prototype Pathfinder had a traditional centre gear change for the same Morris 'box but by the time it went into production it sported a hang-over from the 1920s, a right-hand gear lever set on the floor; one review described it as a 'plum-shaped knob' on a 9in (230mm) rod, with a cut-away in the seat to accommodate it. 'By no means unfamiliar on cars of the highest class' said the *Motor* in orotund fashion of this development, though Morris, who had not used it since 1916, revived it briefly for the 1957 Isis. Pathfinders for left-hand-drive countries had the change on the left side.

The right-hand change was regarded as a sign of quality as it had been employed by Rolls-Royce on manual gearboxes since the 1920s – the ostensible reason being that a right-hand change allowed a gentleman to disembark onto the kerb without getting the gear lever up his trouser leg.

It was still being used by Rolls-Royce at the time when the Pathfinder was being planned, most notably on the vastly more expensive Bentley Mark VI and on the R-type Continental that ran from 1952 to 1955, though left-hand-drive versions of the Continental had a column change.

Archaic it might have been, but it allowed three-abreast seating at the front when a bench seat was specified and, of course, quality by association. It was also easy to engineer the linkage in the Pathfinder as the Morris 'box had side selectors. *Motor Sport* liked it: 'Add a good mark to Riley for using a right-hand gear change on the Pathfinder, which is the former 2½-litre in new, inflated guise.'

The familiar Riley torsion bar front suspension was used at the front. The coil spring set-up at the rear was designed by Palmer, but put into practice by Terry Mitchell at Abingdon and was sufficiently revolutionary for its time for the *Motor* to remark that 'it breaks away from the conventions of this country'. Palmer's view of it was that it was something he had been forced to do. 'We had a lot of trouble over Riley traditions. *Every* Riley it seemed had to have a torque tube, but I had to use a Nuffield axle which wouldn't adapt, so I compromised by giving it radius arms and a Panhard rod with coil springs.'

The rear 'live' axle that could move independently was braced against drive and braking torque by the two pivoted radius arms running from the spring mountings to the centre of the car. Almost at the end of production – after much Panhard rod woe – these coils were changed for semi-elliptic cart springs

The all-steel bodies with the curiously named 'turret-type-top' as the publicity leaflets called it, came from Nuffield Metal Products in Coventry and looked much the same as the Wolseley – apart from the different radiator grilles – though the Riley body sat 2in (5cm) lower and there were differences in the wheel arches and sills.

Atop the Riley grille sat the radiator cap – except it wasn't one. The story goes that when Lord Nuffield saw the mock-up that had been designed to have the cap inside the engine bay, he insisted on a traditional chrome cap at the end of the bonnet to provide a sighting line. So it was put back, but performed a totally different function as a bonnet safety catch. He may not have known that the radiator cap on the earlier Riley RMs was also a dummy.

There was also a great debate, before the car was even designed, over what sort of vehicle was fitting to carry on the Riley name and satisfy the enthusiast, and whether it should be a four- or six-seater. There is some evidence that the successor to the 2½-litre could have been another coachbuilt body. Some years later, Palmer said in an interview in *Thoroughbred and Classic Cars* that he had been instructed to use the Riley 2½-litre engine and the big BMC gearbox: 'They must have weighed 700lb (1,540kg) in all so I simply didn't dare propose a unit construction shell. I designed a box section chassis with another Italian-style body on top of it.'

## Palmer takes over

Crucial to the final decision was the sudden death of Harry Rush, Riley's chief designer for many years, begetter of the Big Four and RM and a man of staunch traditional views. On 23 December 1949, he was killed when his 2½-litre hit a telegraph pole between Coventry and Oxford.

At the Cowley design office, where he was still concerned with Riley matters, he had shared a room with Palmer who was to become chief engineer, chassis and body at BMC, but was then responsible for MG and Wolseley design.

By the time Christmas had passed, Palmer had taken on the Riley brief as well; whether what eventually appeared as the Pathfinder would have been different had Rush survived is a matter for conjecture.

One option for Palmer to keep the Riley flag flying would have been to produce a Riley version of the ZA Magnette, also designed by him and announced at the same 1953 Motor Show. It was not a real MG but very similar to the Wolseley 4/44 and powered by the same 1489cc Austin B-series engine.

So it is interesting to note that after Nuffield decided in June 1950 to replace the MG YB saloon and work started on the Magnette, there was at some stage a proposal to fit the Magnette body with the 1½-litre Riley engine and badge it as a Riley. Peter Tothill, then in the experimental department, also remembers a two-door Magnette saloon being built with a Riley engine.

These plans eventually foundered on what the company minutes describe as 'very strong resistance' from the sales department to fitting the Riley engine – though they do not elaborate on the reasons.

At this early stage of the Nuffield rationalization and later after the BMC merger, there were all kinds of proposals for engine/body combinations, including one to fit the MG TD Midget with the 1496cc Riley engine.

Palmer now had to operate with certain constraints; he was charged with producing a related family of MG and Wolseley saloons – one medium-sized and one large – using as many common parts as possible.

### Gerald Palmer

The Pathfinder designer, Gerald Palmer, is better known for his two other outstanding post-war designs, the Jowett Javelin and the MG Magnette.

He began his career at Scammell the lorry makers, then moved to the Morris drawing office before the war where he worked with Alec Issigonis on suspension designs.

In 1942 he was recruited by Jowett in Bradford, where he fulfilled his ambition to design a new car from scratch and created a milestone in post-war car design with the Javelin, a sleek six-seater capable of 80mph (130km/h) and powered by a flat-four 1½-litre aluminium engine.

In 1949 he returned to the Nuffield empire to work on Rileys, Wolseleys and MGs. 'There was no product planning', he recalled many years later, 'all I had to do was to come up with ideas which I hoped would be accepted.'

With a staff of ten, he produced from the Morris drawing office at Cowley a very pretty unitary construction MG roadster prototype that was cleared for production. But the Abingdon management, experts at the 'not invented here' syndrome, temporized until they could get their own car, the MGA, signed off and Palmer's car was cut up. He did, however, have some input into the MGA as he designed its original twin-cam engine.

He also designed the Wolseley 4/44, of which nearly 30,000 were produced up until 1956; it was the last car to use the famous MG 1250cc XPAG engine from the T-type Midget – albeit with only one SU carburettor.

He began work on the Magnette in 1950 and it was announced at the 1953 Motor Show – the long lead time being to do with the fact that it was to be the first car to use the new BMC B-series 1½-litre engine that had been developed.

There were immediate and predictable hoots of derision from the same MG enthusiasts who decried the MG TF. They disliked the pre-war Magnette name being used on a saloon of unitary construction, not a sports car, and that it used the B-series engine – an Austin product rather than a Nuffield design.

Nevertheless, it became a great success, as it was a well-made and comfortable sporting saloon. It sold nearly 37,000 between 1954 and 1958.

But Palmer's time at Oxford was running out; the warranty costs of the Riley Pathfinder and an adverse review in a motoring magazine of his Wolseley 6/90 led to his sacking in 1956 by BMC's chairman Len Lord. He could have accepted demotion, but left with a £7,500 payoff and, fittingly, a Magnette.

There is also a view that Lord wanted to remove him to make way for the return from Alvis of Alec Issigonis – whom Palmer was wont to call 'the Noel Coward of the British motor industry'.

Although he went to an executive engineering position at Vauxhall, and did work such as anglicizing the Opel Kadette into the Viva HB, he never again achieved the same prominence in the motor industry.

Apart from that work, he will also be remembered for designing a hoist for disabled people and a portable anaesthesia device.

He also designed in 1950 his own home, Orchard House, at Iffley, Oxford, where he lived until his death in 1999 at the age of 88 and where he had worked on his prized cars – a Bugatti T43/4 and a 1920s Targa Florio Mercedes in which he competed.

Three years before his death in 1999, he attended a meeting of the MG Car Club's ZA Magnette Register, when the five cars he had designed – a Pathfinder, Magnette ZA, Wolseley 4/44 and 6/90, and a Jowett Javelin – were brought together in a display for the first time.

Gerald Palmer was charming and self-effacing, which comes through in the autobiography he wrote in 1998 with Christopher Balfour's help. He was also kind enough to invite me to Orchard House not long before he died to talk about his life at Morris and BMC.

*Gerald Palmer at his home in Oxford shortly before his death.*

The Riley portfolio gave him extra creative impetus; he recollected that he took soundings at home and on the continent about what dealers and enthusiasts wanted and finally conceived the new Riley to be a large six-seater in the style of the *grands routiers* that he thought could compete with Jaguar. John Thornley, Abingdon's general manager, recalled it rather differently in an interview in 1985 with *Thoroughbred and Classic Cars*. He said Palmer's original brief was to design a modern Riley, as a replacement to the RMF, a close-coupled, standard-sized four-seater saloon.

But with half the design work done, Jaguar brought out their large MkVII in 1950 – the six-cylinder XK120 engine of 3442cc produced 160bhp at 5,200rpm, enough to propel it over 100mph. It was a huge car, 16ft 4½in (4,990mm) long and 6ft 1½in (1,867mm) wide.

'There was consternation at Nuffield when they realized what a strong competitor they had … immediately they put pressure on Palmer to blow up the Pathfinder, to make it into a five-seater (*sic*) car to compete with the Jaguar. The car ended up over-bodied of course.'

This theory is given weight – though for a different reason – by an interview in *Classic and Sportscar* in 1985 in which Palmer declared that he had originally schemed the Pathfinder as another Riley coach-built model, but Nuffield liked the car so much that they decided to have it made entirely in steel.

So Palmer went ahead with his *grand routier,* designated DO999 by the Cowley design office, drawing a peripheral frame to seat the passengers as low as possible – it was a car that one stepped down into – and utilizing a hypoid rear axle secured to the chassis by two radius arms and a Panhard rod – all this to give the axle as much stability as possible, though not quite enough as we shall see.

The decision to use a proper chassis was forced on him by the weight of the power unit, though his contemporaneous Magnette was unitary construction, something Nuffield had been using as far back as 1939 with the Morris 10 Series M.

## The unhappy Wayfarer

There was also a proposal to put the 1½-litre engine into the heavy Pathfinder chassis. Work went as far as the building of an experimental car, project number DO988, that might well have been called the Wayfarer had it gone into production and would probably have been the missing RMG in the RM sequence. It was said to be deathly slow as it was so underpowered; the car weighed over 500lb (227kg) more than the RMA.

Arnold Farrar, then workshop manager at Abingdon, used to tell the story of how he was called off the factory floor to a meeting of department heads standing around what appeared to be a Pathfinder, but underneath the bonnet was a 1½-litre engine, with twin carburettors. Asked his opinion he replied: 'I hope it never gets built – it'll be overtaken by every Austin Seven on the road.'

Separate chassis were already being abandoned by the major motor manufacturers, though they were retained by small-scale producers such as Alvis, who could not afford the costs of tooling for monocoque bodies. The MGA was another notable exception.

Palmer wanted to use rack and pinion steering, which the RMA had pioneered after the war, but this option was ruled out because he had to develop the steering to suit the Wolseley as well, which used the much longer C-series engine that would have fouled the rack, so the less-precise Wolseley cam and lever had to be used.

The old 2½-litre Big Four was pressed into service, with even more power squeezed out of it, thanks to an increase in compression ratio from 6.8/1 to 7.25/1 using a thin steel head gasket, high-crown pistons and changes to ports and the twin-carburettor inlet manifold. In addition, the crankcase was stiffened in the central web that supported the centre main bearing and the bearing shells were modified.

The Four was now giving 110bhp at 4,500rpm, compared to 90bhp at 4,300rpm in 1946 and 83.5bhp when the engine was first introduced in 1937.

There is a story that old Abingdon hands tell of the new BMC boss Len Lord touring the factory for the first time, finding Palmer's wooden mock-up of the Pathfinder pushed into a corner beneath a sheet and declaring curtly: 'Build it'.

By early 1953 the first prototype TFC 226 had been built. Apart from the reinstated radiator cap, it had a curved one-piece windscreen instead of a divided one and the longitudinal grille across the front of the car had been replaced with chrome trims and integrated driving lights. TFC and two other prototypes performed well, according to Palmer, so the project was authorized.

But the Pathfinder was put into production much too early. Many of the Abingdon staff said more development work was needed – Morris's chief engineer, Charles Griffin, put one version through a hedge on a test route – but the BMC management decreed that the car should be ready by the 1953 Motor Show, as sales of the 2½-litre were in decline, though not precipitately so.

Abingdon was at full stretch in 1953 with the new Riley, a new MG Magnette and design changes to the MG TF. Everything was done in a great rush to meet the BMC's demand for new products at the Motor Show.

The very first production Pathfinder, chassis 501, was begun on 5 October 1953, only days before the show opened. It appeared on the stand in green with biscuit upholstery, but was obviously in no condition to be driven very far, since it went back to the factory afterwards to be rebuilt; it was subsequently despatched on 19 May, 1954[1]. Despite being a lash-up, it won a silver prize at the show for coachwork.

Abingdon's other product, MG, had similar problems; the two Magnettes on the show stand had also been completed only a short time before it opened and they were not even to specification. Quarter lights were missing, so was the walnut facia, due to shortages of supplies of wood, which didn't appear for another six months. Early owners were consoled with free overriders and fog lamps.

'There is little doubt', said *Autocar*, 'that this entirely re-designed Riley will live up to the performance that has been an exceptional feature of this marque for many years and will still further enhance its reputation.'

Cecil Cousins, works manager at Abingdon, knew that the Pathfinder had fundamental faults. 'They put it in the Motor Show … and then we found you couldn't stop it and you couldn't steer it.' After a test driver refused to take it for a 1,000-mile proving run, Cousins says he drove it himself for a mile, went back to the works and told John Thornley it should not go into production. He was overruled.

It was typical of BMC that the launches should have been a rushed and botched job, leaving any problems to be sorted out later.

Cousins always thought that he was blamed unfairly for the Pathfinder deficiencies; the fault really lay with the BMC management at Cowley who took a cavalier attitude to the small works just down the road. The director responsible for Abingdon, S.V. Smith, a former Wolseley body inspector, turned up only once a week as he ran the operation from the Morris works at Cowley. He was widely known as 'Hitler Smith' or 'Sack 'em Smith', whose forte was engineering administration rather than car manufacture.

## Painful production

BMC would create a demand and then be totally unable to meet it. Anyone wanting to buy a Pathfinder at the show would have been severely disappointed, though after years of shortages of new cars, and diversion of resources to export markets, the British driver was stoical in the face of shortages and incompetence.

Only four cars were finished in the two months until the end of 1953 and all were rebuilt. The fifth was started on 18 December, but was not finished until 21 January 1954. After that, limited production began with cars for export markets – largely as demonstrators for distributors in Canada, New York, Copenhagen, Geneva and Stockholm.

## The problems

Difficulties began with the very first builds at Abingdon where the bodies from Coventry were mated to the chassis that had been welded by John Thompson's at Wolverhampton, who also supplied MGA frames to Abingdon.

The problem was that they did not fit, and a great deal of hammering, swearing and welding was necessary to get them to come together. The Abingdon management, alarmed at this setback, sent a deputation to Wolverhampton to discover the cause.

Initially, Thompson's were reluctant to show them where the frames were being welded, according to Peter Tothill, then in the experimental department at BMC. What they discovered was certainly alarming. The production facility was in an earth-floored tin shed, thick with welding smoke, and the chassis were being welded on wooden trestles, not the metal jig they had been paid to use by BMC.

This was likely to have caused the major problem in early production cars of the loss of rear axle control, due to shearing of the bracket anchoring the Panhard rod to the chassis. A Panhard rod is a horizontal steel rod attached to the rear axle housing at one end and the chassis at the other. It is crucial for the car's stability as it affects how much it rolls; its purpose is to keep the centre of the car directly above the centre of the rear axle during cornering. The Riley publicity called it an anti-sway bar.

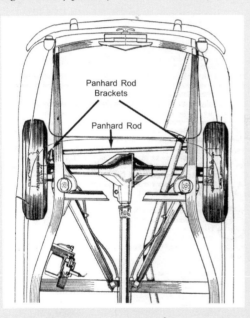

Panhard Rod
Brackets

Panhard Rod

*ABOVE:* The thin locating screw at the end of the Panhard rod has a small thread and can rust and break as did this one. Dave Rowlands

*LEFT:* The two Achilles' heels of the Pathfinder – the Panhard rod and, on the left, the Clayton-Dewandre servo. David Pipes

Because the welding had not been done on the proper jig, the brackets at either end of the rod were misaligned, putting excessive force on them during cornering. The rod was also attached to the brackets with small-thread screws and even if the bracket remained secure, the rod could come adrift if the bushes became worn and the screw threads rusty. There is a story that Vic Oak, BMC's engineering director, passed a drawing board on which the Pathfinder's rear end was being schemed and said: 'That rod will break, you know.'

It was the failure of this vital component as it tore away from its mountings that earned the car the unhappy soubriquets – 'Ditchfinder' or Hedgefinder' – that persists unfairly to this day. The terms were first used, according to Cecil Cousins, by the Abingdon test drivers and later by the Sussex police who discovered their patrol cars heading in unexpected directions during hot pursuits. Many police forces had been used to the sharp rack and pinion steering of the RMB and must have been surprised at the vague cam and lever action of the Pathfinder.

*continued overleaf*

## The problems *continued*

Palmer, recalling the Panhard rod setbacks in his autobiography *Auto-Architect*, said: 'I am sure these disastrous failures were caused by poor quality or inadequate welding on early production frames.' To solve the problem, additional transverse tie-rods were fitted retrospectively and on production cars from chassis MA/3498, which was well into 1955.

Rectification was very expensive; BMC told dealers to remove the body from the chassis to deal with the Panhard rod issue – did they all do so, or did some cut corners and still claim the warranty costs? The service memorandum from Abingdon in January 1956 told dealers: 'it should be introduced retrospectively on earlier Pathfinders at your discretion'.

If it were potentially dangerous – as it was – should it not have been mandatory? Today's recall notices for potentially lethal automotive faults – thanks to Brussels' legislation – would demand it.

Similar welding failures occurred on the Wolseley 6/90 as it was, of course, using the same chassis, but these did not seem to dent its reputation in the same way as the Pathfinder's – whose drivers tended to press on perhaps more than the Wolseley's.

There were many fewer occurrences and one explanation might be that the Wolseley went into production eight months later. The 6/90 was certainly thrown about by the Metropolitan police as enthusiastically as was the Pathfinder by provincial forces.

It's interesting to note that Palmer's MG Magnette that appeared for the first time at the 1953 London Motor Show also had severe problems with the rear axle, which wound up under heavy braking; one prototype went through a hedge near Oxford, but the fault was sorted out before the car went on sale.

There were also complaints of clutch judder from the 10in Borg and Beck – a recurrent issue with 2½-litre RMs due to the torque from the Big Four. It took until January 1956 to introduce Pathfinder modifications, the most important being hydraulic rather than mechanical operation of the clutch and the addition of a vertical steady to the gearbox extension. This was said to reduce judder to an 'acceptable level', which a service department memo defined as being a smooth take-off in first and reverse on smooth, level ground.

It continued: 'A slight tendency to judder when reversing uphill or on a loose surface is only to be expected'. Presumably this message was to be passed on to owners to deter them from pursuing the matter further, but in many cases the hydraulic operation cured the fault. However, the service department did admit that in some cases further work was needed that was fairly fundamental, in that it included fitting a one-piece flywheel, a slotted clutch plate and a new timing cover. Further service difficulties arose from rainwater leaks that penetrated the engine compartment, passenger space and boot. Bad pressings were blamed; the Wolseley body, almost identical but made in a different factory, had no such problems.

The Pathfinder's body made by BMC subsidiary Fisher and Ludlow had so many leaks that a service bulletin, issued to dealers in October 1954 by service manager Arnold Farrar, detailed ten areas where water could penetrate the body. In one of those areas alone, the scuttle and dash panel, there were seven separate places that had to be sealed. Bostik sealant and Dum-dum putty were prescribed to be lavished on crevices and crannies.

Jacking points were another area of difficulty; they proved unsafe and had to be replaced under warranty.

But a more major problem was with the braking system. Palmer was persuaded by Girling to adopt their new two-trailing shoe system – a competitor to the Dunlop disc, which was now available, but which BMC had not adopted; it similarly relied on servo assistance.

To ensure the pedal effort necessary to stop such a heavy car – 1⅛t (1,594kg) – a large Clayton-Dewandre servo (manufactured in the Titanic Works, Lincoln) was necessary and as the car was now in a late stage of development, the only place to house it was for it to be bolted to the chassis under the rear seat, even though this meant long pipe runs to and from the servo.

Depending on how the servo was behaving, braking would be instant and fierce or almost non-existent. Due to problems with the seals in the servo and other malfunctions, a pedal could be quite hard one minute and completely soft the next; the brakes might lock solid or fail – all most alarming.

An early Pathfinder publicity brochure talked of engineering leadership in steering, suspension and brakes: '12in [30.5cm] hydraulic brakes, operating through a booster, are always ready to turn surprise into complete safety.' Or vice versa in many cases.

Palmer recalled ruefully in his autobiography:

It [the servo] was also unduly exposed to the elements and it may be this factor, perhaps caused by corrosion or even physical damage due to flying road debris, which gave rise to a very indifferent service picture, although specific examples of brake failure were difficult to find.

There was much fiddling about with the brakes at Abingdon. There was an attempt to tackle the fundamental problem, which was the servo, by adding an additional vacuum reservoir, though this could have been to ensure enough vacuum for overdrive cars when free-wheeling. There were also at least two different master cylinders and two wheel cylinders tried.

A lengthy service bulletin to dealers in July 1955 more or less admitted that there had been a series of errors:

Some difficulty is apparently experienced in understanding the special features incorporated in the Girling 'Autostatic' braking system of the Pathfinder. This memorandum is an endeavour generally to clarify matters and particularly to obviate the confusion which may have been caused by the necessity for investigating and correcting certain points which have arisen since the commencement of production.

For instance, modifications from car number 1978, to try to avoid a clanking noise from the brakes when released from stationary, led to new and different problems, so the original system was reverted to from car 2376. Presumably owners had then to live with the clanking. There were two reasons why brakes were binding and much information on overhauling the servo.

Peter Tothill was responsible for some of the extensive Pathfinder brake testing at the MIRA track. With driver Ted Higgins he did a series of brake fade tests, accelerating from 20mph to 80mph (32km/h to 130km/h), braking hard down to 20mph again, then repeating this twenty or thirty times, constantly measuring brake temperatures.

We thought we'd go to the canteen for lunch and as Ted drove into the courtyard, the car lurched and we lost the brakes and were heading for the wall. Ted whipped the nose around and buried in it a pile of builder's sand up to the top of the radiator grille. As we walked into the canteen we got a round of applause.

Then Norman Dewis (Jaguar's former chief test engineer) who'd seen all this, asked discreetly if we were having problems with the Girling Autostatic system. When we said we were, he went off in a terrible rage as Girling had assured him that it was only the Jaguar Mk VII that was having problems.

Another of the hazards Peter Tothill remembered was boiling brake fluid. The front brakes were self-adjusting, with the shoes in rubbing contact with the drums. After braking they were designed to shake back a couple of thou, but this didn't always happen and the heat generated was transferred to the brake fluid. Resolution of braking problems was to come only when the 2.6 went over to a Lockheed system and their Brakemaster servo.

There were also several gearbox changes, though these were not for service reasons. The original Morris 'box was superseded by a unit mated to the C-series engine cars and in late 1956, the Austin-Healey or Austin Westminster 'boxes were installed.

There were three different tyre sizes: the first cars had 6.70 × 16 tyres, most of the 1954–56 cars had skinnier 6.00 × 16 tyres and the final cars had 6.50 × 16.

The total number of modifications made to the Pathfinder in four years was 162, though most were trivial. The extent of the fiddling about with the car was evidenced by the fitting of no fewer than three different facias in its short life.

But two of the very early cars, MAA/511 and MAA/518, were taken off the line and sent off to the chassis engineering department under the code names EX231 and EX232, to try to sort out the variety of problems that had emerged[2].

Chassis MAA/525 a works demonstrator registered JMO 854, was also sent to development.

Production was painfully slow at the outset; in January and February 1954, only two or three a week were being produced.

It was not for some months that the pace quickened and then only to a leisurely ten or so cars a day; in fact many of the cars were assembled in bays by a few workers, to allow the higher-production MGAs and Magnettes to roll down the main lines.

Despite apprehension at Abingdon, the Pathfinder was a fine-looking 100mph car – the fastest saloon car in the BMC stable and with a host of luxurious features. The full-width bodywork made the car look much bigger than its low-slung Riley predecessors, the 2½-litre RMB and RMFs; it was 3½in (89mm) wider at 5ft 7in (1,702mm) and had a wider track but was half an inch higher than the RMF at 5ft 0in (1,524mm).

It contrived to look sleek, even though compared with the 2½-litre it was shorter in length by 2½in (64mm) and had a wheelbase 5½in (140mm) shorter. Although it was the fastest Riley production car, topping 100mph (161km/h) – some 9mph (14km/h) faster than the 2½-litre – the other performance figures were not dissimilar, as the typical specimen figures from *Motor* tests in the table below show.

Overdrive, which became available later, slowed the car down because of the extra weight, but gave it a very relaxed cruising gait of 28.71mph (46.19km/h) at 1,000 revs in overdrive top.

At the 1954 London Motor Show, Nuffield had the audacity to announce the Pathfinder as 'an entirely new and spacious saloon of imaginative body design', despite the fact that it had won a prize in the coachwork section at the show the year before. They were perhaps hoping that people would forget it had already been launched. Certainly few cars had

been built – even by June 1954 only about 200 had been made – as production was hampered by the time it took to sort out the problems. The only visible change in 1954 from the previous year's model was the deletion of a chrome strip along the bonnet, under the windscreen and of the two chrome flashes behind the headlamps.

In some ways, the old Big Four was an anomaly in such a large modern car in 1953, despite the fact that with its great torque it could accelerate the bulky Pathfinder away in top from 12mph (19km/h) and could peak at 5,500rpm in the intermediate gears – remarkable for a long-stroke engine. The first seventy or so cars to be built had a 102bhp engine, which was soon uprated to 110bhp.

But BMC had another big four in its engine line-up, the 2660cc unit used first in the Austin Atlantic and then in the Austin-Healey 100s up until 1956. Sophisticated it wasn't, having commercial origins, but it was very powerful and if Palmer had not insisted on keeping the Riley engine, it would have made more business sense to standardize on one engine.

The trend was for cars of 2¼ litres or more to have six-cylinders – as did the Wolseley 6/80, though there were a couple of other Big Four survivors such as the Sunbeam 90 Mk IIA of 2267cc – soon to be replaced.

The Riley long-stroke engine with a stroke-bore ratio of 1.49 to 1 (120mm × 80.5mm), though loved by its devotees, looked old-fashioned in comparison with the new and efficient fours and big sixes that – thanks to the abolition of the RAC rating – were beginning to appear with a bore and stroke ratio that was almost equal. Although an

| Performance results: Pathfinder versus the 2½-litre | | | | |
|---|---|---|---|---|
| | *0–60mph (sec)* | *Standing ¼ mile (sec)* | *Top speed (mph)* | *Overall mpg* |
| Pathfinder | 16.8 | 20.8 | 100 | 19.5 |
| 2½-litre (1952) | 16.4 | 20.8 | 94 | 20.8 |

*RIGHT AND BELOW RIGHT: Overdrive was a late and not particularly successful option. Note how the chassis member has been kinked to accommodate it compared to the bottom picture, something that might have been thought of at the design stage.*

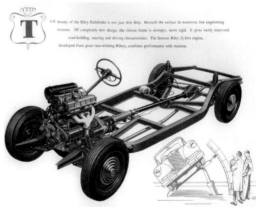

industry norm these days it was not a new idea; the innovative engineer Lanchester had produced such a square engine in 1899.

It took more than half a century to become adopted in Britain. In 1953 Vauxhall's new big sixes – the Crestas and Veloxes – appeared with 'over square' engines – the bore of 79.37mm was actually larger than the stroke of 76.2mm. There was considerable debate around this time about the advantages or not of square engines. Vauxhall claimed that there was much less wear on these new engines, citing the fact that in terms of piston travel in feet per mile the figure for the new engine was 1,873, compared with the old model's 2,335.

Correspondents to *Autocar* dismissed this as nonsense and humbug, saying the real problem with engine wear was on the bottom end rather than cylinders and pistons.

Ford's Zephyr Mark 1 of 1953 was a large comfortable car, an understressed six that had the same engine size as the Vauxhalls. In 1953, you could buy the Zephyr for £754; the Riley was £1,382.

According to Bank of England figures, buying the 1956 Pathfinder with all the options at 2004 prices would cost £25,460 – about the

same as an entry-level BMW 5-series. The Ford would be just under £17,000.

These are false comparisons of course, because those who bought Rileys were a specialist breed, unlikely to buy a Ford. BMC saw the opposition as Jaguar, whose larger and faster MkVII was £400 more expensive than the Pathfinder at the 1953 London Motor Show.

The Jaguar looked over-bodied and bulbous compared with the Riley, but it was considerably more successful, particularly in America for which it was designed. It sold more than 30,000 in its seven-year production run.

## The other influences

Palmer's *grand routier* dream was possibly nearer to a larger version of the Lancia Aurelia, a car that both Issigonis and he admired and which lent some styling cues to the Pathfinder and certainly to the Magnette, though Palmer suggested that the Pathfinder had been more influenced by a Pinin Farina-bodied Bentley he had seen.

Then again, others have seen resemblances to the 1947 sedans of the American Kaiser-Fraser company and to the Singer SM 1500 of 1951.

Whatever the origin, it was said to be the first Riley to be produced without the drawing of its predecessor being overlaid on the design, though there are similarities in various angles of the elevations.

So what did the Riley faithful expect to get for their money when they saw the Pathfinder at the Motor Show in October 1953? What did Palmer's 'discerning Riley owner' seeking that magic cachet expect, apart from Percy Riley's PR head and torsion bar front suspension?

- A fast, fine-handling car that allowed owners to believe they were rather different from those who drove mundane mass-production vehicles.
- Sporting heritage – well, yes, but mainly pre-war.
- Innovation – though what there was of that caused more problems than it was worth.
- Quality – there was certainly an attempt to provide everything the discerning driver of 1956 wanted.

As the *Autocar* remarked: 'It is unusually well-equipped in terms of instruments, controls and lighting and the lavish nature of the furnishings and fittings is evident'.

The leather seats were deeply upholstered, with the front seats recessed at the back to give more knee-room for passengers in the large rear seat, which had a large folding armrest.

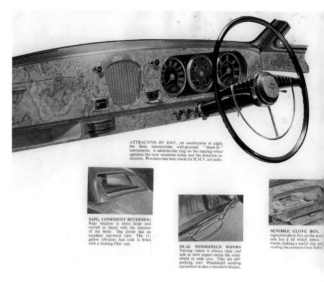

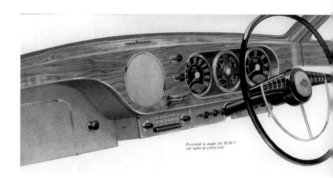

*Two of the three different dash treatments. For such a low-volume model it hardly seemed worth the effort to make these minor changes. The round loudspeaker grille identifies the 1954–55 car and the other the final version.*

Twin roof lights came on when the doors were opened. The polished wooden dash had three large circular dials, read through the top half of the steering wheel, which included a rev counter, oil pressure and water temperature gauges. Illumination of the instrument panel was by 'black lighting', something Saab employed in the nineties; in the Pathfinder's case, only the instrument needles and the numerals were illuminated, and there was a two-position switch to illuminate the speedometer alone.

From graceful radiator to sweeping tail the new Riley Pathfinder brings a host of exciting, exclusive features. The tasteful interior trim and wide leather-covered seats with spacious room for six adults to ride in relaxed comfort typify the impeccable luxury to be found in every inch of this fine car. Polished walnut facia and garnish rails testify to the lasting elegance of an individually built car. A heating and ventilating unit is also provided, keeping you cool when the weather is warm and snug when it is cold. The Riley Pathfinder is a car built for those who want to enjoy motoring *always*.

SEATS FOR RELAXED DRIVING. Whether you specify individual bucket seats or a bench-type front seat, the gear lever, being recessed into the driver's seat, allows him full control of the car always, even with three people in front.

TRAVEL IN COMFORT. You ride in style, in perfect comfort, in the wonderful Riley Pathfinder. The interior has a new spaciousness with deep, wide seating for complete relaxation. Cushions and seat backs are covered with leather; upholstery and trim are in tasteful colours harmonising with the body finish. Ventilating air control keeps the interior fresh and cool in hot weather, and you have a choice of either a one-piece front seat or two bucket seats. Notice the convenient position of the gear lever.

*The interior of the Pathfinder was luxurious by any standard. The side-mounted gear lever is seen here in both right- and left-hand drive versions.*

Also provided as standard were self-cancelling indicators, two-speed self-parking wipers, heater, map-reading lamp, twin fog lamps and 'in-built windscreen washing and demisting equipment'.

All these features sound commonplace today, but fifty years ago they denoted luxury and it's difficult to believe now that even until many years later, a heater had to be paid for as an extra on most cars.

Apart from the right-hand gearchange, there were two other curiously old-fashioned touches, perhaps to maintain the Riley mystique.

One was a hand throttle – useful, thought the *Autocar*, for manoeuvring under difficulties (what sort was not specified) and for warming up in the morning. 'Useless', said *Country Life*'s man of the same feature, which had been carried over from the previous series of cars.

The other was an advance/retard control that could override the distributor setting. The *Motor* had observed in a road test of the Riley 1½-litre in 1954 that this control was now rare on cars, though it conceded that it might be

useful if only low-grade fuel was available. This might have happened in remote parts of Europe, but was unlikely in the UK, though the star system for defining octane ratings was not introduced until 1967.

Also rather outdated was the use of semaphore indicators that were operated by touching the semi-circular horn ring on its right or left. Flashers were now becoming common and could be fitted on export cars.

Starting would be quite a handful, for two hands were already needed to bring the engine to life as the ignition switch was to the right of the steering wheel and the choke and starter button to the left. It's ironic that starter buttons, which were phased out to make life simpler for drivers, are now making a return in high-priced sports cars because they add to the 'driving experience'.

After the engine was running, the driver would release that curse of the 1930s, the spindly umbrella-grip handbrake under the dash – which had been imposed on Rileys after the Nuffield take-over – and accelerate away.

133

**Pathfinder specification for 1955**

ENGINE: Four cylinders, bore 80.5mm (3.169in), stroke 120mm (4.725in), capacity 2443cc (149cu. in), brake horse-power 110 at 4,400rpm. Machined hemispherical combustion chambers; inclined valves actuated by short push-rods and rockers from twin camshafts mounted on each side of engine and chain-driven from crankshaft; sparking plugs centrally situated; gear-type oil pump; full-flow renewable element oil filter; sump capacity 12.1pt (7ltr); three-bearing balanced crankshaft; aluminium alloy pistons; large diameter gudgeon pins with burnished finish.

IGNITION: 12-volt battery and heavy-duty coil; Champion 14mm sparking plugs.

COOLING SYSTEM: Pressurized; cooling system capacity 17¾pt (10ltr).

FUEL SYSTEM: 13gal (59ltr) tank with a concealed filler cap is provided; twin SU carburettors; rear-mounted SU electric fuel pump.

CLUTCH AND GEARBOX: Borg and Beck single-plate dry clutch and four-speed gearbox with synchromesh engagement on second, third and fourth gears. Ratios: first 13.59, second 8.446, third 5.88, top 4.1, reverse 18.42.

TRANSMISSION: Hardy Spicer tubular propeller shaft with needle-type universal joints.

REAR AXLE: Semi-floating with final drive by hypoid gears; rubber-mounted torque arms and transverse anti-sway bar.

SUSPENSION: Riley Torsionic independent front suspension with torsion bar springing controlled by telescopic hydraulic dampers.

Rear suspension: long coil springs and concentrically mounted hydraulic dampers.

BRAKES: Servo-assisted Girling hydraulic fully-compensated brakes operate in 12in (30cm) drums.

STEERING GEAR: A cam-type steering gearbox; two-spoke steering wheel.

ELECTRICAL EQUIPMENT: 12-volt positive-earth system and 63amp/hr battery; hand-operated headlamp dipping switch; headlamp main beam warning light; sidelamps; twin tail- and stop-lamps; twin reverse lamps with automatic switch; number-plate lamp; two fog lamps; map-reading lamp; non-glare instrument panel illumination; ignition warning lamp; dual-arm self-parking windshield wiper; twin Windtone horns; trafficators or flashing direction indicator equipment according to market; suppressor equipment; two roof lamps with individual switches; cigarette lighter.

BODY: All-steel construction with turret-type top; bucket-type or bench-type front seats, three-place rear seat with folding centre arm-rest; arm-rests on front passenger's and rear doors; Triplex safety glass throughout, four winding windows; ventilating hinged windows on front doors; one-piece curved windshield and large curved rear light; inbuilt windshield washing equipment; heating, ventilating and demisting equipment with fresh-air intake on scuttle; 11cu. ft (0.3cu. m) luggage container with counterbalanced lid; two-position non-glare rear mirror; two sun visors; polished wood facia and garnish rails; large glove box with map-reading lamp and switch on passenger's side; door check straps with automatic catch to hold doors in open position; spare wheel under boot floor on special carrier; full-width bumpers with overriders front and rear; provision made for HMV car radio.

WHEELS: Disc-type wheels with 6.00-16 tyres, five-stud fixing, and large plated hub discs.

COLOURS: Finished in: Black with Maroon, Green or Biscuit upholstery. Maroon with Maroon or Biscuit upholstery.

Green with Green or Biscuit upholstery. Blue with Grey upholstery. Grey with Maroon or Grey upholstery.

DIMENSIONS: Wheelbase 9ft 5½in (2,883mm); track 4ft 6½in (1,384mm); ground clearance 7in (178mm); overall height 5ft 0in (1,520mm); overall width 5ft 7in (1,702mm); overall length 15ft 3in (4,648mm); unladen weight 30½cwt 3,416lb (1,550kg) approximately.

Source: *Riley brochure*

It was a sign of how badly the Pathfinder's launch was planned and the besetting problems it had in early production that it was not until more than a year after its debut that BMC allowed Britain's two premier motoring magazines to road test the car, although they had waxed enthusiastic about it in their October 1953 Motor Show issues – without having driven it.

The test car, KJB 372, was in the hands of *Motor* in November 1954. 'The most comfortable Riley so far made', it declared, praising the beautiful upholstery. By this time the car had the 110bhp uprated engine. None of the British motor magazines had had the 102bhp version for test, though *Wheels* in Australia did. The performance figures were almost identical, though the later version's top speed was about 5mph higher at the 100 mark.

*Wheels* was impressed with its outstanding high-speed ability, making the point, as did other journals, that it was a 100mph car at a cost (£875 basic without tax) well below any other saloon rival. It saw it as a fine touring car, highly suitable for long-distance high-speed travel. There was a lengthy explanation of the braking system, which it said provided really powerful effort with a somewhat indirect feel, though it discovered the somewhat recondite fact that a powerful self-servo effect in reverse might lead to the front wheels locking up if the car was backed down an icy gradient.

But it was a 'safe car on corners'. The Panhard rod was obviously still holding firm at this stage.

There were also 'small blemishes'. The tool lockers at the rear filled up with water, which could lead to rust; the under-facia handbrake was poor and in an awkward position and *Motor* discovered a problem that can still catch out an inexperienced hand at the gear lever.

As there was no synchromesh on first, many drivers started in second gear since there was plenty of torque, but reverse was so close to second that it was easy to unexpectedly start going backwards. Similarly coming down from third and failing to select second properly could lead to horrible noise.

Nevertheless, with a flourish of trumpets, *Motor* proclaimed that this was the best Riley yet, built by motoring-minded engineers for enthusiastic motoring owners. 'The name Pathfinder can be placed at the head of the illustrious roll of model names which have been borne by one of the oldest motor manufacturing concerns in the world.' Alas, the name was soon to be tarnished.

*Motor* did have some reservations about the slow steering response, which may have planted a seed about the car not being as good in this department as its predecessor.

*Autocar* tested KJB 372 in February 1955 and was in its 'jolly good' mode – enthusiastic without being quite as declamatory as *Motor* though it noted that the road test had been a long time coming since the 1953 Motor Show. Nevertheless, it was worth the wait.

Phrases like 'a particularly good all-round car', 'very good value for money', 'a first-class sports saloon', peppered the report. John Bolster in *Autosport* talked of the car's 'all-round excellence' and of its being the best Riley he had ever driven.

'I shall remember it most', he wrote, ' for the easy 100mph, that *dear* little gear lever and the way it held the treacherous roads of winter.'

## Over the ton

The Pathfinder was not to everyone's taste – this letter-writer to *Autocar* in July 1955 thought it undistinguished: 'Its profile is quite well-balanced and it has very distinctive wheels but otherwise it is uninteresting. It is altogether most un-Riley-like, looking more like a family saloon and it certainly qualifies for the "suet pudding" class.'

Pudding indeed – a fully-loaded Pathfinder was hurled around Montlhéry in 1955 by Bob Porter, who averaged 108mph (174km/h).

Nearly 3,000 Pathfinders were built before overdrive became an option from chassis MA/4288, in the 1956 model. The chassis had to be slightly modified to take the bulge of the overdrive, and a polished chassis with a sectioned overdrive was displayed on the Riley stand at the 1955 Motor Show, at which the 1½-litre no longer appeared, having been phased out.

The Borg Warner overdrive was an extra £63 15s and was not taken up with any great enthusiasm as it was specified in only 179 home market cars and thirty-two export models – about 10 per cent of the two thousand or so cars built from then until the end of production.

*More than 290,000 miles (466,500km) have been covered by this Pathfinder, first registered in January 1956. It's an overdrive version now owned by Dave Rowlands who uses it every day. The colour scheme is light blue over dark.*

*A much bigger heater blower replaced the puny efforts in earlier RMs.*

The overdrive was operated by a push–pull control under the dashboard, so could be switched in or out for second, third or fourth gear. With overdrive engaged, which cut in at around 32mph (51km/h), the car would hold its gear and accelerate to the rev limit in that gear. If the accelerator were lifted above 32mph, it would move to the next gear; if speed dropped below 26mph (42km/h), the overdrive disengaged and the car free-wheeled, something that could catch out the unwary. For quick acceleration, there was a kick-down switch under the throttle pedal that resumed normal drive until pressure was released.

## Pathfinder chassis change points

| | |
|---|---|
| 501 onwards | First basic chassis. |
| 1354 | Frame modified for R2 gearbox, not used by the Pathfinder at this stage but probably for the Wolseley 6/90 and its hydraulic clutch that had a revised bell housing. |
| 3676 | R2 gearbox with hydraulic clutch now fitted to Pathfinder, but original Morris-type still recurs. |
| 4288 | First recorded overdrive car with altered side member to accommodate extra gearbox size. Parts List states that this happened from car 4379. |
| 5176 | Workshop manual says overdrive cannot be fitted before this chassis number – perhaps because old frames were still being used as well as the new altered version. |
| 5554 to end | Final hundred or so Pathfinders are put on the leaf-spring chassis already used by the Wolseley 6/90. |

*Gearbox variants*
Four different types of gearbox were fitted to the Pathfinder.

| Chassis | Gearbox | Designation |
|---|---|---|
| 501  onwards | Morris | R |
| 3676  onwards | BMC C-type | R2 |
| 4703  onwards, occasionally | Austin-Healey | R3 |
| Occasionally in final cars | Austin Westminster | R4 |

Source: *Dave Rowlands*

*For Magnificent Motoring*

The flexibility of the engine was such that if overdrive were engaged in second gear, the car would get up to 70mph (113km/h) with the foot on the floor. Overdrive third was very similar to normal top gear, but overdrive top with a ratio of 2.87 to 1 allowed 90mph (145km/h) cruising at only 3,000rpm.

The overdrive naturally put on a bit of weight; the car was now 3,506lb (1,590kg), compared with the standard 3,486lb (1,581kg), but there was no fuel penalty. *Autocar* tests actually showed it had better overall fuel economy at 23.7mpg compared with their previous test of the standard car that showed 21mpg. Riley claimed it reduced engine speeds by 30 per cent.

The recorded best maximum speed was 102mph in both cases, but the standard car had the edge on the 0–60 time with 16.7sec compared with 18.8sec for the overdrive version.

## The end of the Big Four design

By the mid-1950s, the 2½-litre based on the Big Four design had lasted for nearly twenty years (not counting the war years). It was a fine design, much-loved, but showing its age with the longest piston stroke in the world, being very expensive to produce for just one model in a factory BMC wanted for other purposes, and having no place in the engine line-up of the A engine for small cars, the B for mid-range cars and the C for large cars.

It was clear that Percy's PR head would be abandoned for the Pathfinder's successor, the 2.6, that would have the six-cylinder C-series block, but there was a plan to make it more distinctive by using a double-overhead camshaft head. Gerald Palmer had conceived designs for this, developed from his four-cylinder version, which after many years of development finally appeared in the MGA Twin-cam. He called the Riley version a project to 'out-Jaguar Jaguar'.

A prototype twin-cam six, known in the works as 'the barge', was built in the winter of 1954 and had the Abingdon project code EX 207. It had disc brakes instead of the troublesome Girling units, but it was decided not to proceed, probably because of the cost of the twin-cam head, and it ended its life as a works hack. It was broken up a few years later.

When the C-series finally appeared in a Riley, of course, it was the standard pushrod version in the Pathfinder's undistinguished successor, the Two-Point-Six.

There were other BMC body/engine experimental permutations, such as the six-cylinder Magnette (EX202) and the 'Three-litre Riley' as it's described in the experimental register (EX206). Neither made it into production. Another EX project 185 is described as special parts for a competition Pathfinder.

MG historian David Knowles says it was Abingdon's review of the Pathfinder in July of 1956 that eventually led to the abandonment later that year of the rear coil springs and the fitting of standard semi-elliptics – a suggestion for better handling that came from the MG bosses John Thornley and Syd Enever, who drove a Pathfinder himself, though the set-up had been fitted first to the short-lived Wolseley 6/90 Series II in early 1956.

However, BMC was to claim in its publicity that the Riley's new suspension had improved road-holding 'by a commendable extent' by eliminating all vibration. This announcement was accompanied by much snorting from Pathfinder experts, who had not detected this in the first place. The *Autocar* also pointed out that a saving in unsprung weight

'usually expected' when this change of spring-ing happened, had not occurred, which was an odd thing to say since few cars were on coil spring rears and the leaf springs were going to be as heavy or heavier than the coils.

The general view was that fitting leaf springs to the rear was a cost-saving and ret-rograde step, though it did obviate the rear suspension problems that had given the Pathfinder such a bad name. The *aficionados* would say that once the Panhard rod welding

had been sorted out, the rear end was perfect anyway.

So Gerald Palmer's live rear axle became constrained by leaf springs, something he believed belonged to the horse and cart era. But it was only the final few – some one hun-dred cars – that were put on this chassis.

Final changes, also carried over, from chas-sis MA/5172 were a differently shaped loud-speaker grille and the moving to different positions of the clock and ashtray.

---

### Special requests

The pace of the Abingdon production line, down which cars were pushed by hand, was leisurely enough to allow for customized versions of Pathfinders to be produced by special request. Chassis MAA/2498 for instance had the seat runners put well back 'to suit a 6' 4' driver'. Bucket seats instead of the bench front seat were a common option (at extra cost) as were air scoops – shields fitted to the driver's door to direct air into the car, until rendered unnec-essary by the introduction of swivelling quarter lights. Syd Enever, Abingdon's engineering chief, had a 'special handbrake' on his car. Some export orders occasionally demanded whitewall tyres.

Many police forces bought Pathfinders; MAA/922 in black with maroon trim and a certified speedometer went to the Gloucester police; Norfolk police ordered versions with roof-top aerials and VHF radios fitted. Sussex con-stabulary was a big customer, as was Buckinghamshire, who took delivery of nine in November 1955.

Colours could also be varied from the standard and, once duotone cars became available as standard in Decem-ber 1955, the options widened considerably.

Official BMC duotones had the second colour on the roof only, though the London Riley distributor Jimmy James had cars painted that had the top colour on the bonnet and boot-lid as well. Several present owners have fol-lowed this combination.

A few cars were supplied in primer with varying trim colours to be painted elsewhere. The rarest of the stan-dard finishes was Black with Grey trim. Duotone cars are noted with the upper colour first.

| MAA/ | Paint | Trim | Remarks |
|---|---|---|---|
| 891 | Bristol Red | Biscuit | Capt. Eyston |
| 928 | Blue | Maroon | special trim only |
| 961 | Ivory | Maroon | Nuffield Metal Products |
| 998 | Ivory | Maroon | |
| 1248 | Almond Green | Green | |
| 1262 | duotone Black/Blue | Green | Earl Mountbatten |
| 1305 | Blue | Maroon | special trim only |
| 1593 | ZA Magnette Green | Green | |
| 1600 | Connaught Green | Green | first Conn. Green, Jan. 1955 |
| 1705 | Grey | Green | special trim only |
| 1797 | Blue | Maroon | special trim only |
| 1843 | Green | Grey | special trim only |
| 1855 | Blue | Biscuit | special trim only |
| 1897 | Grey | Biscuit | special trim only |
| 1909 | Special Dark Blue | Beige | works car, development |
| 1977 | Ivory | Grey | personal export delivery |

| | | | |
|---|---|---|---|
| 1996 | Grey | Green | special trim only |
| 2304 | Sandy Beige | Maroon | |
| 2724 | Moonstone Grey | Green | lhd export |
| 2725 | Moonstone Grey | Maroon | personal export delivery |
| 2827 | Sandy Beige | Maroon | |
| 2859 | Blue | Biscuit | special trim only |
| 2878 | Blue | Biscuit | special trim only |
| 2974 | Metallic Grey | Grey | |
| 3009 | Sandy Beige | Maroon | |
| 3010 | Sandy Beige | Maroon | |
| 3017 | Sandy Beige | Maroon | |
| 3162 | Grey | Green | special trim only |
| 3326 | Pale Blue | White | 1955 Earl's Court car |
| 3327 | Pale Blue | Maroon | 1955 Earl's Court car |
| 3328 | Pale Blue | Dark Grey | 1955 Earl's Court car |
| 3367 | Grey | Green | special trim only |
| 4066 | Almond Green | Green | lhd export |
| 4073 | Glasso Blue/Steel Grey | Grey | first duotone, Dec. 1955 |
| 4077 | Maroon/Kashmir Beige | Maroon | ditto |
| 4080 | Kashmir Beige | Biscuit | first Kash. Beige, Dec. 1955 |
| 4086 | Charcoal Grey | Grey | first Charcoal Grey |
| 4087 | Rose Taupe/Kashmir Beige | Maroon | first duotone, Dec. 1955 |
| 4088 | Black/Willow Grey | Green | special duotone, Dec. 1955 |
| 4089 | Maroon/Charcoal Grey | Maroon | special duotone, Dec. 1955 |
| 4090 | Damask Red/Willow Grey | Maroon | special duotone, Dec. 1955 |
| 4091 | Black/Damask Red | Biscuit | special duotone, Dec. 1955 |
| 4104 | Dove Grey/Charcoal Grey | Maroon | special duotone, Dec. 1955 |
| 4109 | Cedar Green/Green | Green | special duotone, Dec. 1955 |
| 4428 | Cedar Green | Biscuit | first Cedar Grn, Feb. 1956 |
| 4429 | Wolseley Maroon | Biscuit | first Wolseley Maroon |
| 4484 | Woodstock Green | Biscuit | |
| 4845 | Rose Taupe/Kashmir Beige | Maroon | new facia, Mar. 1956 |
| 4846 | Swiss Grey/Charcoal Grey | Maroon | new facia, Mar. 1956 |
| 4900 | Duo Green | Green | two Glasso colours; repainted, as are 4902, 4910, 4980, 4986, 5008 |
| 4915 | Kashmir Beige/Maroon | Biscuit | marked repainted, as are 5030, 5047, 5080, 5157 |
| 4967 | Two-tone Blue | Grey | |
| 5069 | Swiss Grey/Charcoal Grey | Maroon | repainted, as are 5124, 5173 |
| 5152 | Rose Taupe/Kashmir Beige | Biscuit | marked repainted |
| 5202 | Birch Grey | Green | lhd export |
| 5301 | Moonstone Grey | Maroon | lhd export |
| 5302 | Almond Green | Green | lhd export |
| 5378 | Birch Grey | Maroon | lhd export |
| 5504 | Metallic Blue/off White | Trim? | lhd export 1956 Motor Show |
| 5648 | Glasso Blue monotone | Grey | colour normally found on roof of duo-blue cars |

Facia changes: original MAA/501–3255; integral glove box 3256–5554; triangular speaker and other minor changes 5554 to end.

Source: *BMIHT*

## Styled in new colours

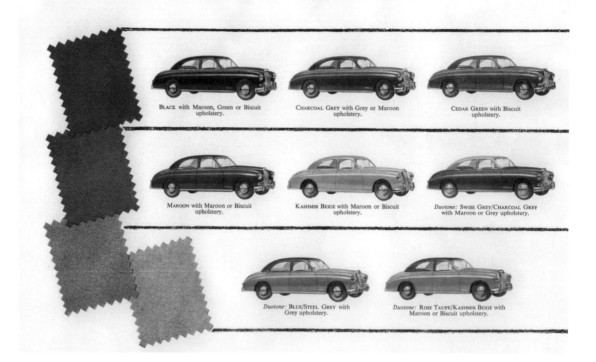

BLACK with Maroon, Green or Biscuit upholstery.

CHARCOAL GREY with Grey or Maroon upholstery.

CEDAR GREEN with Biscuit upholstery.

MAROON with Maroon or Biscuit upholstery.

KASHMIR BEIGE with Maroon or Biscuit upholstery.

*Duotone:* SWISS GREY/CHARCOAL GREY with Maroon or Grey upholstery.

*Duotone:* BLUE/STEEL GREY with Grey upholstery.

*Duotone:* ROSE TAUPE/KASHMIR BEIGE with Maroon or Biscuit upholstery.

The *New*

**Riley**

**1½ LITRE and PATHFINDER**

**T**HE RILEY PATHFINDER is a car built for those who want to enjoy motoring *always*. There's craftsman-built quality in every part, which gives a delightful individual character. The spacious locker provides 11 cubic feet (·3 cubic metre) of unobstructed space, whilst the lid is counterbalanced for easy opening. The spare wheel, hidden beneath the floor, is readily accessible from the outside to save disturbing the luggage.

Many luxury refinements add immeasurably to your comfort and motoring enjoyment. The Pathfinder is designed to meet the *particular* requirements of *particular* motorists—those who take a pride in the car they own, and enjoy " Magnificent Motoring " for its own sake.

The rear-mounted fuel pump eliminates vapour locks and the 13-gallon (59-litre) tank is fitted with a quick-release filler cap.

The twin camshafts, chain-driven from the crankshaft, operate the valves through short push-rods and rockers.

Inclined overhead valves and hemispherical combustion chambers are features that contribute towards the 110 b.h.p. and remarkable efficiency of the Riley engine.

*This Monte competitor of the 1990s is now being restored.*

The Pathfinder disappeared slowly from dealers' showrooms after all the remaining stocks of the Big Four engine had been used. The last chassis, MA/5627, was finished at Abingdon in February 1957.

Many tales, some apocryphal, survive – for instance the story that service staff at the works – telephone number Abingdon 251 – would not answer the phone in case it was a lawyer acting for an enraged client whose Pathfinder had found the ditch.

At the London Motor Show in October 1956, the Pathfinder made its last appearance; there were two right-hand-drive cars and one left-hand-drive with white-wall tyres. The cars were finished in a peculiar lilac shade that was not to be offered to the public. One car was displayed on white stones with leaves, toadstools and artificial plants swaying in the breeze. There was also a Big Four engine on display, just as if this and the Pathfinder had a long future ahead of them. But there were only a few months of production left, which would amount to fewer than one hundred cars. BMC though were already planning the successor to inherit the Riley name, so for them it was motor show business as usual.

At a cost of £1,411, the Pathfinder was still £200 dearer that its Wolseley equivalent and only a few pounds cheaper than the brand-new Jaguar 2.4, reflecting perhaps the cost of building the Big Four in such small numbers.

Jaguar, basking in the glory of two successive Le Mans wins with the D-type, was in an ideal position to steal the Pathfinder's market; the 2.4 was a faster car, though not without its own mechanical difficulties.

The argument is sometimes made that the Pathfinder was a failure because 'only' 5,152[3] cars were made. (Those looking for motoring failures should be asked whatever happened to the 2½-litre Lanchester Dauphin, introduced at the same 1953 Motor Show, or the Daimler Conquest introduced at [note the price] £1,066).

The Pathfinder's defenders counter that it was never meant to be a mass market car, because as a Riley it appealed to a select bunch of upper-middle-class sporting drivers, and in fact sold in similar numbers year on year to the RMB and RMF saloons. Nuffield's volume brand was the Morris; between 1952 and 1956 the Minor alone was produced in quantities of about 1,500 a week.

Riley was a niche product and even in the best year of production, 1955, only about ten to a dozen Pathfinders were being made every week.

The plunging sales of the 2½-litre RMF between 1952 and 1953 and its withdrawal should have led to an urgent production and marketing campaign for its replacement. As it was, due to Nuffield incompetence, the market was effectively lost for nearly a year while rectification took place.

As to the Pathfinder's dire, and exaggerated, mechanical reputation, there is evidence that once the Nuffield management at Cowley had ceded day-to-day control of production to its Abingdon satellite at the start of 1955, the problems were rapidly solved by much better management of the project and there are enthusiasts like Dave Rowlands who think it is an outstanding car.

The Pathfinder guru Harry Wright once said it was a very good car – that would have been even better with power steering and synchromesh on first.

**A Pathfinder saga by Dave Rowlands**

In early 1955 I was waiting at the bus stop just up the road from here in Iver, when I saw a beautiful grey-green Pathfinder which had just been bought by a neighbour – he gave me a lift to school in it and I thought 'What a marvellous car, one day I am going to have one of these.'

But it was quite some time, not until 1961, and by then they had dropped quite a bit in value from about £1,300 new to £250. Even then I couldn't afford it – it was a year's salary for me – but my mother bought it for me. It had had the Panhard rod problem and had very nearly killed its owner when it rolled over; he was a broken man for the rest of his life. But the car was rebuilt, though I had to sell it when I got married, so I was without one for about four years.

Then there was a ring at the door one afternoon and there in the drive there was a Pathfinder with the engine running and a note on it saying 'All yours'. It was the original one that had taken me to school; I'd done odd jobs on it for the owner over the eleven years he had it and it had been absolutely trouble-free for nearly 200,000 miles. I had it for five years and then one day it was stolen from the car park at my work and it never turned up.

I didn't have one for a number of years until about 1990 when I saw a feature about the Pathfinder in a motoring magazine and got one through the RM Club, KJR 718, which I drove down from Northumberland.

I drove it every day for nine years: it was a marvellous car and the only time that anything went wrong with it was when the Panhard rod broke; not the bracket, but the screw thread at the end of the rod – it's very thin and had rusted. It was my fault: I should have checked the bushes. I was going around a roundabout, not very quickly, and the car slewed all over the road. What it must be like at speed I don't know.

People have talked an awful lot of rubbish about the Pathfinder – usually those who have never driven one and certainly never owned one. I have driven Pathfinders every day for around twenty years and of all the cars I have ever driven it's the one I most like to drive. It's fast, it's comfortable, it gives a superb ride and the roadholding is splendid. The only things I criticize about it are the steering, which is heavy at low speeds, and the problems you can have with the original brake servo: once you get rid of this you will never have any more problems.

I've now got two other Pathfinders as well as KJR 718. I've got one for spares and 294 GAA [above], which belonged to Hampshire County Council. They sold it for scrap, but it was saved and it's now done more than 300,000 miles.

For my money, the Pathfinder is a superb car. John Bolster of *Autosport* – who had tested every Riley in twenty-five years of production – said when he was writing about the Pathfinder that it was the best Riley he had ever driven. And I quite agree with him.

### How it all ended

The long-running RM series came to a halt in February 1957, when the last Pathfinder, chassis 5262, was produced at Abingdon. The manufacture of Big Four engines had been stopped in the autumn of 1956 and stocks finally ran out in January 1957.

John Thornley's plan for a replacement Pathfinder with Gerald Palmer's twin-cam head on the Austin-produced C-series six-cylinder engine was not to be realized; the car had the standard 2639cc lump used in the Wolseley 6/90, Austin Westminster and Morris Isis. Pathfinders lingered in the showrooms for months and the car was still catalogued in *Autocar* of September 1957 even though the replacement, called, with a singular lack of imagination, the Two-Point-Six, was ready.

What had distinguished the Pathfinder from the Wolseley 6/90, apart from the engine, was a deliberate design effort to make the Riley look low and the Wolseley look more imposing by using larger sills to make its body sit 2in (5cm) higher.

Now both cars had the same engine, same body and same almost everything else. Apart from the radiator, the styling differences were confined to dashboard, bumpers, and driving lamps and cowled headlamps for the Riley. Beneath the bonnet, the Riley's C-series engine had 101bhp, compared with its clone's 97bhp, and there was a higher final drive ratio. It was probably about 4mph (6.4km/h) faster at a maximum of some 94mph (151km/h), and slightly quicker from 0-60mph at 17.4sec.

For this buyers were expected to pay £1,411 pounds, nearly 10 per cent more than the Wolseley. Unsurprisingly, it was not a success; 2,000 were sold in two years and it was replaced in 1959 with the barge-like Riley 4/68, a version of the Farina-designed Austin Cambridge, which had a 1498cc engine.

There was a final success for the renowned Riley name. The 1.5, launched in 1957 in a body originally designed as a Morris Minor replacement, sold 39,568 before production stopped in 1965. It was by far the best-selling model in the marque's history.

More pallid clones followed: the Elf based on the Mini and the Kestrel based on the Austin/Morris 1100.

The Riley name finally disappeared from new cars in 1969 and is now owned by BMW. There was some excitement in the late 1990s when the firm's then head, Bernd Pischetsrieder, announced that a new Riley was to be built as part of BMW's plans for Rover. He disappeared from Rover shortly afterwards, as did his plan.

---

Perhaps the last word should go to its designer, Gerald Palmer:

Regrettably service problems of varying degrees of severity occurred on this model throughout its production life, many of which remained unsolved. In the attempt to continue the unusual features which would appeal to discerning Riley owners, they were not very well developed.

In 2004 it was estimated that more than 125 Pathfinders were roadworthy.

| | |
|---|---|
| UK | 47 |
| Australia | 60 (many cars still unrecorded) |
| New Zealand | 10 |

The rest are in Europe.

---

1. The other cars on the stand were a blue rhd Pathfinder and a 1½-litre RME lhd in grey.
2. These numbers do not correspond with Abingdon's surviving experimental EX register, which contains project numbers for proposed engineering changes. They are noted in the production records as MAA/EX232/511 and MAA/ EX231/518.
3. Its Wolseley 6/90 Series 1 counterpart on the same chassis sold 5,776.

# 10　Exporting RMs

In the summer of 1948, J.K. Hookes pushed his 2½-litre saloon non-stop from Durban to Johannesburg, sometimes exceeding an indicated 100mph (161km/h) over the 409 miles (658km).

'Riley cars are not only doing their share helping to bridge the gap and safeguard the British breakfast table, but are also showing the flag in an effective manner in many countries', commented the *Riley Record*, demonstrating the obsession with obtaining foreign currency that seized bankrupt Britain after the war.

Despite all the fuss about exporting or dying and the part played by the British motor industry, exports of cars were never more than 3.9 per cent of total British exports in the years 1946 to 1948. But the industry was being built up into one of the main driving forces of the economy, with a reputation for innovation and a huge range of models that were eagerly sought-after.

There was scarcely a country in the world to which RMs could not be exported, from Antigua to Zanzibar, thanks to the enormous scope of the Nuffield group. Take India; as well as distributors in the major cities, Addison and Co Ltd. of Madras also had branches in Bangalore, Trichinopoly, Vizagatapam, Oottacamund, Nilgiri Hills and Coimbatore. Whether you were in Peru, Abyssinia, Iraq or Iceland, Nuffield Exports Ltd., who dealt with any Riley sales outside the UK, were there to sell you a car.

There was no overstatement in the Riley claim of being 'Famous in Five Continents for Magnificent Motoring'.

*The 'black Riley' in the despatch bay at Foleshill. This was a left-hand-drive car for export and it is believed the chrome was painted over to preserve it until delivery. Morris is known to have done this on some occasions. There was also a great chrome shortage in 1951/52 so some Rileys left the works with the Butler lamp rims painted black. Morris at the same time painted bumpers and radiator grilles silver.*

As soon as the war ended, orders from abroad began stacking up, mainly from British spheres of influence unaffected by the war. In April 1946, there were 142 export orders, among them: thirty-five cars for Cairo Motors in Egypt; six for Freeman and Co., Palestine; three for Rogers and Co. in Mauritius; and five for Collis and Co. in Monaco.

There were other Riley distributors agitating for cars in Uruguay, the Canaries, Cyprus, Bombay and Lahore, not to mention Messrs Papageorgopoulos in Greece.

Switzerland became one of the first export markets after the war and Riley exhibited at the Geneva Motor Show in the spring of 1946. By June of that year, 327 cars had been sent abroad, the majority of them going to Europe (135), India (sixty-seven) and Australia (twenty) despite a widespread shortage of steel and other materials. The lack of chrome for plating can be identified in the very early cars, though those having chromed cast bronze bumper blades had black-painted cast bronze bumpers over-riders.

## 100 cars a week

In late September 1947, when 100 cars a week were produced for the first time since the war, the Nuffield vice-chairman Miles Thomas wrote to Victor Riley: 'I am glad to see…that your export orders totalled 40.'

Export customers were often British colonials on leave picking up their cars in London purchase-tax free before returning to their postings, and they got special treatment. When a Mr Thomas went to get his maroon RMB, KLN 261, from the Lex Garage in Park Lane in 1949, he was met by a uniformed Nuffield chauffeur who had brought the car from Coventry. It had also been to Birmingham to have a Weathershields sun roof fitted and to Southend-on-Sea for fitment of an Ecko radio at the works where they were made.

Many of the traditional export markets were right-hand drive, but in 1948 the works began making left-hand-drive cars that, for continental distributors, had speedometers calibrated in kilometres and temperature gauges with Celsius scales. They were also offered with roofs in colours other than black.

At Geneva in 1948, a 1½-litre in grey with a black top was exhibited, as was what one magazine described as a 'black and chromium' 2½-litre. At the Brussels Show, there was a black 1½-litre and a 2½-litre in green with black wings. As part of the post-war currency restrictions that applied across much of Europe, Belgium had a limit of £600 that could be spent on a new car. Rileys were obviously more costly than this, but if the money came from outside the country the restrictions did not apply.

In 1948, a 1½-litre arrived on the west coast of America as part of a Nuffield export mission. International Motors in Los Angeles had been appointed dealers, and to publicize the arrival of the 1½-litre, a pre-war Brooklands was driven across the continent to Los Angeles from New York and pictures posed with the two cars together.

The United States was a prime target for Nuffield exports as there was a desperate need for dollars to keep Britain afloat, but Rileys fared badly, in fact the records preserved by the British Motor Industry Heritage Trust show that no 1½-litres were officially sold in America. When exports did begin there in 1948, only twenty-seven cars were sold, and the following year only thirteen.

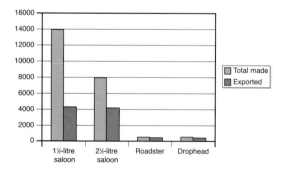

*Riley production and exports by model 1946–54 (inc. CKD).* BMIHT

By 1950 things had improved, the roadster (seventeen) and drophead (127) added to the 2½-litre's figure of seventy-five, made 219. This was the peak year and by 1954 exports to America had declined to four Pathfinders. It was clear from the start that the roadster was never going to be the hoped-for success, and its woes are chronicled in Chapter 6.

The network of Nuffield distributors such as Arnolt in Chicago and Waco Motors in Florida had no trouble shifting large numbers of MG TC and TD models, but the coachbuilt Rileys were not to American tastes.

Arnolt managed to sell only thirteen Rileys between 1948 and 1954 and Waco only three. The greatest success, if it can be called that, was on the east coast where Inskip of New York sold more than 200 cars of the total of 460 or so Rileys that were landed in the United States over a seven-year period.

Austin's car built specifically for the American market, the A90 Atlantic convertible, designed by Dick Burzi, was a similar export flop.

Perhaps the Riley management should have taken notice of Miles Thomas's remarks – before he was ousted by Nuffield – about the American car market. 'There is a saying in America that the average family man would rather have a four-room house and an eight-cylinder car than an eight-room house and a four-cylinder car', he wrote to Sidney Horniblow, a *Daily Mail* hack who had become Lord Nuffield's private secretary.

Far more successful were Riley exports to Australia. Between 1946 and 1957, more than 4,200 RMs were registered there, peaking in 1950 with 1,135 cars. Of Riley export production in right-hand drive, 50 per cent of 1½-litre and 76 per cent of 2½-litre went to Australia – the larger car being more suited to the rugged roads and huge distances. New South Wales took most of the cars, followed by Victoria and Queensland.

It's noticeable that the Pathfinder gave a blip to the declining figures in 1955, but by 1957, which scarcely registers on the chart, only two imported and the following year none. The sharp decline from 1950 to 1952 is almost certainly attributable to British cars now being available direct from an Australian factory, as in the early 1950s BMC opened a large assembly plant outside Sydney on the site of the Victoria Park race track.

In 2002, it was reckoned that there were more than 600 RM series cars in Australia, either on the road or being restored, though it is believed the true figure may be double this with the number of unrestored cars lurking in sheds and garages that may never see the light of day due to restoration costs. However, a three-seater roadster that is being

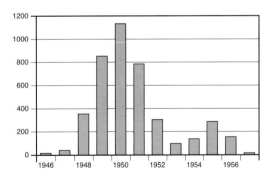

*Australia – new Riley registrations. These chart figures are based on actual registrations and are lower than Nuffield export figures to Australia, probably because some cars were in transit for other countries. Sources: Bob Simpson; 1951 Motor Manual; RTA, Australia*

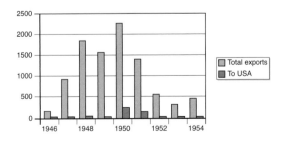

*Riley exports 1946–54.* BMIHT

restored turned up in 2004 in Victoria with only 1,218 miles (1,960km) on the clock. It had not been driven for fifty-two years.

It would be tedious to list all the other countries to which Rileys were sent, as the numbers were small, but it is worth noting that exports to Japan began in 1950, through the Nuffield distributor Dodwell, who had offices in Hong Kong and Japan.

Only twenty-eight cars arrived there over four years, though they were both left- and right-hand drive; two of them were dropheads.

## The Irish RMs

The most curious export market, and the nearest, was Ireland – only just over 200 miles (320km) away in a direct line from Coventry to Dublin – where RMs were made on a special assembly line. The purpose of assembling them in Ireland was that the cars qualified as exports, and that meant more allowances of steel for the Riley works.

In December 1946, assembly of both the 1½-litre and 2½-litre began at G.A. Brittain Ltd, a firm of coachbuilders at Portobello, Dublin, where 312 cars were produced from CKD (completely knocked-down) kits sent from England through Gloucester Docks.

Brittains assembled other cars and tractors for the Nuffield group and were also Riley distributors who imported complete cars, though there were only some twenty of these, including two roadsters and a drophead.

The Irish cars did not have a body number stamped on the bulkhead, but had a chassis number and a Brittain car number on a bulkhead plate.

These Brittain numbers, which are an entirely separate sequence from the Morris Bodies numbers used in Coventry and Abingdon, seemed to run from R1 to R212 for the 1½-litre cars and from R5001 to R5100 for the 2½-litre, though this classification probably included other Nuffield products. Sometimes the R appeared as a P.

Nigel Trotman, registrar of the RM Club, estimates that 212 1½-litres and 100 2½-litres were built in Dublin, all saloons; two of the chassis were used for motor shows.

The highest production years in Dublin were for RMAs in 1946 (forty) and 1947 (sixty); in 1954, the last year of production, twenty-four RMEs were built and the company went into liquidation shortly afterwards.

The RM Club has identified thirty-three of the Brittain cars, and most of these survive.

*Vincent Brittain and Jack Tatlow with the first RMA produced in Dublin in 1946.*

# 11 Sporting success

## Le Mans

In the sweltering June of 1934, six Rileys set off from Coventry to drive to Le Mans to run in the 12th annual Grand Prix d'Endurance. The mixture of Nines and Sixes were to perform the greatest sporting feat in Riley history, coming 2nd, 3rd, 5th, 6th, 12th and 13th overall, being beaten only by a supercharged 1½-litre Alfa Romeo. There were forty-four starters and only twenty-three finishers.

The significance of the Riley win was that the lightweight cars were all in the 1.1 or 1.5 classes and achieved the overall win against opposition by huge cars like the 3.5-litre Lorraine, the 5-litre Bugatti and the 6.8-litre Duesenbergs – none of which finished. Neither did the Aston Martin team nor the Alfa driven by Earl Howe, who later became a 2½-litre owner. The Imp of Kay Petre and Dorothy Champney (Victor Riley's wife) put up the highest overall speed ever achieved by women drivers in the race. When it was all over the six Rileys were driven back home again to Coventry. They all survive today.

There were of course other signal achievements in these glory days up until 1939, that were not to be repeated after the war. The last major sporting achievement of the 1930s was the first place taken by a 1½-litre in the 1939 Crystal Palace sports handicap.

Racing at Le Mans did not resume until 1949 and the Nuffield organization was not interested in setting up Riley works teams to race there or anywhere else. What resources there were went into MGs like Goldie Gardner's EX 135 that broke three international class records at Jabbeke on 15 September 1949.

BMC were very slow in seeing the potential of sport rather than record-breaking for publicity purposes. Things began to change only when the MG drawing office moved from Cowley to Abingdon and the management there began to exercise decisions away from the dead hand of Cowley.

Abingdon's boss John Thornley persuaded Len Lord to let him open a BMC Competitions Department, sometimes called the Racing Department by those who worked there, that began work in December 1954 and was headed by Marcus Chambers.

However, in 1950, the Nuffield board had confirmed that they would give 'reasonable support' to owners of Rileys competing privately. There had already been some support, but this decision validated work that had been going on at Abingdon.

The first fruits of this were seen afterwards that year when Geoffrey Beetson, then thirty-nine and who had owned a prototype Riley Sprite before the war, entered his roadster at Le Mans, becoming the last Riley owner to drive his car there. Beetson was an enthusiast from Bury in Lancashire who was chairman of the Riley Motor Club's local branch. He shared the driving with Robert Lawrie, who was ten years older and who had qualified the previous year in an Aston Martin by coming eleventh.

Beetson's roadster, registered AEN 10, a number that later ended up on an Austin Maxi, was worked on in the development department at Abingdon, the forerunner of the famous competitions and special tuning departments, where the engine was rebuilt, run-in and tested. J.A. Robson, a Riley factory stalwart, described in the BMC magazine *Motoring* many years later the changes that had been made to the car.

There was a close ratio gearbox, a Healey-type rear axle with the higher ratio of 3.5:1 and heavy-duty Girling shock absorbers. Two Lucas Flamethrower lamps were fitted, the brakes modified and a 30-gallon tank fitted instead of the standard 20-gallon tank.

Beetson maintained that the car was standard, other than taking off surplus weight, and was quoted as saying: 'We had done no more to the engine than make sure everything was

working as it should, with lock nuts all round.' In fact, the thermostat and fan were removed to avoid power being sapped at high speed.

The weight reductions involved discarding the bumpers, hood, windscreen and seats and fitting a racing windscreen and seat. The car was painted matt green – even the chrome bits – to avoid reflections at night.

There were a few body modifications to cut down time in the pits, where there was to be a pit boss/mechanic, Ivan Waller, pit crew and a chart analyser. The strap-down bonnet was one-piece and protruding through it were the oil filler/breather, oil level tap and water filler

*The last Riley owner to drive his car at Le Mans, Geoff Beetson (left) with co-driver Robert Lawrie before the race. Note the spare behind the back seat and the twin petrol filler caps protruding from the boot.*

*BELOW: Conference in the pits – wives included. The car was painted matt to avoid reflections. The pit to the right was Aston Martin, who ran three cars.*

*The roadster ran remarkably well, reaching 110mph (177km/h) on some parts of the course and peaking at over 5,000rpm. Autocar*

cap. At the rear, the petrol filler orifices were poked similarly though the boot lid; all the fillers had quick-release caps. The bonnet straps had been tensioned with accelerator return springs, which proved handy when the proper throttle spring broke at 115mph (185km/h).

During the day on both 24 and 25 June 1950, the weather was warm and sunny. Taking four-hour turns at the wheel, car 22 averaged 74.22mph (119.44km/h), including stops for refuelling and driver changes. There were several points on the course where it reached more than 100mph (161km/h), sometimes 110mph (177km/h) – which was more than 5,000rpm; despite these speeds the car averaged 15.3mpg (21ltr/100km)over the whole race.

There were only twenty-nine minutes during the course of the 24 hours when the car was not in motion. By the end it had covered 1,788.455 miles (2,878.161km) without a problem other than the broken spring, a leaking rocker breather and a sudden thirst for oil. Beetson and Lawrie could not have done it without a pit crew, mechanic and chart expert.

There had been sixty starters and there were twenty-nine finishers; Beetson and Lawrie were 17th – a creditable mid-range achievement; they were fourth in the 2000cc to 3000cc class and eighth in the Rudge-Whitworth Cup.

Winners were the Rosiers in a Talbot-Lago T26GS, whose average speed was 89.71mph (144.37km/h). The Riley finished behind a Jowett Jupiter and a clutch of other British cars including a Healey, an Allard and two Jaguar XK 120s. By the following year the pattern of Jaguar domination with the C- and D-type had begun. An enthusiastic amateur in a Riley, even with some factory support, was not in the running and Lawrie himself had switched back to Aston Martin for the 1951 race.

Beetson's car, chassis number 60 SS 5379, was sold on and was last heard of in Devon in 1980, the same year that he died.

## The Monte

The RMs, it has to be said, were not natural rally cars, the 1½-litre being somewhat underpowered for such events and the 2½-litre nose heavy on the Alpine passes, but then Daimler and Armstrong-Siddeley's rather cumbersome models might have been considered even more handicapped.

Nevertheless, there was never any shortage of Riley drivers applying to take part in the Monte Carlo Rally after it was resumed postwar in 1949. It had begun in 1911 as the *Société des Bains de Mer* sought a way of bringing visitors to Monaco in the winter.

In the 1950 Rally, the first in which RMs took part, the starting points were Glasgow, Lisbon, Monte Carlo and Oslo and there was a total of seventy-three British starters of which forty finished. The RAC chartered a steamer, the *Dinard*, on which the Glasgow starters were hoisted for the voyage from Folkestone to Boulogne.

At Lisbon, Brinkman had the misfortune to see his car dropped by a crane from a great height onto the quayside, but seems to have been able to continue.

In the early 1950s, almost all the Riley entrants started from Glasgow then drove to Llandrindod Wells, where they filled up with petrol at the Automobile Palace and then drove down to Dover. The author remembers being allowed to stay up late for the thrilling sight of the cars thundering through the packed streets of his home town with lights ablaze at well above the speed limit. Crowds were often out at five in the morning watching the cars pass. Later Glasgow starters went via Stranraer and then to London and Dover.

Works teams began taking an interest because of the huge publicity the rally received, but not Riley, who at first relied on tweaking the cars that amateurs drove to work every day.

In 1952, for instance, factory teams were fielded by Ford, Jowett and Sunbeam-Talbot, for whom Stirling Moss drove the following year into sixth place. Daimler fielded a team for 1954, Armstrong-Siddeley and Aston Martin followed the next year and finally BMC woke up to the publicity potential.

In the 1956 rally they entered three Pathfinders, two three-car teams of Austin Westminsters, an Austin A50 and two MG Magnettes.

Merrick's Pathfinder had the passenger seat removed and a full-length bed put in its place.

## The Alpine

Riley took part with three RMAs in the 1947, 1948, 1949 and 1950 Alpine Rallies, without overwhelming success. The 1½-litre was rather heavy and underpowered for such excursions and did not cope well with ascents and descents, though in 1950 Slack's RMA achieved 77.3mph (124.4km/h) on the flying kilometre.

The 2½-litre was more successful; in 1949 in the 1949 Alpine Rally, Antonio de Heredia from Lisbon in his 2½-litre Riley, car 107, was fastest in the under 3000cc class in a 5km timed run on the autostrada in 127.2sec. He came 16th in the general classification. In 1948 he had won the Rallye-Soleil in Cannes.

ABOVE: *The 1951 works Alpine rally cars with the good and the great of Abingdon. Tom Sangster, sales director foreground, Alec Hounslow development engineer and at the back, Syd Enever, the legendary MG chief engineer/designer (and Pathfinder driver).*

*One of the works Alpine rally cars rounding the Ginger Hall bend at Sulby on the Isle of Man at the end of a day of TT racing in 1949. The car was driven by Bryan Mylchreest, whose family had the Riley dealership on the island. The duty has been performed since by his son David; the dealership is now Jaguar.*

155

## RM Monte Carlo Rally entries 1950–56

Far more people applied to take part in the Monte than were ever accepted. In the 1950s the RAC, who screened the British entrants, were getting more than 400 applications for some 80 to 100 places allocated to British cars by the Automobile Club of Monaco.

Lyndon Sims turned out almost every year, as did the Sutherland brothers, who won *Autosport*'s Monte Rally Trophy in 1956. Some competitors, like Arthur Bassett of Swansea, were Riley distributors. Placings and car numbers are given where known.

| Names | Car | | Placed |
|---|---|---|---|
| *20th rally January 1950* | | | |
| G.F. Hayward/J.R. Kempe-Roberts | 1½ | GBL 490 | 40th |
| E.H. Channon/P. Channon | | | |
| E.N. Brinkman/J. Ellis | | | |
| | | | |
| *21st rally January 1951* | | | |
| G.F. Hayward/J.R. Kempe-Roberts | 1½ | GBL 490 | |
| S.H. Kevill-Davies and I.H.S. Pelling | 1½ | | |
| John/Ian McLaughlin | 1½ | | |
| Frank Cooper and G.L. Carte | 2½ | KLM 1 | |
| Arthur Bassett and G.J. Fender | 2½ | GWN 646 | |
| Tom W. Dargue and J.E. Haesendonck | 2½ | TML 255 | |
| Press car | 2½ | FMO 165 | |
| | | | |
| *22nd rally January 1952* | | | |
| Mrs O.I. Johnson | 1½ | | |
| Tom W. Dargue/R.F. Frazer | 2½ | TML 255 | |
| Arthur Warren/G.L. Clarke | 2½ | | |
| Bob Porter/G. Patrick | 2½ | OPC 100 | |
| G.J. Fender/E.St.H. Tweney | 2½ | | |
| E.N. Brinkman/M. Johnson | 2½ | | 133rd |
| Press car | 2½ | MLN 410 | |

Driving for three days and nights in the Monte took its toll on Ian Sutherland's trousers. He and his brother William were regular competitors in NS 2525, firstly a 2½-litre and subsequently a Pathfinder. With them is Rex Neate, their technical advisor and Riley dealer in Southampton. Erdé

Herbert Feldman and Joe Strang's 2½-litre at the concours de confort in the Casino gardens at Monte Carlo at the end of the 1952 Monte. It is not recorded whether the leopard-skin upholstery took the judges' eye.

| Names | Car | | Placed |
|---|---|---|---|
| *23rd rally January 1953* | | | |
| A.C. Potier Godinto/W. Baxter | 1½ | | |
| Tom W. Dargue/R.F. Frazer | 2½ | SPD 590 | |
| J.T. Spare/L. Griffiths | 2½ | | |
| R.P. Lane/D. Plant | 2½ | LOH 700 | |
| Arthur Warren/G.L. Clarke | 2½ | SPF 777 | |
| G. Howard–Sorrell/L. Johnson | 2½ | | |
| Lyndon Sims/E.J. Rudd | 2½ | AEU 921 | |
| L.J. Mars/J. Bolton | 2½ | | |
| William/Ian Sutherland | 2½ | NS 2525 | |
| G.J. Fender/E.St.H. Tweney | 2½ | | |
| | | | |
| *24th rally January 1954* | | | |
| John Bremner/Anthony Oldworth | 2½ | | 39th |
| Gordon F. Hayward/Douglas Scott | 1½ | | |
| William/Ian Sutherland | 2½ | NS 2525 | |
| Leslie Griffiths/Robert C. Wingfield | 2½ | | |
| Albert V. Milton/Kenneth H. Elridge | 1½ | | |
| John Campbell/Robert Barrach | 2½ | DRS 1 | |
| Herbert Feldman/Joe Strang | 2½ | LYX 102 | |
| Arthur Warren/Frank Cooper | 2½ | SPF 777 | 38th |
| Lyndon Sims/A.P.O. (Buddy) Rogers | 2½ | AEU 921 | 22nd |
| Tom W. Dargue/Reginald F. Frazer | 2½ | SPD 590 | |
| Alan Stross/Derek Howard | 2½ | | |
| John W. Bowdage/Jack E. Wright | 2½ | NXH 900 | |
| Neil Buchanan/Edward Harte | 1½ | | |
| | | | |
| *25th rally 1955* | | | |
| John/Ian McLaughlin | RME | OOX 870 | |
| Lyndon Sims | 2½ | AEU 921 | 41st |
| Leslie Griffiths/Barry Leavens | | | |
| Miss M. Ireland/J. Mulkearn | | | |
| Ken Fraser/C. Jeffrey | Pathfinder | NGB 2 | |
| William/Ian Sutherland | | NS 2525 | |
| | | (number transferred) | |
| | | | |
| *26th rally 1956* | | | |
| Lyndon Sims/Ralph Stokes | Pathfinder | KRX 820 | 65th |
| William/Ian Sutherland | Pathfinder | NS 2525 | 42nd |
| John Bremner/Anthony Oldworth | Pathfinder | KJB 13 | 69th |
| Arthur Warren/Peter Wilson | Pathfinder | KJB 280 (poss) | 107th |
| R. Merrick/A. Grant | Pathfinder | ROC 554 | |

The last Monte in which RMs competed while they were being produced was 1956. 'Wintry weather expected', announced *Autosport*, to nobody's great surprise. The 1957 rally was cancelled because of the Suez crisis. The days of the enthusiastic amateur entrants did not end until 2001; entries are now restricted to sixty cars.

*continued overleaf*

**RM Monte Carlo Rally entries 1950–56** *continued*

*Monte winners*

Year    Names

1950 – M. Becquart/H. Secret (Hotchkiss)              Starters 282     Finishers 136
1951 – Jean Trevoux/R. Crovetto (Delahaye)           Starters 337     Finishers 283
1952 – Sydney Allard/George Warburton (Allard P1)    Starters 328     Finishers 167
1953 – Maurice Gatsonides/P. Worledge (Ford Zephyr)  Starters 404     Finishers 346
1954 – Louis Chiron/Ciro Basadonna (Lancia Aurelia GT)  Starters 363  Finishers 329
1955 – P. Malling/G. Fadum (Sunbeam Talbot Mk III)   Starters 319     Finishers 273
1956 – Ronnie Adams/Frank Biggar (Jaguar Mk VIIM)    Starters 308     Finishers 233

*Gary Wills had the floor of this Pathfinder strengthened before entering the 1995 Monte with Mike Whitton and Pete Manson. They came 63rd. Wills had competed the previous year in a different Pathfinder, TNG 417. The '95 rally car, once used as garage hack by Davenports of Sandy, Beds, is being restored in Wales.*

## Sporting RMs and their drivers

There were a handful of powerfully fast RM drivers who appeared in events at home and abroad in the 1950s, ranging from international meetings to club events. They cannot all be chronicled so here are some of the highlights of the cars and their drivers, in alphabetical order rather than in terms of skill.

**Frank Cooper** was a scion of the Oxford marmalade dynasty, though he lived at Liphook in Hampshire. He was a keen attendee at rallies around the country and in 1949 he bought in London a red RMB, registered KLM 1, to enter in the 1950 Monte.

The *Riley Record* noted that among the special bits and pieces needed for the rally were: 'a map board, electric kettle, picnic case, snow chains and pick and shovel'. Cooper completed the rally and the car took a coachwork prize.

The car was sold back to Jimmy James in London shortly afterwards and the registration number retained for a second RMB – bought in November 1950, this time in Apple Green

ABOVE: *Harold Grace passing the pits at Silverstone, with Bristol in pursuit.*
BELOW: *Silverstone again, this time in the 1955* Daily Express *meeting. Note the air intake under the front bumper to ram cold air into the carburettors.*

159

*'Regardless', one of the best-known RM rally cars, has recently been restored to its full rally spec. Here it is in 1955 on the Cat's Eye rally.*

with a Green roof. It was modified mechanically at Abingdon in much the same way as the first car and entered for the 1951 Monte. Because of its unusual number, KLM Royal Dutch Airlines was talked into providing some refreshments *en route*.

It was lavishly equipped compared with KLM 1 the first. There was a freshwater tank in the boot that fed a stainless steel washbasin in the rear seat, fitted suitcases, picnic tables and a hinged headlining that folded down to provide a sleeping area in the rear seat. Another notable feature was the 'compressed air apparatus for tyre inflation'. Body modifications included built-in foglamps and Bentley Mk VI-type headlamps.

The Dutch connection proved to be less than a blessing for KLM 1 the second, as the car broke down in Holland, either from water-pump failure or propshaft problems (there's some dispute as to the reason).

Again the car was not long in Cooper's hands. He sold it later that year to the bandleader Billy Ternent and the registration number was eventually sold to a KLM pilot who put it on a Ford.

KLM 1 the second, now VSN 839, languishes in Manchester waiting to be restored. The modifications are mostly still there; the Green roof has been replaced with Tarmac!

**Tom Dargue** not only drove his RMB to and from work in Stratford Broadway, East London, but also hurled it around Alpine passes. TML 255, known as 'Regardless', was – and is – a 1949 2½-litre that Dargue sent back to Abingdon for competition modifications late in 1950.

These included a Healey gearbox, and 3.5:1 rear axle. There were cylinder head and cam changes and neat tricks such as a quickly removable boot lid that enabled jack and wheels to be lifted in and out without delay. Lighting was enhanced with Lucas Flame-throwers and a hand-operated spot on the off-side windscreen pillar. The car ran on Swedish Wittmer tyres that were fine for snow, but overheated and ran hot on the road.

Still with the car that has now been restored, are the original roof rack, radiator muff, special lights and a full set of eight drilled wheels – the holes in the front wheels for brake ventilation are larger than those in the rear.

*ABOVE: Highlight of the Riley Motor Club's year was the winter rally. That inveterate competitor Tom Dargue is on the line here in the 13th rally on 21 February 1953. It began in Ashstead in Surrey and finished at the RAC Club at Epsom.*

*RIGHT: Tom Dargue transferred the gearbox from 'Regardless' into his new 2½-litre. In the 1954 Monte it ran on unusual tyres – Avons with Renold chains in the grooves that can just be seen here.* Chris Hudson

Alas, Dargue, for all his enthusiasm, was not particularly lucky in 'Regardless' in the Monte; in 1951 a broken shock absorber put it out of contention in the first event in Paris. The following year, he and co-driver John Kelshaw – to whom he sold the car and who nicknamed it 'Regardless' – ended up in a ditch near Le Puy for several hours. They had a de-ditching appliance – lengths of double-thickness tarpaulin through which spikes could be driven into the road – but although it worked on other occasions, this time it did not.

Crossway Models in Lincolnshire sell a 1/43 scale version of TML 255 for £85.

Dargue moved on to an RMF, SPD 590, prepared by Boon and Porter in Barnes. The Healey gearbox was transferred from TML 255 and there were many other modifications – notably Marchal head- and fog-lamps and a large central Marchal in front of the radiator. The Wittmer tyres were discarded in favour of Town and Country for the 1953 Monte, and Dargue qualified in the last 100 for the mountain exercise, but alas suffered fuel-pump trouble.

In 1954 Dargue appeared in the Monte again – his fourth event – this time with unusual tyres, Avons with Renold chains in the grooves to cope with snow and ice.

Dargue campaigned the car in the Daily Express, RAC and many other rallies until he part-exchanged it for an MG Magnette in 1958.

**Harold Grace** owned a garage business at Tring in Hertfordshire, which is still run by his son Gilbert, who was his youthful race mechanic and prepared his cars with devices such as a hose under the front bumper to ram cold air into the carburettors. The elder Grace collected some four hundred trophies in his racing career that began when he took his grass track racer to meetings in a pre-war Riley with the passenger seat taken out.

His 2½-litre NRO 341 was a familiar sight at meetings and he fought many epic battles in Pathfinders like KRX 820 at Oulton Park, Brands and Aintree. In 1953 at Silverstone, he won the team award, first in his class and second overall to Stirling Moss. In 1955 in the same race he was second in his class, just ahead of Lyndon Sims, and fifth overall. Gilbert

ABOVE: *Oulton Park, October 1957: Harold Grace with a well-known Pathfinder with a single-seater nearly on his rear bumper.*

LEFT: *Harold Grace with the* Daily Express *team award won at Silverstone on 9 May 1953. He was first in his class and second overall to Moss. He prepared the car in the workshop of the family business G. Grace and Son, which is now run by his son Gilbert, then his youthful race mechanic.*

Grace, a former chairman of the Riley Motor Club, recalled that his father used to get an indicated 125mph. He used special valve springs that enabled the normal maximum rpm to be increased from 4,800 to 6,000rpm, which gave inordinately high piston speeds.

Like many racers they would have boxes of SU carburettor needles to suit different circuits. For instance, they would use a lean setting for fast circuits and a richer one for shorter circuits like Brands Hatch. Boiling brake fluid in the Pathfinder was a known competition problem suffered by Grace. Coming down the Hangar Straight at Silverstone and into Stowe corner required fierce braking.

**Bob Porter** was managing director of Boon and Porter of Castelnau, Barnes, who had the Riley distribution for South London and Surrey all sewn up. He was a keen competition driver taking part in the Monte Carlo rally and in 1952 organizing the Riley team. He is perhaps best known for his attempts to put 100 miles into an hour at the circuit at Montlhéry, 15 miles (24km) south of Paris.

*SPD 590 was bought through Boon and Porter by Tom Dargue for day-to-day use, but more particularly for rallying. Here he is on the 1953 Monte. Note the roof-rack of light alloy with a baffle in front to reduce wind howl and the driving lamps – a centre-mounted Marchal and twin Lucas Flamethrowers. Chris Hudson*

Bob Porter (left) transferred his flying Pegasus mascot from the 2½-litre to the Pathfinder for the Montlhéry run. He usually ran without wheel discs to which he had taken a dislike. With him on the circuit were Ray Jeffs and his wife Molly and sister-in-law Sue, who wore hats even on record attempts.

MONTLHERY
21st October 1955
Standard Riley "Pathfinder" (2½ litre) covered 108.03 miles in the hour, officially controlled.
Driver:- R. C. Porter
Passengers:-
Mrs S. Porter, Mrs M. Porter and Mr R. Jeffs

His first attempt to do so was in 1949 with an RMB, MPL 100, declared to be standard other than that there were no hubcaps or bumpers, but probably tuned by his own mechanic Bing Telfer. It failed, averaging 94.18mph (151.54km/h), though reaching a maximum on the straight of 104mph (167km/h).

But several years later, in October 1955, Pathfinder KRX 820, driven by Porter, covered 108.03 miles (173.82km) at Montlhéry. The timing, as officially recorded by the *Union Technique* as an average speed for 100 miles, was not particularly remarkable in itself, but Porter had three passengers aboard, his wife Mollie, sister-in-law Sue and London insurance broker, Ray Jeffs.

The event was a BMC publicity exercise to show off their 100mph-plus cars and there were five other cars involved, piloted by Abingdon works drivers: Ron Flockhart (Austin Healey 100, 104.3mph/167.8km/h); Ken Wharton (MGA, 102.52mph/164.95km/h) and John Gott, who drove the other three (MGA Series II tune 112.23mph/178.97km/h; Wolseley 6/90 101.19mph/162.81km/h and Austin A90 101.98mph/164.09km/h).

There is a video of the event that appears to show Marcus Chambers, BMC's competition manager, trying to slow Porter down, and it has been implied that Chambers did not want to report to his boss, the fearsome Len Lord, that his beloved Austin was the slowest in the speed tests. However, the official explanation in the desperately dull BMC magazine *Motoring*, which had replaced the *Riley Record*, was that Chambers was trying to flag him down because of the severe weather conditions – there were gale-force winds and heavy rain.

Said Mollie insouciantly afterwards: 'It was just like a family outing. We were dressed quite normally and throughout the hour talked quite naturally.' Porter, with a degree of self-interest, declared the Pathfinder to be the best Riley ever made. But a customer who bought a Pathfinder from his Barnes showroom and expected the same performance would have been disappointed. Porter's car was breathed upon by Bing Telfer, whose reputation was such that even Jimmy James the North London distributor sent cars to Boon and Porter to be tuned by Telfer.

Compare Porter's 108mph, fully loaded, with the maximum speed figures from Pathfinder road tests:

*Autosport* – 101mph
*Autocar* – 102mph.

## Rally modifications

The extent to which cars could be modified for sporting events is detailed in the history of GRX 881, a 1952 RMB, originally owned by Gordon Hayward, joint managing director of Haywards, the Riley distributors of Ashford in Kent.

It was prepared at Abingdon for competition work, with cylinder-head work including especially hardened tappets with extra return springs. The camshafts were those used in the Healey version of the Big Four and the heavy-duty clutch was probably the same as that in the Jaguar XK120.

The wheels had unusual pierced discs to aid brake cooling, which Haywards made themselves – and subsequently made for other Riley owners once they had been seen – also adding the hooks on the chassis extensions to act as tow-out or tie-down aids.

Hayward drove in three Monte Carlo Rallies, but not in GRX 881, although it had been his intention to do so and the car was modified for an event in which it never took place.

There were additional rear lights to conform to rally requirements; other factory modifications included release petrol caps, a rev counter, additional wiring for inspection lights in the boot, under the bonnet and under the dash.

Additional spot lamps were fitted at the front and a sign-reading spot lamp was fitted internally to the passenger's side windscreen. The headlight dip-switch was transferred to the floor, as in earlier RMs, and a vacuum-operated screen-washer fitted with the button taking the place of the dash-mounted dip-switch. Demister/defrosters were fitted inside the windscreen.

Hayward raced it at Silverstone and Goodwood and campaigned it in the *Daily Express* Rally and in 1953 in the RAC Rally – despite the modifications it came 84th.

GRX 881 now has drilled wheels for brake cooling as well, done by the present owner Gwyn Morris, to bring it into line with other competition cars such as SPD 590, JOR 775 and TML 255 'Regardless'. Drilled wheels were a factory option from 1949.

*The special wheel discs aided cooling.*

In 1953, Bob Porter and his Riley team, Gilbert Grace, Buddy Rogers (qv) and Gerald Gelberg, won the team prize in the Production Touring Car Race at Silverstone. The average speed was 69.71mph (112.16km/h); Bristols were in second place at 67.91mph (109.27km/h).

**A.P.O. 'Buddy' Rogers** was a very fast driver in his 1947 RMB, SMX 417. He took part in many rallies and race meetings. He made his money bringing Sun-Pat salted peanuts to Britain, and in 1956 crashed his racer, the Sun-Pat Special, at Goodwood, decapitating himself in front of the crowd.

**Lyndon Sims**, the flying Welshman, was probably the fastest RM driver, who rallied, raced and trialled his 1951 maroon RMB. It was registered AEU 921 in Breconshire – so few cars were registered in mid-Wales that Brecon started using a third registration letter only in 1949, and neighbouring Radnorshire in 1958. It had Healey manifolds and back axle, according to a mechanic at Castle Motors, Cardiff, who fettled the car.

Sims intended to enter the 1952 Monte, but was rejected for lack of experience. After cramming in several other rallies he qualified for the 1953 event.

AEU's first year of triumph was 1954, when at the end of the Monte, in which he came twenty-second in general classification, he took on Stirling Moss in a works Sunbeam-Talbot at the speed event around the grand prix circuit in Monaco. On a wet Saturday morning, cars were despatched in groups of six and Sims duelled with Moss, finishing alongside him, but with a best lap one second quicker at 2min 28.5sec.

He recalled in the *Riley Record* that Moss would not give an inch but 'on the penultimate lap I hung back a bit and allowed him to take a lead…then I went like a dingbat, caught him up again and we crossed the line more or less together…and was I pleased. Stirling didn't think it funny at all!'

Sims took part in three consecutive Montes in AEU 921, from 1953 to 1955, the last with drilled wheels, but since the car was now more than three years old it was ineligible for the 1956 rally. Marcus Chambers at BMC offered him a works Pathfinder, KRX 820. It carried a crew of three, Sims plus Ralph Stokes and Tom Bowns.

On the mountain circuit, with time and petrol running out, Bowns climbed into the boot and while hanging on at high speed running down a col, transferred most of the contents of a two-gallon can into the tank so that the control could be made in time. But alas, though they finished, the penalties for the damage to the car took them out of the reckoning.

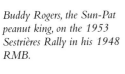

*Buddy Rogers, the Sun-Pat peanut king, on the 1953 Sestrières Rally in his 1948 RMB.*

## Being prepared

Travelling abroad after the war was a hazardous pursuit, even for a car as reliable as a Riley. For those daring enough to take the car abroad for a 'continental rally', a considerable undertaking in those post-war days that involved the Riley being hoisted by crane aboard a channel ferry, there was a suggested list of spare parts for the 1½-litre in 1948.

This ran to no fewer than eighty items and included a crown wheel and pinion set, spare rear spring, piston, rings and con-rod. The total cost was £146 5s 5d – about £3,650 today. There was no suggestion as to where this lot was to be put – perhaps a following truck.

Complete set of engine gaskets
Tappet push rods
Rocker R.H. complete
Rocker L.H. complete
Rocker ball pins
Rocker ball pin adj. nuts
Valve guides
Valves
Split cotters
Valve springs
Cylinder head studs
Piston complete
Piston rings – compression
Oil control rings
Circlips
Connecting rods complete
Tappets
Oil filters complete
Fan belts
Water-pump hose
Bypass joint ring
Water pump sealing plate
Carbon ring
Water pump gland rubber
Water pump gland spring
Oil seals
Oil relief valves
Oil relief valve adj. spring
Petrol pipes
Cylinder head tubes
Hotspot tubes
Hotspot return tubes
Hotspot conduit tubes
Top water hose
Hose clips
Clutch driver plates lined
Carbon thrust complete
Crown wheel and pinion
Rear wheel studs
Rear hub oil seals

Hardy Spicer journal complete
Road wheel nuts
Torsion bar
Front hub oil seals
Front hub felt washer
Steering ball springs
Rear road spring
Main leaves
Rear shackles complete
Brake fork joint pin
Brake fork joint
Engine steady cable
Control ball joints
Master cylinder for front brake
High pressure feed pipes – long
High pressure feed pipes – short
4 brake shoes complete – rear
Oil feed rubber tube
Brake shoes complete, front
Headlamp bulb single filament
Headlamp bulb double filament
Sidelamp bulb
Pass lamp bulb
Waterpump assy, complete
Front damper assy, complete
Front damper bushes
A.C. fuel pump
Lower tubular strut
Inner tube 5.75 × 16
Distributor complete with gear
H.T. Coil
Sparking plugs
Torsion bar rear end brackets

| | |
|---|---|
| Total spares cost: | £146 5s 5d (about £3,650) |
| Price of new Riley 1½-litre in 1948: | £863 (£21,575) |

*Large crowds turned out in town centres to watch rallies in the 1950s. This Swansea-registered roadster is on the starting line of the Welsh Rally.*
National Motor Museum

In eight Montes up until 1961, Sims reckoned that this was the only one in which he damaged a car, hitting a rock and partly demolishing the nearside wing. However, one of the Abingdon development team, Jimmy Cox, is quoted in David Knowles's book *MG – the Untold Story* as saying of one of Sims's Monte adventures: 'He ran out of brakes, they were running metal-to-metal – and I remembered that he finished up grinding the side of the car along the wall at the side of the road as he went down the mountain to try to stop it.'

In May 1954, in the *Daily Express* International trophy meeting at Silverstone, he drove an extraordinary race, considering he was up against 200bhp works Jaguar Mark VIIs driven by Moss and Rolt, with private entrants Adams and Appleyard in similar breathed-upon VIIs.

It was a Le Mans start and Sims had wired starter and ignition together and put the engine at fast idle. At the end of the first lap he was in the lead from Appleyard, but spun off in the second lap at Stowe corner, losing twelve places. Nevertheless, he fought his way back through the field passing the 2½-litres of Harold Grace (NRO 341) and Buddy Rogers (SMX 417) to finish seventh, averaging just over 73mph (117km/h) for the 50 mile (80km) race. Grace was eighth and Rogers tenth.

In 1955, Sims competed again at Silverstone in the Daily Express International trophy meeting in 1955 in a team of Pathfinders entered by Bob Porter. Jaguars dominated and he came seventh after Tony Crook in a Bristol 405 and his team mate Harold Grace who was fifth. A green and cream 2½-litre also ran, driven by Gerald Gelberg, who retired on lap 14. This car still exists.

**Arthur Warren** was a mercilessly fast competition driver, who hammered his cars. It was said that it was best to get out of his way as he approached – good advice for both drivers and ladies. The answer to the question 'would you have bought a used Riley from this man?' would have been 'No'.

## The rest

There were dozens of enthusiastic Riley amateurs who took part in the large number of rallies that took place during the 1950s such as the Cat's Eye, the Little London, the Welsh and the Daily Express. Large crowds would turn out to watch them, particularly at the regular seaside rallies at places like Eastbourne, Blackpool and Morecambe.

The Riley Motor Club's winter rally was the competitive highlight of the club year. *Motor Sport*, observing the antics at the 1952 rally remarked acidly: 'They say competition improves the breed and the Nuffield Organization can be quite certain that the reverse gear jumps out on the present-day Riley.'

The czars of the London Riley dealerships, Jimmy James and Bob Porter, awarded cups for the best open and closed cars in that year. The open prize was won by H.S.M. Wilkinson in a 1950 2½-litre and the closed by C. Audrey in a 1948 RMA.

167

# 12    Buying, maintaining, restoring

1951 RMC Roadster ... Bills for more than
£30,000 ... MoT ... £18,750

Advertisement *RMemoranda* autumn 2004

All RMs, apart from the last Pathfinders, are now more than half a century old and though they were solid enough when they were built, they were never designed to last fifty years. Like other classics, hundreds of RMs disappeared when the compulsory ten-year Ministry of Transport test began in 1960, because drivers could not afford the repairs needed to keep their cars on the road. When this test was reduced from every ten years to every three in 1967 there was another large cull.

The mechanics of an RM are simple and not over-expensive to restore. The body is another matter, as a steel-bodied ash-framed car can have the disadvantages of not only rusting, but having serious concealed problems with wood rot; restoring a complete wreck could cost more than £25,000. Some people want to spend this sort of money, others prefer to restore at home for minimal cost.

One Riley expert in the south of England quoted these figures in the autumn of 2004:

Total engine rebuild RMA to RMF   £3,500
Total bare metal respray, new roof,
correcting minor decay       £6,000 – £7,000
Nut and bolt rebuild of wreck        £30,000

Obviously these figures can vary widely, given the wage rates in different parts of the country and the size of the restoration firm, but it's possible to spend a great deal of money restoring a car that is unlikely to recoup the investment,
let alone the original cost of the car, though it has to be said that most Rileys continue to be rebuilt at home at a much lower cost.

The advice for those considering buying an RM is to buy the best that can be afforded. An RMA might sound a snip at £2,500, but getting it right could cost thousands more. If there's a choice, the advice is to go for the most interesting one, possibly an early car, with some history.

But the most important advice is to join one of the Riley clubs, talk to people who know them and if you are going to buy, take someone with you who knows Rileys well, preferably someone who has rebuilt one. If the work is going to a restorer, get several estimates and ask about for examples of previous work.

Lustrous paint can hide major flaws as two-pack is very good at covering filler. Anyone considering buying an RM should be wise to the pitfalls and ask for receipts for work that has been done, though home restorations will not have these.

There are also a few simple tests outlined below that can detect some problems.

## The body – RMA-RMF

• The wooden A-post that runs from the windscreen down either side of the car at the front is a notorious rot spot as it projects about 4in from the front body mounting under the front wings. Also check that the vent panels open and close properly and that the nails securing the Furflex draught excluder do not pull out readily and show signs of rust. Check that the door lock striker plates are firmly attached to the body. If a plate comes off the occupant will find out why they are called suicide doors!

A-post repair sections are available, but the cost of repairing severe damage can be expensive as in some cases the roof and the windscreen have to come off. Check for scuttle shake when the car is driven.

The steel peak rail above the windscreen, which is covered by the roof material, does not usually rot too badly, but the wood behind often does. This has to be in good condition because it has to retain the nails used to secure the outer roof covering and the interior headlining. Beware again of rusty nails that pull out easily.

Early cars had part of their floors underneath the seats made from wood, up until 1948/49.

• Check that the doors open and shut properly and rock them on their hinges, looking for play in the hinge pins, though over-sized hinge pins can cure this problem. They are hinged on the B-post, which is steel not wood and very strong, but alas, the post is

*The notorious A-post where it protrudes beneath the front wing (above right). If rot in this cannot be repaired, the roof, among other things, has to come off to put in a new post, since it runs right up the side of the car (right).*

*A new A-post is spliced in.*

*The profile of the doors was changed in the RME and the bottoms are prone to rot.*

anchored at the bottom to wooden sill members that run the length of the car. These can rot badly, but cannot really be seen without removing the steel sill above them. Do the chrome strips on the doors line up with those on the body sides?

Tired sills are easy to see as they twist under the weight of the doors and the B-post drops, which manifests itself in gaps between the doors and the body. Look particularly at the front door where the A-post meets the roof. This is often mistakenly attributed to tired body mount packing.

Roadsters can have shown signs of damage on the rear wings due to doors flying open, which can happen to all timber-framed RMs if the front door striker plates fail due to rotten A-posts, so extra catches and even bolts have been used to reinforce the original Silent-travel catches. But the main enemy again is the rotting of the wooden frame due to water ingress, particularly under the boot floor, and the rear wheel arches.

Dropheads tend to suffer from stress-cracking at the top of the doors.

• Check for rust in the rear doors of the saloon at the bottom corners and in the door openings. The doors of the restyled or spatted

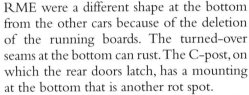

*The sill and bottom of the rear wheel arch inside the car – before and after restoration.*

RME were a different shape at the bottom from the other cars because of the deletion of the running boards. The turned-over seams at the bottom can rust. The C-post, on which the rear doors latch, has a mounting at the bottom that is another rot spot.

• Check for rust where the wings join the body as the hidden edges can rust badly, particularly at the rear where the wing beading can allow in water to rot the wing fixing. There was no sealant on early cars. Repair means cutting off and replacing a 3in strip.

• Front wings rust around the wired edge, but also underneath where they join the front mounting bracket. On more expensive cars like the Alvis, the wings were bolted to the bracket; on the Riley they are spot-welded, which is where the trouble begins. This can be cured by removing the bridging member and fitting the wing directly to the supporting arm with a spacer bolted through the sidelight – except on the RME which has a faired-in sidelight. Rust creeps in here on these cars.

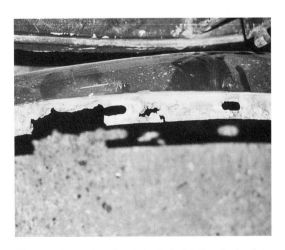

*The rear wing section where it is attached to the wheel arch is a rot spot.*

171

**Which one for you?**

The **1½-litre** is a well-mannered town car, light to drive and easy to corner, that can cruise at 55–60mph (89–97km/h) on the motorway and return an overall 30mpg (9.4ltr/100km). It runs best on cross-ply tyres, but these can bring the penalty of 'tramlining' – the steering seems to take on a life of its own on white lines.

The **2½-litre** is a different proposition, a stress-free long-distance cruiser, that does not like traffic jams and is heavier on the brakes and even more so on the steering. The weight of the Big Four at the front when running downhill can lead to severe understeer if there is a bend at the bottom. Parking requires some strength, particularly with radial tyres. The clutch is heavy and the engine has heavy pistons and can feel lumpy. On the credit side, 2½-litres can cruise between 65 and 70mph (105–113km/h), though overall petrol consumption is unlikely to be more than 20mpg (14.2ltr/100km). One great advantage is that unleaded petrol can be used as a combination of a low compression ratio of 6.7:1 (6.8:1 in later cars) and a long-stroke slow-revving engine make valve seat recession unlikely.

The **Pathfinder**, with the same Big Four engine and front suspension, is a luxurious, fine-handling fast car – once the brake and rear axle locating rod problems have been sorted out, as most of them have by now. The earlier rear coil-sprung versions are favoured by the purists, though the replacement semi-elliptics in the last cars may give more peace of mind. Unseen rust is today's enemy.

The choice between these two 2½-litre Big Four-engined cars is between the wood-framed classic and the all-steel neo-modern. But the earlier RMs will always be worth much more than the Pathfinder and the roadster is always the most expensive.

In styling, the basic RMA to RMF saloons offer small differences – many buyers make up their minds on a preference for the classic round instruments on the dashboard rather than the later square type, which are more reminiscent of the Morris range, and that came in during the autumn of 1949.

In body style, the most significant change affecting both saloons was the larger rear window from October 1952. The other major change, in the 1½-litre saloon only, came in the RME from October 1953 when the running boards were deleted, there were new helmet wings at the front and spats on the rear wings. This curious readoption of the 1930s spat craze came as part of the new vogue for streamlining and is not to everyone's taste, though Riley were not alone in rediscovering it as their neighbours Alvis had adopted it on the 3-litre in 1950 as did Jaguar and Bentley at different times.

The RMB from the 1949 season had increased power and better brakes with twin-leading shoes at the front, though the system was still of the hydro-mechanical type. Fully hydraulic brakes were adopted in 1952 on all models.

*How to tell the difference*
The 'classic' RMs as they are sometimes known, that is, before the Pathfinder, can be difficult to tell one from another. This is a brief guide to some of the major differences. A quick way of distinguishing them, apart from the longer wheelbase of the 2½-litre, is that the 1½-litre had a dark blue radiator badge and the 2½-litre a light blue diamond. All boot badges were dark blue. Badges could be altered to special order and both green and red have been seen.

*RMA 1½-litre saloon*
Production dates: September 1945–52. Total made: 10,504
Chassis numbers: 35S 10001 to 42S 20504.
Characteristics: Running boards, dark blue radiator badge, small rear window (until September 1952), driver's windscreen opens in early models. Round instruments to chassis 39S 17029 in 1949, then square instruments; driver's window now non-opening. From chassis 41S 19635 – twin rail rear bumpers and spare-wheel door now slides upwards; small rear overriders replaced with large versions. Two small separated front bumpers become one-piece full front bumper. There were also a few RMA dropheads.

*RMB 2½-litre saloon*
Production dates: 1946–52. Total made 6,900
Chassis numbers: 56S 2001 to 62S 9910 (note: also includes RMC and RMD chassis)
Characteristics: Longer bonnet and wheelbase, light blue radiator badge, two engine drive belts. Modified engine RMB-2 engine with single belt from chassis 62S 9353. (Arnold Farrar put this at 9332.)

*RMC 2½-litre roadster*
Production dates: 1948–50. Total made: 507
Chassis numbers: from 58SS 2802
Characteristics: Roadster two-door body with bench seat and steering column gear change on early cars, over-blessed with four overriders per bumper.

*RMD 2½-litre drophead*
Production dates: 1949–50. Total made: 503
Chassis numbers: from 59D 5201
Characteristics:
Drophead body, two-door.

*RME 1½-litre saloon*
Production dates: 1952– 55. Total made: 3,446
Chassis numbers: from 42S 20505 to RMS 23950
Characteristics: Large rear window (though some early cars still had the small window), hypoid axle, all hydraulic brakes. Full front bumper from chassis No. 20778. Facelifted from chassis 21855, October 1953, with running boards deleted, new helmet wings with 'trouser crease' and rear spats.

*RMF 2½-litre saloon*
Production dates: 1952–53. Total made: 1,050
Chassis numbers: from 62S 9911 to RMF 10960
Characteristics: Large rear window and full front bumper from chassis 62S 10107. Spare-wheel door now slides upwards, hypoid axle, all-hydraulic brakes.
RMB2 cars – named after the new engine designation are sometimes called RMFs; they had the earlier body, torque tube and hydro-mechanical brakes, but the later 'one-belt' engine.

*RMH Pathfinder*
Production dates: 1953–57. Total made 5,152
Chassis numbers: from MAA/501 to MAA/5652.
Characteristics: Steel-bodied, six-seater, saloon version only.
Similar mechanics to 2½-litre RMF, except for coil-sprung live rear axle.
Overdrive available from MAA/3436. Transfer to Wolseley 6/90 leaf-sprung chassis from MAA/5554.

**The survivors**

The Riley RM Club has an excellent database, maintained by Gordon Webster, that on 1 January 2005 had records on 6,521 RMs.

| Model | Number built | On database | Roadworthy |
|---|---|---|---|
| RMA | 10,504 | 1,726 | 471 |
| RMB | 6,900 | 1,417 | 344 |
| RMC | 507 | 370 | 111 |
| RMD | 503 | 254 | 89 |
| RME | 3,446 | 1,583 | 614 |
| RMF | 1,050 | 456 | 178 |
| RMH | 5,152 | 471 | 115 |
| Unknown | 244 | | |

There are 132 non-standard bodies, mainly coachbuilt bodies on early RMA chassis, such as woodies and specials on shortened chassis.

*ABOVE and RIGHT: The top of the car with and without the steel mesh covering.*

On the 2½-litre's front wings, check for stress cracking – small cracks at right angles to the bonnet sides. The cracks tend not to appear on 1½-litres because the bonnet sides are fixed, whereas the 2½-litre's are removable by unbolting, which led to less rigidity and later cars had a strengthening plate attached to overcome the problem.

- In the boot, look for rust in the gutter channel on the top edge under the boot hinges and down the sides of the boot. In some cases the gutter would rust away completely if the seal were sponge rubber rather than the original solid seal.

The boot also rots at the rear mounting points, which can lead to it settling. Lift the carpet and check the condition of the two bolts that hold the body to the chassis at this point. Check for settling by examining the bumper support irons where they protrude through the body in grommet holes – these should be central and the body should not be resting on them. The body is mounted on the chassis at four points down each side using a rubber-impregnated cork called Kautex, that resembles Weetabix. This can become over-compressed and also cause the body to settle. To remedy the problem, each mounting needs to be repacked separately.

*Taking out the windscreen exposes another common area of rusting.*

- The roof and rear window frame are very prone to water ingress causing wet rot. The roof covering of leathercloth was subsequently changed to Everflex. Both let water in through the stitching to the hessian beneath and the wadding that lies beneath that. The saturated material rots the wooden framework of the roof and corrodes the mesh frame that supports it. There are many synthetic products available to revive and reseal dull roof coverings; the old-fashioned remedy of black shoe polish mixed with boiled linseed oil is cheaper and kinder to the environment and if worked into the seams will prevent damage.

Another result of this water ingress is the rotting of the wooden rear window – check for rot by pressing it with your thumb. If it gives significantly there's a problem. New ones can be bought complete. A roof covering job can be done at home for about £200 using readily available kits.

## The body – Pathfinder

No wood rot problems here as it's an all-steel body, but the Achilles heel is rust and not just in the usual places like sills and wings. Hidden rust is the enemy. Not for nothing do many Pathfinder owners cover the top of their cars with tarpaulins when they are left outside in the rain, as water can seep undetected behind the front bulkhead and rot the panels below. The air vent in front of the windscreen is usually to blame, though leaks through the windscreen and door seals are very common. The rear seat pan is another area to check for rot.

## The chassis

All models have a robust chassis, though the front suspension cradles in cars made after 1948 can be affected by rust. Check the wheels for play by jacking them off the ground, placing a strong lever under them and rocking the lever downwards against a fulcrum to lift the wheel. Top/bottom play means

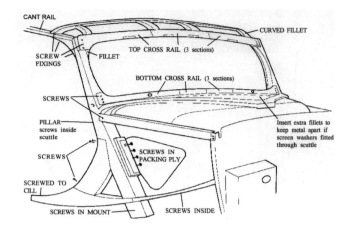

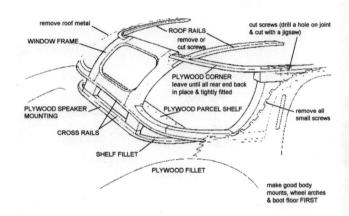

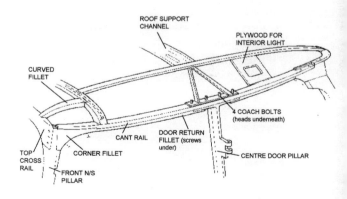

*These excellent line drawings by Alan Dixon show how the complex wooden structure of the coachbuilt cars fits together.*

worn bearings/swivel pins; fore and aft play checks bearings and track rods. At the steering wheel there should be no lost motion of any consequence.

Steering wheels are not an item with which you would normally expect trouble, or even embarrassment. However, the Abingdon cars had a wheel made of mild steel with an acetate coating and when this deteriorates through age and deliquesces it leaves an 'incontinence patch' on the driver's seat. What's worse is that the spokes become detached, which is an MoT failure point. The earlier cars do not suffer from this, having a plastic-coated alloy wheel. The later wheels can be replaced, though at some considerable cost (£280), if a second-hand one cannot be found. Some owners have had their wheels re-rimmed in wood.

Brakes: check for pulling to one side when braking. Worn seals allow oil onto the drums. The rear axle usually has a breather hole to allow pressure inside it to be relieved, but these holes, particularly on the near side, are often clogged with dirt or painted over. As the pressure builds up, oil forces its way past the axle seals and onto the rear drums.

The Bundy hydraulic tubing rusts, particularly where it runs along the chassis, and is best replaced with ³⁄₁₆in Kunifer, which means that modern brake hoses can be used.

There were several different types of Girling brake master cylinder used, though almost all look identical from the outside. The seal retainers and pistons were changed several times to avoid problems with the brakes either failing completely or locking on.

Riley parts supplier Derek Allnutt, who has done a lot of research on the RM's Girling brakes, says that silicone brake fluid should not be used as it can distort the recuperating seal. Although silicone was not around in 1948, the factory identified seal damage at that time done by brake fluid other than the recommended Girling. Today, universal DOT3 and DOT4 glycol-based fluids are recommended. DOT5 is the silicone-based fluid, whose advantage is that it does not absorb water.

## The transmission

The clutch on the RMs has caused incessant adjustment problems due to its tendency to drag if the adjustment is not correct. The rule for getting it right seems to be ¾in (20mm) free play before biting and 4in (100mm) afterwards. This is borne out by a *Sales and Service Bulletin* of January 1947 that points out that this ¾in gives the correct clearance of 1¹⁄₁₆in (20mm) between the clutch release plate and the carbon ring.

But there is a joint in the system that is usually very badly worn, making it impossible to achieve the correct setup angles unless it is either rebuilt or the shaft on which it sits is moved round a spline or two at its end fork. The common result is a clutch rod breakage as the rod bends under load as the pivot locks up.

Clutch judder on the 2½-litre due to the torque of the engine is common, though the whole of the driveline should be checked for sloppiness. Tired engine bearers, broken engine restraining ties, flywheel run out and oil on the clutch are other culprits.

Pathfinder judder was so bad that there was a service revision of the clutch and a revised timing cover that enabled the previous RMB/F front engine mountings to be used. Continuing judder problems in reverse on the Pathfinder can sometimes be traced to play in the live rear axle and prop shaft, but it can be intermittent.

The 2½-litre is prone to half-shaft breakages, due to the high torque from the engine and the fact that there are not enough splines on the shaft. In the last series of production cars, the RMF remedied this problem when the hypoid rear axle replaced the spiral bevel type in late 1952 and another four splines were added.

Many 2½-litre drivers, who often muse how pleasant it would be to have a half-shaft tree in the garden, change up from first gear as soon as possible to avoid the strain on the shafts, which shear at the planet wheel.

Some owners even go to the lengths of trying to park facing downhill rather than uphill, so that they can start in second gear to put less stress on the half-shafts. However, Riley experts like John Joiner suggest that the load that causes the damage to the shafts occurs if the brakes are slammed on, as the inertia of the large flywheel transmits a sudden shock to the rear axle. He says that surprisingly most shafts break under a light load, as fatigue cracks have built up over the years.

Modified shafts with a different taper from the original, giving more flexing capabilities to deal with the load, are available at a cost of some £285, but those with spiral bevel axles do have the advantage that the differential can be repaired easily; not so the hypoid version.

## The engine

The signs of age and neglect are usually obvious; low oil pressure when the engine is hot, blue smoke on acceleration and ominous thumpings from the crankcase. However, high oil pressure can be misleading due to sludging in the crankshaft journal oil galleries, a well-known problem with these cars that keeps pressure high but delivery to the bearings low.

The workshop manual for both the 2½-litre and 1½-litre says that under normal running conditions the oil pressure should not drop below 30lb per sq in and 12lb per sq in should be shown when idling. A *Sales and Service Bulletin* suggested these figures for the 1½-litre:

| | | |
|---|---|---|
| 10mph | 650rpm | 13.5lb per sq in |
| 40mph | 2,500rpm | 31.0lb per sq in |
| 70mph | 4,400rpm | 47.0lb per sq in |

The figures for the 2½-litre were slightly different at 40lb per sq in at 50mph; at tickover it was 12lb per sq in. But the advice tended to vary. A letter from the Riley service department to a customer enquiring about oil pressure in the 2½-litre said that at tickover, pressure could range from 10lb per sq in down to 2–3lb – which might be too low to be measured on the dashboard oil gauge, an instrument of wondrous imprecision.

It went on to suggest that at 40mph it should read 40lb per sq in, which chimes neatly with

many Riley owners' rule of thumb that everything is all right if psi=mph. However, it is best to be wary of an engine that shows a pressure of 10–15lb per sq in at hot tickover unless it has recently been rebuilt.

Rileys need frequent oil changes as the oilways in the crankshaft are very narrow and a build-up of sludge can occur to the extent where they become blocked with material that is so solid that it has to be drilled out. The cleaning-out of sludge traps was a neglected task as new Rileys passed from owner to owner, storing up trouble for the future. The procedure is not mentioned in the Driver's Handbook or the Workshop Manual.

Blocked oilways lead inevitably to big end failure. Some owners have remedied the problem by drilling extra oilways, and indeed the problem was finally acknowledged in the RMF and Pathfinder, which did have an extra oilway in each bearing, though this was largely negated by the insertion of a tube that destroyed the self-cleaning action.

The 1½-litre suffers more than the 2½-litre from this sludging, because it had to be driven harder to achieve cruising speeds and because the oilway in the crank shaft journal is smaller. In new cars, oil was changed after the first 500 miles and then every 1,500 miles with decarbonization done after 2,500. Oil filter kits are readily available from the clubs.

Most cars from the 1940s and 1950s relied on white metal bearings on the crankshaft and indeed some of these seem to go on forever, despite the perils of sludge, but their replacement is becoming more and more difficult as few firms these days have the technology to cast them, though a few die-hards still advertise their services in the *Automobile* magazine.

The 2½-litre had modified con-rods with shell bearings from engine RMB2/945; earlier engines and the 1½-litre can be adapted to take them, again by modifying the con-rod.

The later con-rods had a major benefit; the big ends are split diagonally so the pistons can be extracted though the top of the block.

## Spares

Spares for Riley RMs are plentiful, with the exception of body parts for the Pathfinder. There are several different sources from the one-make Riley clubs to entrepreneurs.

New wooden sections for body repair are available although many can be made at home using simple hand tools. Most of the wood used for the frame is ash but there is also some beech and plywood. Marine ply laminated to produce whatever thickness is required, can make an alternative for many sections such as sills and roof timbers.

Some new steel panels are available but are generally hand-made and relatively expensive. Small repair sections are available that can save a lot of time when repairing a larger panel.

RM Rileys are still being broken as being beyond economic repair so there is still a good supply of cheap second-hand parts, particularly at autojumbles.

*Spares suppliers*

The Riley RM Club scheme is probably the most comprehensive and has been in operation for nearly thirty years. During that time a stock worth £300,000 has been amassed. 'What matters in spares is instant availability off the shelf', says John Kirby, who runs the Riley RM Centre Ltd on behalf of the club.

There are more than 1,200 different part numbers available, from a 2½-litre exhaust at £300 to a 2p washer. 'There isn't anything I couldn't have manufactured, I even have a source for engine blocks, though they are not required', says John.

Almost everything is re-manufactured; much is made in Hong Kong and Taiwan but the best source for engineering components is the Czech Republic, where the quality is excellent. Steering rack gaiters that would have cost a fortune to be made in the UK were made in the Czech Republic for a tenth of the price.

Needle rollers for gearboxes were not available commercially, so the club persuaded an Italian manufacturer to do a one-hour production run of 30,000 needle rollers.

Not everything is made abroad: wooden frame parts and new semi-elliptic leaf springs for example, are made in Yorkshire.

There are some things that are not remade – new front wings for instance would be extremely expensive and it is almost always possible to patch old ones.

One problem with older cars is the cost of windscreen glass, which often has to be to cut to order; the club has laminated windscreen glass at £22 (exVAT, 2004 prices). Among the hundreds of other different parts available are a set of replica Butler driving lamps at £97.50 and a new steering wheel at £280.

Because of the club's mutual trading structure, parts can be sold only to current club members.

**The Riley RM Centre Ltd**
Cotebrook House
Dam Hill
Shelley
Huddersfield HD8 8JL
Tel: 01484 607744
Fax: 01484 604339

**The Riley Motor Club** spares scheme covers all Rileys, and supplies spares for them to its members worldwide. The biggest volume of sales is to RM and 1.5 owners. Pathfinder, 2.6 and some pre-war parts are also available. Typical prices in 2004 were:

| | | |
|---|---|---|
| Exhaust systems | 2½-litre £140, 1½-litre £148 | |
| Prop shaft | 2½-litre £19 | |
| D lamps | Black £32 | Chrome £45 |

Unit 3, Doynton Mill
Mill Lane
Doynton
Bristol BS30 5TQ
spares@rileymotorclub.org

There are several other suppliers of new or second-hand spares, several of whom also undertake restoration. Some, but not all of their services are detailed below.

**Dave Brown** – services include boring/grinding and white-metalling
3 New Mill Lane
Mansfield Woodhouse
Mansfield
Notts NG19 9BL
Tel: 01623 460511

**E B Mould** – ash frames/panels supplied
31 Sandbach
Great Lumley
Chester-le-Street
Co Durham DL3 4LL
Tel: 01740 621145

**Donnington RMA Services** – shell-bearing conversions, brake overhaul, roof replacement kits, and new headlinings.
52 The Street
Bunwell
Norwich
NR16 1NA
Tel: 01953 789014

**Lundegaard Spares Co.** – one of the longest-established firms specializing in the RM Series
Alec Gatherer
6 Hill Crescent
Higher Blackley
Manchester M9 8EX
Tel: 0161 795 8164

**R. Wren**
The Acorns
Front Road
Murrow
Wisbech
Cambs PE13 4JQ
Tel: 01945 701009

*Mainly restoration*

**Glen Kingham**
1 Leydenhatch Cottages
Birchwood Road
Swanley
Kent BR8 7PX
Tel: 01322 614930

**Gavin Lumsden**
Red House
Bowsers Lane
Little Walden
Saffron Walden
Essex CB10 1XQ
Tel: 01799 522330

*There are plenty of wooden repair sections available; the vulnerable rear window frame is on the top.*

## Clubs

Names and contact numbers of officials are not given since these tend to change. These websites giving current contact details were active at the start of 2005.

The Riley RM Club was born in the summer of 1969 – a group had come together to discuss the problem of getting spares for their RMs. The club maintains a register of more than 5,000 known RMs from a total production of some 28,000. Magazine: *RMemoranda*
www.rileyrmclub.org.uk

The Riley Motor Club caters for all Rileys including RMs. It is the original Riley factory club founded in 1925. Magazine: *The Riley Record*
www.rileymotorclub.org

Scottish Riley Enthusiasts founded in 1991, to provide a local focus for the Scottish members of national Riley clubs.
www.sre.gb.com

The Riley Register is for pre-war cars.
www.rileyregister.com

Riley Club Holland – all types of Rileys.
home.hetnet.nl/~riley50/pages/rileyeng.htm

Riley-Club Switzerland founded in 1979, has about 90 members.
www.riley-club.ch/en/factsfigures.htm

Riley Motor Club of South Australia is one of several Riley clubs in Australia.
www.bold.net.au/~leighj/html/rileysa.htm

Riley Motor Club of Western Australia.
www.rileywa.org.au

Riley Club – Victoria, also caters for Tasmania.
users.bigpond.com/rileyclubvictoria/index.html

Rileys in Australia is a website developed by Phil Soden from the New South Wales Riley Club. It includes a lot of technical information and links to information and contacts related to the Australian Riley world.
www.phil.soden.com

The Queensland Riley Club were developing their website at the time of writing.

ACT Club – email: fairey@ozemail.com.au

Woodie Car Club UK – www.sitegarden.co.uk/woodies

There was plenty of meat originally in the crankshafts if they needed to be reground. Modern shell bearings are available down to 40thou for the 1½-litre can and 48thou for the 2½-litre. Crankshaft breakage is almost unheard-of due to the strength of the forgings.

Normal running temperature of both engines should be between 70–80°C (158–176°F). The 1½-litre head had hotspot tubes within it and had two in the block, but these corrode and many owners have sealed them off during engine rebuilds.

The 2½-litre engine tends to run rich when new carburettor jets or needles are required.

*There are probably some forty roadworthy Pathfinders, some like this restored to a very high standard.*

## Modifications

Conversions to unleaded fuel, involving cylinder head modification, are fairly common, as are canister oil filter kits for the 1½-litre, as the original fitment became unavailable many years ago.

Purists may mock but some RMB/RMF owners have fitted five-speed gearboxes for more relaxed cruising, typically a Getrag box from an Opel Manta GTE. This can provide 80mph (130km/h) cruising at 3,000rpm. One roadster was converted with a five-speed box from a Volvo 740. As another example, a drop-head has been modified to take a Rover V8 engine and SD1 five-speed gearbox.

Others have used a different final drive ratio. The axles Riley supplied to Donald Healey had a ratio of 3.5:1 instead of the standard 4.1:1, a reduction in engine speed of nearly 15 per cent and some of these sets have been recommissioned.

Conversions are very popular in Australia where vast distances have to be covered in hot weather. One Riley club run in 2004 was 1,000 miles (1,600km) over a long weekend. Apart from the different versions of RMs – from station wagons to short-wheelbase racers – nearly all are modified mechanically, usually with louvred bonnet side panels, electric cooling fans and oil coolers. Some have disc brakes and five-speed gearboxes.

## Further help

There is an excellent series of guides on RM maintenance and repair that is produced by John Joiner, a noted Riley expert, who has helped with this chapter. They can be found at www.rmriley.funurl.com. In addition, he has produced a series of maintenance booklets that are also available on CD at £10.

# Appendix I: RM production

The chassis numbers of most of the Riley RMs up to the Pathfinder follow the Riley system of classification laid down in Coventry in 1936. The numbers are based on a production year from October to September, not the calendar year. This was largely to coincide with new models being launched at the London Motor Show.

The system is rather perverse as it depends on adding or subtracting 10 from the year of manufacture. A typical chassis number for a 1948 RMA saloon would read:

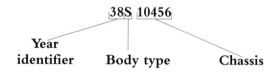

**1½-litre** The initial two-digit chassis number is 10 *fewer* than the last two digits of the calendar year, because 3 denotes a 1½-litre chassis in the 1940s and S stands for saloon, which is followed by the number itself. In the 1950s the first number becomes 4. Thus chassis prefixed 35S to 45S are 1½-litre.

**2½-litre** The initial two-digit chassis number is 10 *more* than the last two digits of the calendar year. Chassis prefixed 56S from 1946 to 62S in 1953 are 2½-litre.

Body types
S  =  saloon
D  =  drophead
SS =  roadster

This body nomenclature was introduced after the Nuffield takeover in 1938. Under the old

regime S had stood for Special series twin-carburettor engines and SS for Sprite series. Thus the pre-war 1939 Nuffield chassis were:

| 29S | 1½-litre | 49S | 2½-litre |
| 29D | " | 49D | " |

In 1952, RM cars, particularly the RMEs and RMFs, maintained the year reference but prefaced it with RME/F on a bulkhead plate:

Car number:     RME 42S 20564
Engine number:  RMA 10702 (signifying a 1½-litre car)

This lasted until the end of 1952, when the year signifier was dropped, and the chassis were labelled RME ★★★★. Similarly the RMF dropped the year signifier so that by 1953 all numbers were RMF ★★★★.

It should be noted that many chassis without bodies left the Riley factory between 1946 and 1948; details of these are in this appendix under chassis numbers.

There are three different types of chassis plates by which the car can be identified:

| Small diamond | up to 1948 | on nearside scuttle cross member |
| Small oblong | up to 1950 | " |
| Large oblong | to end | on offside scuttle cross member |

(also shows engine number)

The following figures are courtesy of the British Motor Industry Heritage Trust, with interpretation by the Registrar of the RM Club and, in the case of the Pathfinder, by the author.

### Chassis numbers and production – 1½-litre RMA and RME

| Year | Number built | Chassis from | to |
|------|-------------|--------------|-----|
| 1945 RMA | 8 | 36S*10001 | 10008 |
| 1946 RMA | 1,312 | 36S 10009 | 11322 |
| 1947 RMA | 2,720 | 37S 11323 | 14042 |
| 1948 RMA | 1,925 | 38S 14043 | 15967 |
| 1949 RMA | 1,498 | | |
| | of which | | |
| | Coventry 408 | 39S 15968 | 16375 |
| | Abingdon 1,090 | 39S 16376 | 17465 |
| 1950 RMA | 1,356 | 40S 17466 | 18821 |
| 1951 RMA | 1,164 | 41S 18822 | 19985 |
| 1952 RMA/E | 1,050 | 42S 19986 | 21035** |
| 1953 RME | 819 | RME 21036 | 21854 |
| 1953 RME | 320 | RME 21855*** | 22174 |
| 1954 RME | 1,747 | RME 22175 | 23921 |
| 1955 RME | 29 | RME 23922 | 23950 |

* First chassis was not registered until late 1946, so would have had the original 1945 chassis number overstamped with 36S before registration. The yearly totals do not quite match the final production figures due to factory miscounting.
** Chassis changed to RME at 42S 20505 – all-hydraulic brakes, hypoid rear axle, open transmission shaft
*** Facelift model – 'the spatted RME' from 21855 – rear spats, helmet front wings, no running boards.

| Total | RMA production: | 10,504 |
|-------|-----------------|--------|
| | RME | 3,446 |
| Total | 1½-litre | 13,950 |

### Chassis numbers and production – 2½-litre

| Year | Number built | Chassis from | to |
|------|-------------|--------------|-----|
| 1946 RMB | 76 | 56S 2001 | 2076 |
| 1947 RMB | 613 | 57S 2077 | 2689 |
| 1948 RMB | 1,307 | 58S 2690 | 3996 |
| 1949 RMB | 1,517 | | |
| | of which | | |
| | Coventry 315 | 59S 3997 | 4311 |
| | Abingdon 1,202 | 59S 4312 | 5513 |
| 1950 RMB | 2,232 | 60S 5514 | 7745 |
| 1951 RMB | 1,457 | 61S 7746 | 9202 |
| 1952 RMB/F | 1,059 | 62S 9203 | 10261* |
| 1953 RMF | 699 | 63S 10262 | 10960 |

*RMF begins at chassis 62S 9911
Note that roadster and drophead chassis numbers are included in these figures, as there was no separate series for them.

Total: 8,960

---

**Chassis numbers and production – RMC 2½-litre roadster**

| Year | Number built | Chassis start/end |
|---|---|---|
| 1948 | | 58SS 2802 |
| 1949 | 259 | |
| | *of which* | |
| | *Coventry 121* | |
| | *Abingdon 138* | |
| 1950 | 241 | |
| 1951 | 7 | Not known |

The two-seater roadsters were given a chassis prefix 2S as in 60 2S 12345

Total: 507
Exported: 190

---

**Chassis numbers and production – RMD 2½-litre drophead**

| Year | Number built | Chassis start/end |
|---|---|---|
| 1949 | 20 | 59D 5201 |
| | *of which* | |
| | *Coventry 2* | |
| | *Abingdon 18* | |
| 1950 | 375 | |
| 1951 | 105 | Not known |

Total: 500
Exported: 416

Actual body production seems to have been 503, based on bodies produced; one was put on an RME, another onto an RMA; this was involved in an accident and subsequently transferred to a 2½-litre chassis by John Kirby in the 1980s.

---

**Chassis numbers and production – Pathfinder**

Chassis numbering for the Pathfinder changed completely from the old Riley method and adopted the Abingdon standard. Thus a typical chassis number reads:

MAJB135505 where
M     =  2.5 litres
A     =  4-door saloon
J      =  the top colour of a duotone car, in this case Dark Grey
B     =  the bottom colour, in this case Black
1     =  right-hand drive, home market
3     =  type of paint, in this case cellulose
5505 =  chassis number

The following figures, like those above, are based on an October–September production year. Cars produced in 1953, such as those for the Motor Show, are subsumed into the following year's figures.

| Year | Number built | Chassis from | to |
|---|---|---|---|
| 1954 | 889 | MAA/501 | MAA/1390 |
| 1955 | 2,719 | MAA/1391 | MAA/4110 |
| 1956 | 1,477 | MAA/4111 | MAA/5588 |
| 1957 | 67 | MAA/5588 | MAA/5652 |

Total:  5,152

These figures are based on the calendar year dates that the Pathfinders came off the finishing line, not the dates the chassis were laid down, although the total is the same. There is some element of overlap of dates and numbers at the turn of the year, so that in some cases cars had been allocated chassis numbers in one calendar year but were not completed until the next.

| Year | Number built | Chassis from | to |
|---|---|---|---|
| 1953 | 4 | MAA/501 | MAA/504 |
| 1954 | 877 | MAA/505 | MAA/1381 |
| 1955 | 2,718 | MAA/1382 | MAA/4099 |
| 1956 | 1,504 | MAA/4100 | MAA/5603 |
| 1957 | 49 | MAA/5604 | MAA/5652 |

Total:  5,152

## Engine numbers 1½-litre and 2½-litre

A much simpler system than chassis classification, as numbers for both 1½-litre and 2½-litre began initially at no. 2001

1½-litre engine numbers prefixed   A
2½-litre                                            B

There is no correlation, as there is with many other makes, between engine and chassis numbers. Anders Clausager, who was archivist of the British Motor Industry Heritage Trust, has pointed out that no cars built at Abingdon ever had matching engine and chassis numbers, except for the early Austin-Healey 100/6, whose numbers were allocated by Austin at Longbridge and who took as an engine number after installation whatever number was on the chassis.

Later 1½-litres had a bulkhead plate that gave the chassis number prefaced by RME and the engine number prefaced by RMA.

The first engine in the Riley 2½-litre sequence was B1, which was produced for the 16hp range in 1938/9. Some fifty of these were produced, so when the 2½-litre chassis began at 2001, there was a disjunction of about 1,950 between engine/chassis numbers. This gap grew smaller as more engines were made for spares and sent to Healey. The Healey engine numbers also have the same Big Four prefix and range from a very early B7 to B8223, with huge gaps in between.

This numbering system continued until the revised engine of 1952, which began:

RMB2/1

The owner's handbook for the early cars said that the engine number was stamped on the starter motor mounting flange, but on Coventry-built cars this is the chassis number. The engine number is stamped on the timing case just below the distributor.

The engine number itself can be found in several other different places – on a diamond plate in a variety of locations, such as on the block beneath the air cleaner. The diamond plate, making the numbers easier to see, is said to have been introduced so that exported cars could have their engine and chassis numbers checked quickly during import formalities.

Reconditioned 1½-litre and 2½-litre engines have the prefix R for early cars; later there is a C before a five or six digit number and yet later a prefix like AEH 4A. If the engines were genuinely factory reconditioned, they were sleeved back to standard bore size. However, it was quite well known at Abingdon for 'reconditioned' engines to be in some cases brand new. It was certainly the case for MGA Twin-cam engines that blew up with some regularity in the warranty period.

All Riley engine blocks and heads are stamped with the date of machining. The dates are on the top face of the block and at the rear of the head.

## Body numbers

These are stamped, not very carefully, into the wooden bulkhead cross rail and are often indistinct or even unreadable.

As all the Riley production records were lost long ago, the task of piecing together how body numbers were created and estimating how they relate to chassis has been undertaken by experts like Gwyn Morris of the RM Club.

He has discovered that the bodies, built in batches by the Morris Bodies Branch in Coventry, were supplied as chassis became available, in runs of up to 1,400, though the usual batch was 1,000.

Of the first batch of 1,000 bodies, for instance, numbered A2000 to A2999, 935 were placed on the 1½-litre chassis from 35S 1001 to 36S 10935, and sixty-five on the 2½-litre from 56S 2001–56S 2065.

Both 1½-litre and 2½-litre saloon bodies are in the same number sequence and not delineated separately like the chassis. This is because the main structure of the body is the same for both models, and other than the longer bonnet, the 2½-litre needed only slight changes in the bulkhead to accommodate the higher steering column and the SU fuel pump.

The run of body numbers is ascending but not consecutive, so the next series of saloon bodies, after the first thousand, begins not at A3000, but at A8600 and runs to A9999, a set of 1,400 bodies. The sequence after that, of 800 bodies, runs from A15600 to A16399.

The reason behind this disparity, which continues throughout production, is probably to do with the fact that Bodies Branch was producing other bodies for MG and Morris, and that the Riley gaps are in fact filled by others.

It is also not clear whether there were small runs in a sequence to accommodate left-hand-drive models. However, roadsters had a separate batch of numbers – A34500 to A35000, as did dropheads from A50001 to A50500. These would not have been produced in a straight production run of 500 but built to order.

Trying to match bodies to chassis numbers is further complicated by the fact that between 1946 and 1949, there were many chassis that were sold without bodies, to be turned into vehicles such as woodie estate cars, as factories had restricted supplies of steel for their own bodies.

In a few cases, chassis were bodied as dropheads by outside coachbuilders; then there were the factory prototypes of the six-light saloon and the bodies sent for assembly to Brittains in Dublin, that were not included in the Bodies Branch numbering system but given their own Brittains number (*see* Chapter 10).

In 1953 there was a change to the system of allocating five-digit numbers prefaced with A, with a sequence that ran without a letter before it from 5601 to 6150.

Then, at about the time the 'spatted' RME was introduced, the sequence changed again and now ran in two blocks of 1,000, from 10000 to 10999 and 15000 to 15999. The final sequence of ninety in 1954/55 was from 20000 to 20089.

It is estimated that the works turned out 22,833 coachbuilt RM bodies (312 for Brittains) and seventy-six chassis that were bare.

# Appendix II: colour schemes

## From 1946 to 1948

Many early cars were black, but some cars were painted in two-tone colour schemes – typically wings and upper body panels in black, lower body panels in colour. The roof fabric was normally black, but was seen coloured, e.g. Mrs Victor Riley's 1½-litre saloon, and on some cars delivered to Australia. Some cars for hot climates were delivered with white roofs, as was one to an RAF officer in Aden. The actor Charles Victor, who made 126 films, had an Ivory 1½-litre with a white top, that it seems was recovered in black, probably because of the task of keeping it looking clean.

Cars were sometimes painted to special order, such as Lord Mountbatten's 2½-litre that was blue and black, with the two-tone split that became known as the Mountbatten split. This was quite different from the split of black cellulose with the side panels in a different colour.

Trim was usually brown in early models.

## From December 1948

| Body colour | Trim |
|---|---|
| *Saloons:* | |
| Black | Red, Green, Brown or Beige |
| Maroon | Red |
| Green | Green or Beige |
| Ivory | Red, Green or Brown |

*Drophead coupé as saloon but also in:*

| | |
|---|---|
| Scarlet | Beige |
| Light Green | Beige |
| Ming Blue | Beige |

| Body colour | Trim |
|---|---|
| *Roadster:* | |
| Ivory | |
| Red | |
| Black | Red |
| Scarlet | Beige |
| Light Green | Beige |
| Ming Blue | Beige |

On open models, the hood colour matched the upholstery.

All coloured cars were available with black wings.

Ivory cars were available with black wings and roof.

## From July 1949

| Body colour | Trim |
|---|---|
| *Saloon and coupé:* | |
| Black | Beige, Maroon, Green or Brown |
| Autumn Red | Beige or Maroon |
| Almond Green | Beige or Green |
| Sun Bronze | Maroon |
| | |
| *Roadster:* | |
| Black | Beige, Red or Green |
| Clipper Blue | Beige |
| Almond Green | Beige |
| Red | Beige or Red |
| Ivory | Red or Green |
| Sun Bronze | Beige |
| Autumn Red | Beige |

## From September 1951

| Body colour | Trim |
| --- | --- |
| *Saloon:* | |
| Black | Beige, Maroon, Green or Brown |
| Autumn Red | Beige or Maroon |
| Almond Green M | Beige or Green |
| Grey M | Maroon |
| Grey (particularly RMFs) | Rust, Maroon, Green |

On metallic cars, wings were sometimes to tone, such as an Almond Green metallic body with Woodland Green wings.

## From October 1952

| Body colour | Trim |
| --- | --- |
| *Saloon:* | |
| Black | Beige, Maroon, Green or Brown |
| Woodland Green | Beige or Green |
| Autumn Red | Maroon or Beige |
| Silver Streak Grey M | Red |

## From January 1954

| RME saloon only: | |
| --- | --- |
| Black | Maroon, Green or Red |
| Green | Green or Red |
| Maroon | Maroon or Red |
| Blue | Grey |
| Ivory | Rust or Maroon (Maroon only from Dec. 1954) |
| Grey | Rust, Maroon or Green (Maroon only from Dec. 1954) |

## Wheels and hubcaps

Wheels were usually painted using the body colour, as were the hubcaps between the outer ridge and the centre. Where two-tone schemes were used, the predominant colour was utilized. However, all-chrome hubcaps became a no-cost option.

Roadster hubcaps were usually chrome.

This information came from an article written by Brian Palmer in *RMemoranda* March 1973 and an article in *Rileyfax*, reproduced by permission of the Riley Motor Club of U.S.A. It appears by courtesy of the Riley RM Club in whose magazine it appeared in June 1982.

## Pathfinder colours

There was a choice at launch of five basic body and four trim colours:

| Paint | Trim |
| --- | --- |
| Black | Maroon, Green or Biscuit |
| Maroon | Maroon or Biscuit |
| Green | Green or Biscuit |
| Blue | Grey |
| Grey | Maroon or Grey |

There were often permutations of these five body and trim colours. This lasted until the spring of 1956 when they were replaced from MA/5234 by a new range of solid shades and the introduction of duotone colours.

| Monotone paints | Trim | Carpet |
| --- | --- | --- |
| Black | Maroon, Green, Biscuit | Maroon, Green, Brown |
| Cedar Green | Biscuit | Green |
| Wolseley Maroon | Maroon, Biscuit | Maroon, Brown |
| Charcoal Grey | Maroon, Grey | Maroon |
| Kashmir Beige | Maroon, Biscuit | Maroon, Brown |

| Duotones (upper colour first) | Trim | Carpet |
|---|---|---|
| Rose Taupe/ Kashmir Beige | Maroon, Biscuit | Maroon, Brown |
| Blue/Steel Blue–Grey | Grey | Blue |
| Swiss Grey/ Charcoal Grey | Maroon, Grey | Maroon |

Wheels were normally painted to match the bodywork – the upper colour on two-tone cars.

The colour code was included in the chassis number, as was the type of finish. These are the basic codes. For duotone cars, the top colour was the first letter in the chassis designation.

| | |
|---|---|
| A | Black |
| B | Grey |
| C | Red |
| D | Blue |
| E | Cedar Green |
| F | Beige |
| G | Brown |
| H | Primer only |
| J | Dark Grey |
| K | Light Red |
| L | Light Blue |
| P | Ivory |
| R | White |
| S | Mid Grey |
| T | Light Green |
| U | Dark Green |

| | |
|---|---|
| 1 | Synthetic |
| 2 | Synobel |
| 3 | Cellulose |
| 4 | Metallic |
| 5 | Primer |
| 6 | Cellulose body Synthetic wings |

# Appendix III: 1½-litre major modifications – chassis and engine

**To late 1949**

**Chassis**

| | |
|---|---|
| 36S/10001 | Commencing number. |
| 36S/10157 | Serrated clutch bottom shaft. |
| 36S/10632 | Clutch pedal stop and second pull-off spring added. |
| 36S/11000 | Clutch plate with black and green springs. (Engine A1246) |
| 36S/11304 | Hydraulic carburettor dashpot fitted. |
| 36S/11360 | Modified centre bearing to torque tube. |
| 36S/11782 | Larger roller on brake compensator. |
| 37S/12053 | Horns moved to wing stays. |
| 37S/12440 | Stitched roof lining. |
| 37S/12560 | Narrow gearbox tunnel; floorboards modified to fit. |
| 37S/12646 | Machined differential box. |
| 37S/12800 | Strengthened lower front suspension struts. |
| 37S/13127 | Stiffener to front number-plate. |
| 37S/13925 | Mk. II Lucas headlamps and modified cowl. |
| (From engine A3100) | Static balanced clutch and flywheel. |
| 38S/14565 | Bolt replaced in trunnion housing. |
| 38S/14740 | Longer anti-roll bar brackets. |
| 38S/14581 | Clamp bolt on torque tube deleted. |
| 38S/14544 | RYZ clutch plate and light bowl assembly. |
| 38S/14685 | 2½-litre swivel arms fitted. |
| 38S/14903 | Semi-hydrostatic HNS.1 brakes, lined MR.41 added. |
| 38S/15001 | Second Series commencement, including Ley's crown gear housing. |
| 38S/15072 | Second Series body (lower front floor). |
| 38S/15306 | Extruded door-surround rubbers. |
| 38S/15151 | Internal bonnet locks. |
| 38S/15355 | Hand dipper-switch. |
| 38S/15454 | High trunnion 'B' member lowered. |
| 39S/16156 | Softer rubbers on trunnion mountings. |
| 39S/16223 | PV6 type rear dampers in place of PR. |
| 39S/16692 | Blanked-off swivel bush housing. |

| | |
|---|---|
| 39S/17120 to 17124 (inc)<br>39S/17126 to 17128 (inc)<br>to 17135 (inc)<br>39S/17142 to 17159 (inc)<br>39S/17161 to 17193 (inc)<br>39S/17195 to 17209 (inc) | 1½-litre rhd with new body trim and door cappings. Con- 39S/17130 cealed visors, new floorboards and gearbox cover, but fitted with old type (1949) facia and round instruments. |
| 39S/17010<br>39S/17011<br>39S/17012<br>39S/17125<br>39S/17194<br>39S/17210 onwards | Common bodies 2½-litre and 1½-litre rhd with new body trim and door cappings, concealed visors, new floorboards and gearbox cover, but fitted with new type (1950) facia board and square instruments. |

39S/17210     Previous to this chassis number, headlamps had a cut-off rear body to clear the wing blade. The wings have now been indented and will take a standard domed rear body. Cars with the old wing should be serviced with the old lamp.

The new lamp part numbers:

| Home | H.8228 (N/S 1 off) |
|---|---|
| | H.8229 (O/S 1 off) |
| Export | rhd H.8229 (2 off dip left) |
| | lhd H.8230 (2 off dip right) |

39S/17314     Improved venting for rear axle. ³⁄₃₂in hole drilled in top of casing 8in off centre on the right-hand side and fit new filler plug No. 500004 or blank off hole in existing plug.

39S/17420     New front suspension rebound rubbers (taper type) (Part No. A.2728).

39S/17420     Improved tubular-type lower front suspension links with new long web plate (replaces all older type of links).

New Part Nos.

| 500043 | Bottom link assembly (RH) (1 pair comprising). |
|---|---|
| 500045 | Bottom link assembly (rear RH). |
| 500047 | Bottom link assembly (front RH). |
| 500044 | Bottom link assembly (LH) (1 pair comprising). |
| 500046 | Bottom link assembly (rear LH). |
| 500048 | Bottom link assembly (rear LH). |

From engine A.7449     New type starter (Lucas 25521A) (without switch) (Part No. R.1556). New ST.950 solenoid, switch on bulk-head.

40S/18652     New water sealing of floorboards.

From 1950 the format of change points altered, giving in some cases the reason for the change.

| | |
|---|---|
| BRAKE LINING (FRONT) | From chassis 40S/18484; front suspension 1337<br>Front brake lining shoes shortened by 1in at the leading edge on both leading and trailing shoes. Linings riveted with two rivets at these points.<br>*Reason: To prevent front brake grab.* |
| BRAKE HOSE (FRONT) | From chassis 40S/18867<br>Brake pipes re-run to allow hoses to be fitted behind suspension links, instead of in front.<br>*Reason: To prevent chafing of hose on rim of road wheel.* |
| OIL PIPE (ENGINE TO ADAPTOR) | From engine A10292<br>Oil pipe – engine to adaptor new part H7132.<br>*Reason: Fitting of flexible pipe to prevent chatter in oil gauge.* |
| BRAKES | From chassis RME/20505<br>Introduction of full hydraulic brake gear. |
| FRONT HUBS | From chassis RME 20505<br>Introduction of front hubs incorporating ANF threaded studs. |
| FRONT SUSPENSION | From chassis RME 20505<br>Introduction of front suspension unit with twin leading brake shoes. |
| REAR AXLE | From chassis RME 20505<br>Hypoid rear axle with open propeller shafts and hubs with ANF threaded studs and stronger road springs. Hypoid 90 oil now used for rear axle and gearbox. |
| VALVE SPRING (OUTER) | From engine RMA 11280<br>Introduction of valve spring (outer) part 166553 replacing valve spring. (outer) R647.<br>*Reason: To improve valve spring crash that is too low with 8 × 14 axle ratio.* |
| WHEEL CYLINDER (FRONT) | From chassis RME 20505<br>Now ⅞in diameter instead of 1in |
| FACE LIFT | From chassis RME 21855<br>Alterations to body, wings, bonnet, head, side and fog lamps, front and rear bumpers, main wiring harness, etc. Running boards deleted.<br>*Reason: Improved design.* |
| CYLINDER HEAD | Cylinder head gasket part AEB123 with increased water apertures replaces part R1396.<br>*Reason: To obviate tendency to scuffing of pistons and bore distortion.* |

ENGINE          Separate RH and LH rear engine mounting brackets replace single mounting support bracket. Exhaust system support brackets now Meta-lastic instead of links and rubber bushes.
*Reason: To reduce engine vibration.*

Source: *BMIHT and* Riley Record

# Appendix IV: 2½-litre major modifications – chassis and engine

This list, from works documents, is not exhaustive and does not, for instance, mention the early change of petrol pump in April 1947 from AC mechanical to SU electrical.

| | |
|---|---|
| 56S/2001 | Commencing number first sanction. |
| 56S/2019 | Round air filter, with carburettor elbow and rocker boxes to suit. Ninety jets, EE needles for carburettors. |
| 56S/2020 | Battery reversed (terminals to rear). |
| 56S/2043 | 18in steering wheel replaces 17in. |
| 56S/2056 | Strengthened lower struts on front suspension and aluminium crash pads, shorter clutch pedal. 'A' member with added bracket. |
| 56S/2089 | 10in clutch (previously 9in) and flywheel bell housing to suit. (Engine A 139.) |
| 57S/2169 | Corrected speedometer. |
| 57S/2196 | Four-core radiator block. |
| 57S/2202 | Heavier rear springs (13-leaf D.5704). |
| 57S/2414 | Stiffener to front number-plate, modified rockers and shafts. |
| 57S/2511 | Weak top spring on front brakes. |
| 57S/2642 | MK. II headlamps and cowls. Hardened clutch centre. (Engine 650.) |
| 58S/2582 | Clamp bolt on torque tube deleted. |
| 58S/2861 | Screwed oil retainer to front hub. |
| 58S/2863 | Brake linings MR4I front, Don rear. |
| 58S/2959 | 100bhp engine introduced[1]. Larger inlet valves, cylinder head modified. Engine No. 699 solid tappets, modified push-rods with ball pins. |
| 58S/2976 | RYZ clutch lined plate, light bowl, moulded friction ring. (Engine 789.) |
| 58S/2998 | Longer anti-roll bar with brackets to suit. |
| 58S/3001 | Commencing number second sanction. |
| 58S/3047 | MR41 linings front and rear. |
| 58S/3071 | 2 leading shoe front brakes adopted. |
| 58S/3225 | ¼in longer propeller shaft (A.1857) to straighten shackles. |
| 58S/3275 | Internal bonnet locks. |
| 58S/3352 | Extruded rubbers to doors. |
| 58S/3397 | Hand dip-switch. |
| 59S/4119 | Ley's crown gear housing to rear axle. |
| 59S/4203 | Softer rubbers to trunnion mountings. |
| 59S/4611 | PV6 type rear dampers in place of PR6. |
| 59S/4766 | Blanked-off swivel bush housing. New part numbers A.2712 and A.2718. |

| | | |
|---|---|---|
| 59S/5131 to 5135 inc. | | |
| 59S/5138 to 5145 inc. | Common bodies 2½-litre and 1½-litre rhd with new | |
| 59S/5147 to 5158 inc. | body trim and door cappings, concealed visors, new floor- | |
| 59S/5164 to 5210 inc. | boards and gearbox cover, but fitted with old type (1949) | |
| 59S/5212 to 5217 inc. | facia and round instruments. | |
| 59S/5219 to 5234 inc. | | |
| 59S/5241 | | |

| | | |
|---|---|---|
| 59S/5004 | 59S/5235 | |
| 59S/5005 | 59S/5236 | |
| 59S/5095 | 59S/5237 | Common bodies 1½-litre and 2½-litre rhd, with |
| 59S/5096 | 59S/5238 | new body trim, door cappings, concealed visors, new |
| 59S/5137 | 59S/5239 | floorboards and gearbox covers. New type (1950) facia |
| 59S/5146 | 59S/5240 | board and square instruments. |
| 59S/5211 | 59S/5242 | |
| 59S/5218 | (onwards) | |

59S/5235 — Cars now filled at works with Lockheed No. 33 brake fluid. Girling or Lockheed may be used and will mix. Girling is suitable for arctic conditions.

59S/5256 — Previous to this chassis number, headlamps had a cut-off rear body to clear the wing blade. The wings have been indented and will now take a standard domed rear body. Cars with the old wing will still be serviced with the old lamp. The new lamp part numbers are:

| | | |
|---|---|---|
| Home | | H.8228 N/S. |
| | | H.8229 O/S. |
| Export | rhd | H.8229 dip left. |
| | lhd | H.8230 dip right. |

59S/5363 — Improved venting for rear axle. ³⁄₃₂in hole drilled in top of casing 8in off-centre on the right-hand side and new filler-plug Part. 500004, or blank off hole in existing plug and drill as indicated.

59S/5437 — New type starter M459/L5/26038.A (without switch) Part No. S.811 replaces S.64, and new dynamo Lucas C.45PV/4-LO S.812 replaces S.63 (Engine No. B.3896). New solenoid (ST.950) switch on bulkhead. New control box RF/95/2 Lucas 37076.E must be used.

59S/5490 — New type front suspension rebound rubbers (taper type) Part No. A.2728.

59S/5490 — Improved tubular type lower front suspension links with new long web-plate (replaces all older type links)

New Part Nos:

| | |
|---|---|
| 500043 | Bottom link assembly. RH, 1 pair comprising: |
| 500045 | Bottom link assembly. (Rear RH) |
| 500047 | Bottom link assembly. (Front RH) |
| 500044 | Bottom link assembly. LH, 1 pair, comprising: |
| 500046 | Bottom link assembly. (Rear LH) |
| 500048 | Bottom link assembly. (Front LH) |

59S/5510

The exhaust manifold on rhd cars, Part No. S.490, has now been replaced with Part No. S.668, the lhd manifold. rhd and lhd cars now use a common exhaust manifold. The front exhaust pipe assembly H.6194 has been replaced with H.8281, now common to rhd and lhd cars.

Connecting rods S.553 changed to connecting rods S.863 (with wider big-end bolt centres) commencing Engine No. B.3157.

Rods should be serviced singly for the respective engine numbers (as they are different weights) or as either a set of four S.553 or a set of the latest S.863.

| | |
|---|---|
| 500047 | bottom link assembly (front RH) |
| 500044 | bottom link assembly M (1 pair, comprising) |
| 500046 | bottom link assembly (rear LH) |
| 500048 | bottom link assembly (front W |

*Reason: Improved type.*

5510

Exhaust manifold on rhd cars, pt. no. S490 replaced by lhd manifold, pt. no. S668. Front exhaust pipe H6194 replaced by H8281 now common to RH and lhd cars.

*Reason: To use common manifold on rhd and lhd models.*

59D/5006 to 60D/6576

Trouble has been experienced of excessive hood covering wear and damage caused by friction of the fabric when travelling with the hood folded down. A service scheme has been prepared to rectify this trouble, details from the factory.

59S/6095

11in brake drum, rear, replaces 12in brake drum.
*Reason: Improved braking.*

60S/7337 (saloon);
60S/7564? (drophead)

Floorboards, gearbox cover and ramp plate have been modified to a flanged and bolted-down type in place of the previous clip-down gearbox cover. All floorboards, ramp plate and gearbox cover flange joints are now made with a strip of ¾in wide Prestik jointing material. This material is supplied in rolls suitably cut off and stuck to all floorboard and gearbox cover edges, the parts fitted on top and the bolts pushed through the Prestik during assembly. Redundant holes in ramp plate (on cars without heater fitted) are covered up with leather cloth fixed with Bostik 'C' adhesive. An additional steering column grommet is added to steering column on the front face of the bulkhead. The ramp plate sound baffle board and felt backing are done away with and new padded carpets are added. Full modification details from the factory. Pressure-type radiator cap now fitted to radiator and the top radiator to cylinder-head hose externally reinforced. New hose pt. no. X6255. Vacuum release valve opens at 1lb/sq. in. Pressure release valve 6¼ – 7¼ lb/sq. in. Brake pipes re-run so that brake hoses are now fitted behind the suspension links instead of in front. New part nos are:

| | |
|---|---|
| A7005 | front suspension assembly |
| 500193 | assy of pipe, tee piece to OIS hose (RH) |
| 500194 | assy of pipe, tee piece to NIS hose |
| A7008 | front suspension assembly |
| 500219 | assy of pipe, tee piece to NIS hose (LH) drive |
| 500218 | assy of pipe, tee piece to OIS hose |
| 500188 | assy of hose bracket RH |
| 500189 | assy of hose bracket LH |
| 500245 | front brake carrier plate RH |
| 500246 | front brake carrier plate LH |

*Reason: To prevent chafing of front brake hose against rim of road wheel.*

**60S/7681**

Front shock absorber pt. no. D5670, Girling DA6/6 1in bore telescopic have been superseded by pt. no. 500157 Girling type CDRS 1½in bore telescopic. New part numbers:

| | | |
|---|---|---|
| 500157 | Front shock absorber | 2 off |
| 500110 | Anchorage sleeve | 2 off |
| 500113 | Nut for anchorage sleeve | 2 off |
| FB108/18N | Bolt ½in B.S.F × 2¼in (additional) | 2 off |
| 500111 | Front shock absorber bottom lug RH | 1 off |
| 500112 | Front shock absorber bottom lug LH | 1 off |
| 500114 | Dowel pin bottom wishbone | 2 off |

**7937**

Telescopic rear shock absorbers type DAS9 replace PV6 piston type. This also necessitates the fitting of a new exhaust tail pipe and expansion box assembly. New part numbers:

| | | |
|---|---|---|
| 500158 | Rear shock absorbers | 2 off |
| D5636 | Washer | 4 off |
| FNI08Z | Nut | 4 off |
| SW108Z | Spring washer | 4 off |
| PW110Z | Plain washer | 2 off |
| 500036 | Assy of shock absorber mounting bracket | 2 off |
| 500213 | Shock absorber bracket RH | 1 off |
| 500214 | Shock absorber bracket LH | 1 off |
| 500171 | Expansion box and pipe assembly | 1 off |
| 500155 | Tail pipe | |

*Reason: Improvement to design.*

**From October 1950**: Introduction of carburettor jet with two feed holes, 0.140in diameter replacing jet with ten feed holes of 0.093in diameter. Jets are interchangeable, the old part number is retained.

**From November 1950**: Introduction of a modified door lock incorporating a stronger bolt spring pt. no. RS41349. When modifying earlier locks, in addition to stronger spring pt. no. RS41349, the existing bolt assemblies must be replaced by the following parts:

Front door lock (with one stud on the bolt assembly acting between the operating lever and spring reaction lever)
LH side new bolt assembly pt. no. L3321fA
RH side new bolt assembly pt. no. L3321/B
Rear door lock (with two studs positioned across the bolt assembly)
LH side new bolt assembly pt. no. L3320/B
RH side new bolt assembly pt. no. L3320/A

61S/8481    (approx) body no. 69593. Scuttle ventilator modified by moving the pivot from the central position to the extreme rear.
*Reason: To increase opening and improve interior ventilation.*

8605    1in dia. front brake wheel cylinders pt. no. 300741/2 LH and RH replace pt. no. 300319/20 LH and RH.
(1 and ⅛in dia).
*Reason: To improve ratio between front and rear brakes.*

8413    Export lhd – as above.

62S/9353    Introduction of RMB/2 type power unit, incorporating the following modifications:
1. Water pump mounted on the top front of the timing chain enabling the fan to be mounted on the water-pump spindle and driven by a single belt.
2. The oil relief valve is now preset and requires no adjustment. It is incorporated in the oil pump body and a floating type oil filter employed.
3. The camshafts will have ½in wide ramped cams resulting in much quieter valve gear operation. Note, however that the first 200 engines will be fitted with camshafts having ¾in wide cams.
The tappet setting is 0.011in (hot) in either case.
4. The new camshaft results in a slightly different valve timing:
inlet valve opens          12deg B.T.D.C.
inlet valve closes          53deg A.B.D.C.
exhaust valve opens     55deg B.B.D.C.
exhaust valve closes     20deg A.T.D.C.
5. The compression ratio has been reduced from 6.85:1 to 6.7:1.
6. The direction of rotation of the distributor has been altered to anticlockwise.
7. The location of the front engine mounting has been changed to allow for the new fan-belt run, the front suspension cradle and engine mounting cross tube having been modified to suit.

62S/9304    Air scoops pt. nos. 500531 (RH) and 500532 (LH) of swivelling type are now available for attachment to the front doors and are fitted as standard from the above chassis number. (This seems not to have happened.)
*Reason: Improved ventilation control.*

| | |
|---|---|
| 8873 | New type steering wheel pt. no. 500677 introduced, incorporating a collet-type clamp with fluted lock ring in place of split clamp with bolt and lock nut. |

**RMF**

| | |
|---|---|
| 62S 9911 | Introduction of full hydraulic brake gear.<br>Introduction of hypoid rear axle with open propeller shafts and hubs incorporating ANF threaded studs and stronger rear road springs. Hypoid 90 oil now used for the rear axle and gearbox as well.<br>Introduction of front hubs incorporating ANF threaded studs. |

**Engine numbers**

| | |
|---|---|
| B3157 | Connecting rod assembly S553 replaced by S863. S863 has wider big end bolt centres. Rods should be serviced singly for the respective engine numbers (as they are different weights) or as a set of four S553, or a set of four S863. |
| B6020 | Piston and bore sizes changed from millimetre to inch measurements. Pistons now marked with the correct size of cylinder bore for which they are suitable. The marking on the block should correspond accordingly. |
| B7339 | Guide for dipstick fitted to crankcase.<br>New Part Nos:<br>Dipstick       166086<br>Dipstick ferrule  13454  166087<br>Dipstick washer  13455<br>Dipstick guide  166085<br>*Reason: Improvement to design.* |
| B7644 | Cylinder head with increased depth of combustion spaces pt. no. 166160 replaced pt. no. S810.<br>*Reason: Change to lower compression ratio.* |
| B7736 | Timing chain adjustor, pt. no. 166336 replaces pt. no. S136.<br>Timing chain adjustor bolt, pt. no. 23160 replaces set screw, pt. no. 1114 (to block).<br>Timing chain adjustor bolt tab washer, pt. no. 166337 and timing chain adjustor plug, pt. no. R50 are both deleted. |
| B8126 | Cylinder head stud (short) pt. no. 166344 replaces S335.<br>Cylinder head stud (long) pt. no. 166345 replaces S336.<br>Push-rod tube, pt. no. 166346 replaces S235.<br>Push-rod assembly pt. no. 166347 replaces S748.<br>*Reason: To compensate for increase in height of head.* |
| B8126 | Introduction of high output dynamo pt. no. 164439 (Lucas type C45.PV-5). Improved dynamo adjusting bracket and dynamo split pulley with the |

addition of combined dynamo fan and blanking plate for better cooling.
Dynamo pt. no.164439 replaces pt. no. 164422
Dynamo adjusting bracket pt. no. 166097 replaces pt. no. S2B.
Dynamo split pulley front pt. no. 166103 replaces pt. no. S19.
Dynamo split pulley rear  pt. no. 166104
Dynamo fan with blanking plate pt. no. 164450 added.

RMB2/1

Special batch of 200 RMB2 engines built using inlet camshaft pt. no. 166257 and exhaust camshaft pt. no. 166258 with the width of the cams increased to ¾in. Tappet setting hot is 0.011in.
*Reason: Test purposes.*
1in diameter tappets with angular holes pt. no. 166256 replace ¹⁵⁄₁₆in diameter tappets pt. no 166117.
*Reason: Improved drainage for foreign matter.*

RMB2/531

Introduction of water pump assembly with modified spindle and one pair of split cotters replacing spindle with circlip. The water pump spindle collar pt. no. 166139 has been modified to accommodate the use of the split cotters, and a modified collar must be set out if it is wished to fit the modified spindle and cotters prior to engine no. RMB2/531.
Water pump spindle pt. no. 166511 replaces water pump spindle pt. no. 166136.
Water pump split cotters pt. no. 166512 (1 pair) replaces water pump circlip pt. no. 166138 (1 off).
*Reason: Improvement in design.*

RMB2/884

Introduction of a new oil pump relief valve guide pt. no. 166551 in case iron replacing pt. no. 24118.
*Reason: To prevent noise made by flutter of the oil pump relief valve ball.*

RMB2/945

Introduction of split type connecting rod pt. no. 166165 with renewable bearing shells pt. no. 166519 bottom half steel backed, white metal lined and pt. no.166520, top half copper lead. Con-rod bolts pt. no.16629 with U.N.F. threading ⅜in A/F also fitted.
*Reason: Improved design enabling connecting rod to be passed up cylinder bore.*

RMB2/1288

New distributor incorporating suction operation – Lucas 40336A

RMB2/2050

Gearbox no. CA495. A special batch of 100 gear boxes have been fitted with a new mainshaft pt. no. 166552 having 0.008in extra clearance with the top and 3rd speed hub.
*Reason: To obviate synchromesh rattle.*

RMB2/1280

Oil level indicator pt. no. 166557 replaces pt. no. 166076 with increase in oil capacity of gearbox from 2 to 2⅜pt.
*Reason: To raise oil level.*

| | |
|---|---|
| RMB2/1288 | (rhd) RMB2/LX/1316 (lhd). Distributor pt. no. 166250 with suction-operated advance and retard control unit replaces distributor pt. no. 166182. Carburettor pt. no. 166348 including auto-ignition adaptor fitted to suit. *Reason: Improved design.* |
| RMB2/1332 | Introduction of water pump spindle pt. no. 166561 in harder material replacing water pump spindle pt. no. 166511. *Reason: To avoid possible breakage due to imbalance of fan blades and overhang from pulley drive.* |
| RMB2/1332 | Cast iron fan pulley pt. no. 166517 replaces aluminium fan pulley pt. no. 166145 necessitating the fitting of water pump spindle of greater hardness (*see* water pump spindle modification). *Reason: To eliminate the tendency of hub bore wear.* |
| RMB2/7226 | Deletion of oil hole in timing chain oiler pt. no. S285. The pt. no. remains unchanged though the part is now known as the timing chain case damper stud. *Reason: Oil bleed to timing chain not necessary.* |
| | For service purposes pt. no. 166516 has been allocated for gudgeon pins 0.002in oversize, the pistons with slack gudgeon pin holes must be reamed out to suit. |
| | The timing chain tensioner bracket pt. no. 5309 (mod 2) has been modified with slots 2⁄₆₄in × ⁷⁄₁₆in long in place or the two holes of 0.328in dia. When the modified bracket is fitted in lieu of the original type, a plate pt. no. 166554 together with longer bolts, pt. no. FS104/4Z replacing pt no. 4214 must also be fitted. *Reason: To give added adjustment on tensioner.* |

## Gearbox numbers

| | |
|---|---|
| CA 37 | approx. 17.6.52. Introduction of gearbox mainshaft pt. no. 166241 with an indent added and an additional retainer ball in the synchro hub. The seven balls will be retained by peening into the hub to prevent any chance of ejection. |

Source: *BMIHT and* Riley Record

---

1. The *Motor Trader* published an exhaustive mechanical analysis of the 2½-litre in February 1949, which was checked with the factory. This gives the changeover point to the 100bhp engine in April 1948 from engine 1226, chassis 58S/2976, rather than 58S/2959.

# Appendix V: Riley repair times schedule

|  | 1½-litre<br>Hours | 2½-litre<br>Hours | Pathfinder<br>Hours |
|---|---|---|---|
| **Engine** | | | |
| Engine and gearbox unit- remove and refit | 12 | 16 | 15 |
| Engine and gearbox unit – R/fit replacement | 15½ | 20 | 18 |
| Air cleaner(s) -remove, clean and refit | ½ | ½ | ½ |
| Cylinder head or gasket -remove and refit | 4½ | 5 | 5 |
| Cylinders -rebore, fit new pistons | 17½ | 18 | 20 |
| Decarbonise, grind valves, tune and test | 12½ | 12½ | 12½ |
| Flywheel -remove and refit | 8½ | 9 | 16½ |
| Oil pump – remove, overhaul and refit | 3½ | 5 | 9 |
| Piston – replace one complete | 9 | 9 | 7¾ |
| Piston rings -fit new to all pistons | 8½ | 9 | 10½ |
| Pulley (crankshaft) -remove and refit | ½ | ½ | 5 |
| Timing chain – remove and refit | 7 | 11½ | 8½ |
| Tune engine | 3½ | 3¾ | 4 |
| Valve – replace one | 4¾ | 5¼ | 5¼ |
| Water pump -remove and refit | 2¼ | 1¼ | 4 |
| | | | |
| **Gearbox and Clutch** | | | |
| Gearbox – remove and refit | 7¼ | 5 | 15½ |
| Strip and reassemble after removal | 3½ | 3½ | 5 |
| Clutch – remove, overhaul and refit | 8½ | 9¼ | 17 |
| Clutch housing – remove and refit | 8¼ | 9¼ | 171 |
| Clutch thrust block – remove and refit | 7½ | 8¼ | 15¾ |
| | | | |
| **Front Suspension** | | | |
| Unit complete -remove and refit | 17 | 17 | 10 |
| Unit one side – remove, overhaul and refit | 7 | 7 | 6½ |
| Hub bearings -replace (one wheel) | 1¾ | 1¾ | 1½ |
| Torsion bar – remove and refit | ¾ | ¾ | 2¼ |

|  | 1½-litre<br>Hours | 2½-litre<br>Hours | Pathfinder<br>Hours |
|---|---|---|---|
| **Steering** | | | |
| Rack and pinion assy – r/refit and overhaul | 9 | 9 | 5½ |
| Ball socket & joints (inner) – replace each | 1½ | 1½ | 2½ |
| Ball sockets and joints (outer) –replace each | 1 | 1 | ¾ |
| Steering wheel – remove and refit | 1 | 1 | 1 |

Source: *I.C.M.E. Manual 1974*

# Appendix VI: RM prices

|  | 1½ litre | 2½ litre | Drophead | Roadster | Pathfinder |
|---|---|---|---|---|---|
| | | | **Prices** | | |
| 1945 | £709 | | | | |
| 1946 | £863 | £1,125 | | | |
| 1947 | £863 | £1,125 | | | |
| 1948 | £863 | £1,123 | £1,214 | £1,125 | |
| 1949 | £913 | £1,127 | £1,272 | £1,225 | |
| 1950 | £913 | £1,224 | £1,240 | £1,225 | |
| 1951 | £1,168 | £1,491 | | | |
| 1952 | £1,339 | £1,642 | | | |
| 1953 | £1,205 | | | | £1,382 |
| 1954 | £1,205 | | | | £1,382 |
| 1955 | | | | | £1,240 |
| 1956 | | | | | £1,411 |
| 1957 | | | | | £1,411 |

Pre-war prices: 1940 model year
1½-litre 12hp saloon       £341
2½-litre 16hp saloon       £423

Prices from 1948 are based on the October price each year at the London Motor Show. Prices in earlier years, when there was no motor show, are based on factory announcements.

All include purchase tax that, in the 1940s and 1950s, could see-saw wildly. Apart from its revenue-raising capabilities, it was a blunt Government weapon to stifle demand at home and encourage manufacturers to export.

For instance, in 1951 the 1½-litre's basic cost was £750, but purchase tax was above 50 per cent, adding another £418. The total of £1,168 at 2004 prices is about £23,000.

At one time, cars whose basic cost was above £1,000 were subjected to double purchase tax. This did not affect Rileys, as the factory was careful to keep the basic cost below the threshold, but buyers of expensive cars paid very dearly. The Bristol 401's basic cost in 1951 was £2,095; with purchase tax added it came to an enormous £3,260, equivalent to some £65,000 at 2004 prices. Bristol cars have become stratospherically expensive since then – the Blenheim Speedster in 2004 was £149,418.

It was these penal rates of taxation, even on ordinary saloon cars, that led to the rise of the company car market in Britain and has distorted prices for private buyers for decades.

# Bibliography

Balfour, C. (ed.), *Auto-architect – Autobiography of Gerald Palmer* (Magna, 1998).

Barker, V.E., *Riley 12/4 Production Cars, 1934–1940* (Riley Register, 1993).

Barker, V.E., *Riley 16/4 Production Cars 1937–40* (Riley Register, 1999).

Clarke, R.M. (ed.), *Riley 1½ and 2½-litre Cars 1924–1939: Gold Portfolio* (Brooklands, 1993).

Clarke, R.M. (ed.), *Riley 1½ and 2½-litre Cars 1945–1950: Gold Portfolio* (Brooklands, 1989).

Culshaw and Horrobin, *Catalogue of British Cars 1895–1975* (Veloce, 1997).

Jenkinson, D., *From Chain Drive to Turbo-charger. The A.F.N. Story.* (Guild Publishing, 1985).

Knowles, D., *MG: The Untold Story* (Windrow and Greene, 1997).

Pressnell, Jon, *Citröen Traction Avant* (Crowood, 2005).

Robson, G., *Sporting Rileys* (Oxford Illustrated, 1986).

Rowlands, D., *Riley Pathfinder* (RMH Publications, 2000).

Springate, L., *A Nostalgic Look at Riley Cars.* Pictures from the National Motor Museum (Silver Link, 1996).

Styles, D.G., *As Old as the Industry* (Dalton Watson, 1992).

Styles, D.G., *Sporting Rileys – the Forgotten Champions* (Dalton Watson, 1988).

Thomas, D., *An Underworld at War* (John Murray, 2004).

Walker, N., *A–Z British Coachbuilders* (Bay View Books, 1997).

Volumes of *Autocar, Autosport, Motor, Motor Sport, RMemoranda, Riley Record, Motoring.*

# Index